Early
Too Go

"*Does this one have the F*

"*Thank goodness my prologue isn't in this one*" —Beth Feldman

"*Can you, like, summarize?*" —someone named Chloe

"*And? ...*" —Fran Lebowitz

"*Fuck him*" —Elon Musk

"*Sophia is a hottie. You couldn't throw more pictures of her in?*"
—author's straight friends

"*Is that the fat little boy who complained about the
size of the Vogue closet?*" —Anna Wintour

"*That the little shit who wrote my lines?*" —Usher

"*You'll hear from my lawyer!*" —every person not included in the book

"*You'll hear from my lawyer!*" —most people in this book

"*Finally, I get a paragraph, you cu—*" —Robert "Bobby" Konjic

"*He set the bloody room on fire!*" —manager of posh London hotel

"*There is much more context to the story but yea, I said that*" —
Dominick Dunne, before

"*You have NO idea*" —Super P, world's best publisher

"*I styled the wardrobe, I know nothing else*"
—every stylist who worked on shoots

"*I know everything*" —Champers the Cat

"*I care about your book; I care more about your liver*" —author's doctor

"*How drunk were you when you hit send?*" —author's lawyer

"*I can sell this!*" —author's agent

"*I wouldn't sell this*" —author's entire network

"*He's an HR nightmare!*" —the HR community

TOO GOOD TO FACT CHECK

Flying the Skies with Stars, Scotch, and Scandal (Mostly Mine)

Jeremy Murphy
with Sophia Paulmier

A POST HILL PRESS BOOK
ISBN: 979-8-88845-148-9
ISBN (eBook): 979-8-88845-149-6

Too Good to Fact Check:
Flying the Skies with Stars, Scotch, and Scandal (Mostly Mine)
© 2024 by Jeremy Murphy
All Rights Reserved

Cover design by Jim Villaflores
Author photos on cover by Mark Grgurich

Post Hill Press
New York • Nashville
posthillpress.com

Published in the United States of America
1 2 3 4 5 6 7 8 9 10

This book is dedicated to Marni, my guardian angel.
Thank you for being, well, you.
My life is infinitely better with you in it.

And to Yogi, our missed furry friend who brought joy, warmth,
and love into Marni's home and heart, and to her friends, as well.

"Chance favors the prepared mind."
—Louis Pasteur

TABLE OF CONTENTS

JEREMY MURPHY

Author Jeremy Murphy. Photo by Mark Grgurich.

I originally intended this book to be a fun, dishy chronicle about celebrities and a decade of traveling with them around the world. As the creator and editor of a glossy entertainment magazine called *Watch!*, I brought TV stars to glamorous destinations like Paris, London, Milan, Berlin, Shanghai, and nearly everywhere in between.

In recounting these experiences with my co-writer, Sophia Paulmier, I realized that the celebrities were the most well-behaved people on our shoots. As the productions got bigger, antics got wilder—mostly because of me. This is what happens when you lead an otherwise ho-hum life and then turn thirty and have the world at your fingertips. I lived the life I'd missed in high school and college, but now I had access to first-class travel, five-star hotels, and celebrities. Much of this will be extremely surprising—even shocking—to people who know me, as I kept my reckless lifestyle somewhat secret. But as things got crazier, it became more evident.

Too Good to Fact Check weaves these experiences through the lens of the over-the-top photo shoots we were doing with stars. In between trips with LL Cool J, the cast of *The Big Bang Theory*, Harrison Ford, and so on, I'd managed to throw a party in a hotel where guests set the room on fire, get into a bar fight in an Irish pub, get banned by the King Cole Bar for defending some very respectable prostitutes, drunkenly sing the *Nightline* theme song to a very scared Ted Koppel, cover up a colleague's arrest on a commercial airplane, among other hijinks. Frankly, I'm surprised I'm still alive.

This book has plenty of stories featuring celebrities, who for the most part are endearing and well-behaved. A few are assholes, which you'll see by reading between the lines. I've kept several instances as "blind items" because the culprits have lawyers and I have overdue balances, collection notices, and a pen pal relationship with the IRS.

I've also kept the names of several companies anonymous because it takes away from the story. My baggage is already heavy, and it's my fucking book anyway.

Enjoy, at my expense, these insane memories and anecdotes, and remember: don't wait for someone to hand you an opportunity because they won't. Instead, create it yourself. Just don't screw it up. And if you do, at least have fun doing it.

PROLOGUE

·····★·····

SOPHIA PAULMIER

Sophia Portrait.

"That's Jeremy. He's a writer, you'd like him," Amanda tells me as she extends my drink. She points to a man with parted brown hair and square-frame spectacles.

"YOU'RE A WRITER?" I shout from across the bar.

It's not a particularly loud bar, and there's not a great deal of people around since it's the middle of a post-pandemic summer. But because I'm from Philadelphia, I project at a higher volume than the average person.

"I am," Jeremy replies.

I quickly pick up my denim Stella McCartney bag and Casamigos soda and move to the seat closest to Jeremy.

"Tell me more," I inquire. His eyes pop out.

"Is she for real?" he asks Amanda.

Either no one has ever approached him like this, or I have invaded the six-feet social distancing rule.

"No one has ever had anyone approach me like that," he admits. "What brought you here?"

"Amanda," I answered, pointing to my best friend and the bartender at Felice on East 83rd.

That night, I got to know about Jeremy's new book and his theories on millennials and marketing. We discussed everything from the long list of pronouns and sexual preferences to the marketing budget of every identifying group. He astounded me with his deep views on life and death. The death of the fashion industry. The death of the print world. The death of Hollywood.

"You know who killed everything?" he questioned me.

"Um, Mark Zuckerberg?" I guessed.

"Memes. Memes changed everything," he said, assuredly. If I hadn't met him in real life, I'd subscribe to his subreddit for all the interesting stories and shared love of critique.

A couple of months later, I found myself giving notes on a TV script he'd written: a seventy-page pilot about an Italian family with political and historical ancestry and a hidden art collection. After studying pilots, pitch-decks, show "bibles," and having written my own pilot scripts, I've become quite the "go-to" for notes on these kinds of screenplays. Jeremy's script had potential, and I had a lot of notes that he was eager to hear.

"Let's meet at the King Cole Bar," his text read. I had never heard of it, so I looked it up on Google Maps on my iPhone—East 55th Street and Fifth Avenue. Buried deep to the left of the lobby, I walked in, and a waiter recognized me immediately.

"Sophia, right?" he asked. "Any friend of Jeremy's is a friend of mine." And just like that, I was escorted through the dark, mahogany room dominated by a mural that instantly stole my gaze.

Jeremy, sitting in the corner booth, greets me with a hug and the story behind the mural and its namesake, Old King Cole. The history lesson is interrupted when the waiter brings a cocktail menu; Jeremy introduces him as George.

Jeremy can tell you the history of historic bars, lounges, and restaurants: how each came to be; names of chefs, bartenders, and waiters; famous people who have been; and important people who walk through. This would kickstart his influence of New York whereabouts and famous knowabouts on me.

After a few drinks, we go over his script. I tell him it should start on page thirty-five; since the story is about his protagonist's Robin Hood actions to take back his family's art, he should have the audience meet the protagonist for the first time decoding a safe. Jeremy is unexpectedly quiet. It's a packed house at King Cole, but suddenly, all I hear are crickets. Jeremy's eyes float to the ceiling for this brief pause. I fill the awkward silence by explaining this change of action.

"Everything the audience has learned in these first thirty-five pages is backstory," I tell him. "You can use it for the rest of the season. But they don't need it here in episode one."

He suddenly looks me dead in the eyes and says, "That's *brilliant*."

My mind is suddenly at ease. He can't believe he's never thought of this story change until now.

Months would go by where he'd continually thank me for this one note and state no one's ever suggested this. I really had nothing to lose by sharing this note, but as an actor myself, I am very sensitive to hurting a fellow creative's feelings with critique. I feel so lucky to have a friend who appreciates good writing and strives for it.

When the opportunity came about to co-write his remarkable stories, I happily signed on.

In *Too Good to Fact Check*, you will experience a myriad of places, hotels, bars, cities. You will hear about a lot of actors, writers, musicians, photographers, stylists, managers, publicists, CEOs—both the talented and ego-talented—but what you will really hear is a friend speaking about a time and place when you could be anything, go anywhere, hang out with anyone, and no one would know about it. The social attention of sharing on the internet didn't exist. The need to brag about it instantly didn't make any difference.

The moment was all that mattered, so you could make as many mistakes as you could manage.

And my friend Jeremy did just that.

CHAPTER 1

......★......

Harrison *Bored*

This is the chapter that's going to get me in a lot of trouble, so why not start with it! I seem to run away from everything—responsibility, the right decisions, poly-blend—*but* trouble. So here it comes: Harrison Ford was being an asshole.

Now, a caveat: he's also a legend. No one deserves to be a dick, but if there's a success criterion for getting that license, Harrison's application was approved years ago. Just look at his repertoire: *Star Wars, Indiana Jones, The Fugitive, Jack Ryan* (*Patriot Games* and *Clear and Present Danger*), among many other hits. He even made interesting that movie in which he's a ruthless attorney who gets shot in the head, turns special, and paints Ritz cracker boxes. I also enjoyed him in *Presumed Innocent*, the legal thriller that overcame his abysmal Caesar haircut: pre-Clooney and not as good-looking.

Worse looking was the movie he was then promoting—an unintentionally hilarious medical drama about dying children.

At the time, I was into my fourth year as editor of the magazine and jumped at the chance to work with the A-List star, no matter how shitty his latest film was.

The problem: it was off-the-charts shitty. Despite his best efforts, *Extraordinary Measures* was extraordinarily bad. Ford played Dr. Robert Stonehill, a medical researcher in Nebraska (zzz...) who concocts enzyme treatments (zzzz...) for people battling rare diseases (zzzzzzzzzzzz). Brendan Fraser and Keri Russell portrayed parents of a child battling the real-life Pompe disease, a genetic anomaly affecting children before their tenth birthday. They start a biotechnical company, a natural response to hearing your child is dying, and hire Dr. Stonehill to help find a cure.

Not my kind of flick, for sure. The word was this was going to flatline, which meant he'd be doing as much press as possible to help salvage its chances. But there were several restrictions, including shooting in Los Angeles. God forbid we interrupt yoga, lunchtime kale with Calista, and herbal meditation. Thankfully, the Beverly Wilshire hotel, famous for its roles in *Beverly Hills Cop* and *Pretty Woman* ("Reg...Bev... Wil"), agreed to host us.

This is essential when you're running a magazine with little to no budget: lining up hotels, airlines, restaurants, and other hospitality to sponsor (i.e., give for free) in exchange for putting them in the editorial and/or ad pages. Our publication existed on these types of arrangements, as you'll read throughout the book.

In this case, everyone was game to feature Harrison Ford ... except Harrison Ford.

The star knew better than everyone that this was going to bomb. I soon did as well. The day before we were scheduled to take the photos, the marketing-PR-consultant-gofer-receptionist-whatever for the studio delivered a "private screener" to our hotel. I should have known something was off because she was dressed as a cowgirl, complete with spurs, rhinestone-studded denim skirt, and a cowgirl hat—in Beverly Hills. She also acted as if it was top secret. Really? I couldn't give that away on Canal Street.

Why?

It was worse than expected, and really fucking funny for a tear-jerker about children dying.

First, Harrison Ford is a lot more believable flying spaceships next to human-sized dogs than playing a scientist. In one scene that was supposed to be very tense, the actor announces, "I have to take a shit."

In another compelling scene, Harrison asks Brendan's daughter— trapped in a wheelchair with minimal use of her hands or feet—what was her favorite school subject. Her reply? "PE."

As in physical education. He then races her electronic wheelchair down the street.

The howls coming from our room got louder the longer the movie played; I'm surprised we weren't asked to leave.

The next morning had a weird energy. I'd dealt with major celebrities before, but from corporate headquarters in New York where you can roll your eyes and raise your finger shielded by the phone. Not so in Los Angeles, where I was just an inconsequential, overweight executive who looked half my age. Being in Hollyweird is a very sobering experience. Everyone is blond, plastic, sample size, tan/orange, with perfect skin, teeth, and the latest trend in eating disorders. I've never felt fatter, uglier, less cool, and more out of place.

Harrison was due at 9:00 a.m. at the valet drop-off, which was located in a thruway between the Beverly Wilshire's two buildings off Wilshire Boulevard. His publicist met us on the steps and stood waiting for the actor for thirty minutes, then forty-five. Suddenly, the PR lady revealed the delay: he'd gone to the wrong hotel. The Beverly *Hilton* is nearby and where all the second-tier award shows—Golden Globes and the like—are held; also where Whitney Houston died taking a bath. I'd stayed there before, and it's swanky for a hotel but hard to confuse with the Beverly Wilshire. I keep envisioning Harrison going to the wrong styling suite and finding Jim and Suzy Suburbs expecting room service.

"You're not eggs Benedict!"

Mistake corrected, he drove his Prius to the correct hotel and arrived surly, carrying his own wardrobe in a garment bag. I bounded down the steps to greet him and got a grunt. He only looked at the PR girl, who directed us all to the elevator.

Standing in such close quarters with this vaunted figure from my childhood was a huge moment becoming smaller and smaller each passing second. At one point, Harrison looked at me, rolled his eyes, and asked his publicist, "Why are they dressed up?" To which the PR lady replied, correctly, "They're from New York." As a sign of respect, my staff always dressed professionally; I was in a Giorgio Armani Made-to-Measure suit, sucking my gut in so it fit. Cue another eye roll from Harrison.

I guided them to the "styling suite," which was rendered useless because he brought his own clothes and passed on grooming. In all candor, he didn't need it. At this point, he still looked rugged and handsome.

After a few minutes, we brought him to "set" and had our shooter, Cliff Lipson, take photos. We had minimal time because Harrison had to do an interview afterward. Cliff was a natural and even got him to smile a few times. Cliff has a disarming quality and got talent to relax and lower their guard.

The interview—in a different suite next door—lasted less time, and we got press release quotes out of the actor. Perfect for a cover story!

After less than two hours—*if that!*—we bid Harrison Ford farewell. By this time, no one really gave a shit; we were soured by his sourness. Once his Prius had cleared the property, our crew high-tailed it to a restaurant called 208 Rodeo across the street, where we ate truffle fries while recounting the absurdity. It's telling that not one of us asked for an autograph.

The movie did worse than anyone expected.

Back in New York, I began to put the issue together. The photography was good, which I owe to Cliff. The story almost made interesting the world's least interesting movie star. Still, we had *twelve* pages slotted, which is a lot of real estate to give to a shitty movie with an unintentionally comedic storyline.

Then, a voice from God above (the sixth floor): my publisher who I called Super P. He worked in the sales department and sold all the ads in our magazine. More than anyone, he was my partner in this crazy experiment. Super P put up with me, and I was very happy he put up with me because not a lot of people do.

Magazines work, or worked, on an edit/ad ratio; a good balance is fifty/fifty. For example, if the page count is one hundred, that means there are fifty pages of editorial—the content the magazine produces—and fifty pages of advertisements for cars, cell phones, clothes, pharmaceuticals, etc. Super P and I had a deal: the first half of every issue could not feature *anything* unsightly. I was spending a lot of money on photographers and designers, and the last thing I wanted was the Geico Gecko next to a Demarchelier portrait.

There were no ads at that point more hideous than pharmaceutical ones. It's like they go out of their way to find the ugliest people and put them in wheat fields, bathtubs, golf courses, wherever. And then there are the following pages of text listing all the ways in which these drugs can kill you. Those are less ugly to me, and here's why: it's an extra page the pharmaceutical company has to buy. This is the hidden secret of drug ads: for every word on the front of the ad, there are more words they need to list to justify, not to mention the contraindications listing every possible reaction or side effect. The more dangerous the drug, the more words they need—which means more space, and that means more pages.

The most dangerous of all are the "Black Box" drugs—just thinking about or pronouncing them can kill you. In publishing, we love these because they come with many, many, many pages of contraindications.

Super P called with a huge buy: a six-page ad for Seroquel XL (otherwise known as quetiapine fumarate). The ad included a full-page image of a woman in what looks like an acid-washed denim suit looking solemn as she sits on a dirty staircase (I would be depressed wearing that too).

"Bipolar depression doesn't affect you. It can consume you," blared the headline.

The other five pages of the ad list how you'll die just by touching it.

For me, it was relief: I lost six of the twelve pages I had devoted to Harrison Ford, and I had an excuse.

Who can disagree with money? We probably made more than the movie.

Q&A WITH SOPHIA PAULMIER

Sophia: I could watch a whole doc-series on pharmaceutical ads and their marketing budgets.

Jeremy: They're the only ones spending. Pharma is the crack cocaine of the media industry; it's keeping everything afloat. Despite how ugly the ads are, the money is good, and magazines need all the money they can get. We sure did!

S: How did Harrison Ford's publicist feel about this?

J: She didn't have a say on that. We gave personal publicists approval on images and text, but never layouts. The movie bombed so badly he was probably relieved.

S: If you could have asked Harrison one truth about working on that movie, what would it have been?

J: You don't need the money. Why the fuck are you making this turd?

S: Do you have any regret about meeting him?

J: None at all. It's a story I can tell for the rest of my life. I'm Irish and love holding court with these kinds of memories. People love hearing about celebrities and what they're really like.

S: Favorite underrated Harrison Ford film?

J: *Frantic.* It's a thriller from the '80s in which he plays a husband whose wife disappears in Paris. Roman Polanski directed it, and you have no idea where it's going right through the end.

CHAPTER 2

One Broke Editor

A before and after of Beth Behrs and Kat Dennings, from TV's *2 Broke Girls*, in Milan for the magazine's cover shoot. Taken in Galleria Vittorio Emanuele II, the actresses posed in the public venue, knowing spectators would be removed digitally from the "before" picture. Photo by Andrea Varani.

The next big thing in 2012 was the TV sitcom *2 Broke Girls*. The comedy, starring Kat Dennings and Beth Behrs, had become a hit and was moving to a plum time slot the next season. Kat played a sassy, wise-cracking diner waitress, and Beth was a trust-fund baby who winds up working next to her after Daddy MoreBucks gets sent to Club Fed.

Our team began planning out the year's covers, and I thought they'd be perfect for our summer travel theme. It was now several years after

Harrison Bored, and we'd grown to the point where every spring we would go overseas for three weeks to shoot issues in advance. That year, we had offers to bring stars to Florence, Paris, and London; all that was missing was Milan, Paris's well-dressed cousin. Imagine two attractive women in its fashion triangle? Perfection!

Three years before, I visited with my mom and couldn't believe the "sprezzatura" bathing its men, all wearing fitted Italian suits tailored to an inch of their lives. Women looked great too: tight pencil skirts, chic designer blouses, and Gucci stilettos. They all looked like David and Victoria Beckham but nourished. We, conversely, stuck out like typical Americans, highlighted by fanny packs, sandals, and gelato. We'd built our own fashion *heptadecagon*.

Planning to return, I fretted how we'd cover the cost of the shoot in a city not known for its discounts. Our magazine had *no* brand awareness in Italy, and finding somewhere to host us would be mission impossible. Even Tom Cruise would have trouble, but he's got enough with *Mission Impossible*'s writing—it's incoherent (I had to Google the last one to understand what the fuck I'd spent thirty hours watching). I contacted nearly every upscale hotel in Milan to no avail until an email popped up on my screen from Olivier Gerber, marketing director for the Four Seasons Milan, who saw an opportunity to promote his hotel. Olivier is among the smartest PR reps I've ever worked with.

We'd won the lotteria; the hotel is not only the best in town, but also where all the "in" people stay during Fashion Week. Located in the center of the fashion triangle, its housed in a former convent known as the "Conventino delle Cappuccine," which dates back to the 15th century. Completely renovated, it's now a five-star hotel that features a large courtyard, manicured garden, fountains, and a Renaissance-meets-neoclassical décor and ambiance. Olivier offered to host our entire crew as long as we did the majority of the photography on property, as well as write a separate feature about its location and amenities. Getting this offer—which included a food and beverage allowance—made me happier than when Tom Ford suits in my "one day!" closet magically fit, which is a rare occurrence on par with winning the lottery.

We arrived a day earlier than the talent and passed most of the time at the "you're lucky to be here" foyer bar, which served the freshest mozzarella I'd ever tasted. Photographer Andrea Varani, who had just shot *How I Met Your Mother* stars Neil Patrick Harris and Cobie Smulders for us in Florence, joined us in the lounge, a useless exercise considering he didn't speak English.

We had to hire locally for a wardrobe stylist, which is not hard in Milan. Mireille Comstock, an incredible talent with a strong eye for sense of place, spent a lot of time before pulling pieces from brands like Dolce & Gabbana, Prada, and Armani, among others. The clothing was "elegante" supreme.

Kat and Beth arrived the next day with their boyfriends, and they were tired after an all-night flight from LA. Still, Beth was bubbly and excited; Kat less so, but would warm up after a full night's sleep. Actresses in-house, I looked forward to a stress-free night. *Of course*, it would be interrupted by drama. A publicist from the show we'd brought to Milan texted me an SOS: many of the clothes were ill-fitting. Someone in LA decided to translate sizes from American to Italian, but mathematics isn't a particularly well-developed skill in Los Angeles unless it's box-office scores, recovery days after plastic surgery, or the cost of good coke. That's when they go Isaac Newton.

It was a weekend, so contacting design houses for *new* items was impossible. And the next day was a holiday; shocking for a country that doesn't burn the *day* oil. Our only option was to buy clothes, but it was now 5:00 p.m., and stores were either closed or about to. Mireille raced us to Dolce & Gabbana, where she and the girls picked out dresses and accessories that fit our theme. Meanwhile, I had a nervous breakdown at the register, unsure how I'd cover the expense. As Kat and Beth played *Pretty Woman*, I played Stressed Human and finally hit the panic button: get approval. This is an activity I loathe; "It's easier to ask forgiveness than permission" is my mantra. Stunningly, a helpful bean counter in NY suggested I use the "P Card," a signed confession disguised as a Mastercard. I hated touching this heinous piece of plastic because it never got approved and almost always triggered an audit.

My sweat went from tropical storm to hurricane when I saw what the girls had chosen. While the clothes were perfecto, I was a puddle handing my thermoplastic to the cashier because the cost was five figures. As the saleswoman swiped the card, I stared at the register and did the Jedi mind trick: gently rub your temples and chant, "You will approve, you will approve." This works with your Bloomingdales card too.

In situations like this, you do the math, which might as well be in Aramaic because I can't add or subtract either. But this was simple: do the shoot or you're fucked. We'd already accepted free airfare and hotels, and we'd be liable if we *didn't* finish. That, too, added up to five figures, but much higher. Buying clothes was cheaper than *not* buying clothes. *This* is math I could get into.

Keeping the talent happy, especially on shoot day, is the number one priority of the editor. I've done it well and I've done it atrociously. This was one of my better performances, and D&G gave an incredible start. The girls looked stunning in every setup, and we worked them the whole day with setups in the hotel, Fashion Triangle, and famed boutique store 10 Corso Como. The cover: Kat and Beth coming out of the Galleria Vittorio Emanuele II, Milan's historic shopping center next to the Duomo. Its glass-roof dome is now iconic.

The setup was going to be difficult for several reasons: my photographer didn't speak English; the girls had become celebrities and would surely be noticed in one of Milan's busiest attractions; and someone back in New York insisted we get model-release forms—like a permission slip—from anyone who walked by the camera, even though they'd be *edited out* of the images. I was surprised with the dictate because it was stupid. Can you imagine?

"Hi, Italian person we don't know. Just in case our photographer got you in a frame of a picture that will never be used, can you sign this American legal document with no Italian translation?"

We arrived at the Galleria and walked Kat and Beth to their positions. The girls were wearing plush Four Seasons white robes to conceal their wardrobe, which, looking back, was absurd. *Surely*, no one would question women in bathrobes roaming the arcade. Andrea shot them fast, and for good reason: they attracted huge crowds as we shot them walking back and forth toward the camera. I worried if we even got the shot but had no choice but to leave.

All the images are striking, colorful, and capture a genuine joy both ladies brought to the day. Andrea may have spoken Ewok, but he knocked this one down the runway.

Back in New York, I saw Kat and Beth at a TV function and felt like a star myself: in front of everyone, they gave me giant hugs and expressed their appreciation and excitement.

"You must be important," said 2 Broke Girls executive producer Michael Patrick King.

In that moment, I was.

Q&A WITH SOPHIA PAULMIER

Sophia: I imagine Kat and Beth to be genuine and funny. Like two people you'd want to be stuck on an elevator with.

Jeremy: Genuine, yes. Beth is funny and sweet. I didn't get to talk or bond with Kat much.

S: There's a question I use with actors: Were they shy or were they just tired of trying? Would you say Kat's shy or just tired of trying?

J: It was an all-night flight from LA to Milan; I was surprised Beth was so bubbly. The next day they were both very kind. I used to assume the best but after ten years with celebrities I assume the worst, and if they're nice you're pleasantly surprised.

S: Just out of curiosity, how often did clothing pieces not fit male talent in you ten years of photoshoots with the magazine?

J: Once. A very large actor from *Guiding Light*. Built like a football player. Men are easy—it's not hard to see something won't fit. Women have breasts, which adds another factor to sizing.

S: *Shopping with the 2 Broke Girls, give me details! Did they both go crazy in Dolce and Gabbana? Did they have their own personal likings or did one pick out an outfit the other wanted? And more importantly, how many outfits and pairs of shoes did they go home with?*

J: This was fourteen years ago, so I don't remember what they got, but it's a lot. The bill, I do remember. I will say it was well deserved because they crushed the shoot. Beth posted the cover to Instagram all these years later.

S: *Do you think the fashion industry would be different on paper if editors in chief took their talent shopping and let them keep their outfits instead of using pre-selected sample sizes? And what effect do you think it would have on the public?*

J: It's just not technically feasible. Designers need editorial in magazines at the same time the collections hit stores, which requires samples to use in advance. They've tried that see-on-the-carpet, buy-now strategy and it doesn't work.

S: *Did you have any favorite meals at the Conventino delle Cappuccine?*

J: Anything with bread and cheese, which is basically everything!

CHAPTER 3

························★························

"Non!"

NCIS actress Pauley Perrette recreates Edgar Degas' "Dancer in Front of a Window" in the Michelin-star restaurant at the Hotel Plaza Athénée. Photo by Cliff Lipson, provided by CCG Ventures, Inc.

"He iz in ze swamp with ze alligators," said the French PR contact, vetting celebrities we could shoot at the Hôtel Plaza Athénée Paris.

Specifically, she was referring to Jeff Probst, the host of *Survivor*. I was pitching stars we could bring for a big fashion spread/cover, and Jeff was one of the talents we hadn't shot. Not intentionally. The filming of that series is brutal, and what promo time he had needed to be prioritized and not for us (read: barrel, bottom).

I was also glued to a one-week window—between pret-aporter and a big trade show—where we could shoot at the property, a super chic hotel in the 8th arrondissement of Paris on the famous shopping destination Avenue Montaigne. Its historic connection to Christian Dior, views of the Eiffel Tower, chic Louis XVI design, Michelin-star restaurant, spacious rooms and suites, proximity to Paris's best shopping, and a quintessentially French staff explain its $1,254-per-night room rate.

I had been lobbying its PR rep, Isabelle Maurin, since visiting four years prior. Doing a photo shoot there was always a dream.

Every magazine has a "must" list—the stars you want for the cover. Probst was high up, as was Billy Petersen from *CSI*, Mark Harmon from *NCIS*, Jennifer Love Hewitt from *Ghost Whisperer*, and Simon Baker from *The Mentalist*. The hottest network TV talent at the time was NPH—Neil Patrick Harris, the former child star (*Doogie Howser*) who saw fame again as Barney Stinson on *How I Met Your Mother*. We'd just traveled with Neil to Italy the previous year, and the experience put him at the top of our list.

The Plaza Athénée liked him too and agreed to host our shoot. But Neil got a huge offer to host a primetime awards ceremony, and it conflicted with our dates.

I was heartbroken: not only does he take a good photo, he's also friendly and funny. I was determined not to lose this window and instead pitched a new list of stars to shoot at the hotel.

Non. Non. Non. Non. Non.

Isabelle has incredible panache (I call her "My Flawless Friend") and brings smarts and sophistication to everything she does. She's fiercely protective of the hotel's brand and circumspect with every offer. There's a reason why so many magazines, beauty and fashion brands, and movies and TV shows want to feature the Plaza Athénée: they rarely allow it and approve very few (*The Devil Wears Prada*, *Sex and the City*, and *Emily in Paris*).

I almost got the OK on Jeff, who didn't even know we were pitching him. My idea was something very sleek and timeless—007 meets the Rat Pack. Tuxedos, martinis, big-band music, the works. "Survivor" was the opposite, which is the whole idea. It's unexpected.

Isabelle couldn't risk it, which is understandable. We hadn't shot there yet, so we did not have much of a working relationship.

Convinced I was going to lose this very rare opportunity, I reached for the impossible: Pauley Perrette from *NCIS*, where she played punk lab rat Abby. I wanted her as soon as we started the magazine, but the word was she didn't like to travel. Our shoots had become more international, and Pauley wasn't keen to fly that far. Or so we heard.

I didn't care. Somehow, I sold Isabelle on shooting her throughout the hotel despite her misgivings about the punk/tattoo look. We just had to make it glamorous and reflect the hotel as such.

In this type of situation, many magazines opt to do a standard fashion shoot, photographing celebrities standing in designer wear throughout a location. It's about the clothes, after all.

We were still explaining *what we* were about. I needed something bigger.

I also needed Pauley. She was in New York attending fashion week with two friends—designer/artist Darren Greenblatt and educator Sam Hunt—and got the offer at the perfect moment. Her friends convinced her to go.

Celebrity behavior rarely surprises you, but this one did: Pauley offered to fly coach if she could bring Darren and Sam. She could have brought anyone, but I was shocked at the modesty of the request.

Hotel and star in hand, and AA as our travel partner, I now needed a theme/storyline behind the photos that was a double taker. *Vanity Fair* editor Graydon Carter calls it "the nudge factor"—when what you've read has you nudging the person next to you.

I decided to pay homage to Paris and French culture through the eyes of the last person you'd expect considering her character and show. The idea was to recreate French impressionist paintings with Pauley dressed as the subject. But for this I'd need a wardrobe stylist who could bring the paintings to life with clothing that matched, and with a modern twist. It's not an easy ask, but I knew who to call: The Jackal. It's a silly name we gave her because she could accomplish the impossible, no matter the ask.

"Jackal, get me a frog with side pockets, unicorn, red muffin, and next week's newspaper by 7:00 a.m."

The Jackal is a jack of many trades—fashion, style, marketing, branding—but it is her exquisite eye that distinguishes her in a profession dominated by fake-it-till-you-make-its. She never had to. She can put together an outfit in her sleep, and regularly run circles around her competitors.

She and I began to develop the story and pick paintings. We chose nine, including "Lise with a Parasol" by Pierre-Auguste Renoir (1867), "A Bar at the Folies-Bergère" by Édouard Manet (1882), "Young Woman in Grey Reclining" by Berthe Morisot (1879), "Dancer in Front of a Window" by Edgar Degas (circa 1874–77), and "Woman on a Staircase" by Renoir (1876), and a few others. Each were famous, had French history, and more importantly, could be recreated with the right wardrobe and accessories. We also matched each painting to a location at the hotel that could be photographed in similar style.

Everyone loved the concept—including Pauley and the hotel—and I felt I had crossed the last hurdle.

HAHAHAHAHAHAHA.

The first issue arose at the last minute: all Pauley's identification had been lost. As in, no photo ID to travel. This is one you can't charm your way out of.

Once again, I thought I'd lost the shoot on the one-yard line. We called every rush service, but the timeline was too close.

That's where desperation meets ingenuity; Pauley had the highest Q rating—a score that measures someone's likeness and recognizability—on television, and *NCIS* was number one in viewership. I was willing to bet *someone* at the US State Department was a fan. I called our parent company's Washington, DC, office and asked if we knew anyone in the government who could rush a passport for Pauley in two days. Oh, and she has no ID to prove who she is. Our DC guy was intrigued by the challenge and agreed to give it a shot. A few hours later, he called back with news: someone at the State Department *was* a huge fan.

Pauley was invited to go to a federal government building in Los Angeles the next morning to get a new passport, but there was another hitch—she needed to bring her own photo, and it had to be passport-appropriate (read: boring). Pauley didn't have time, so we raided our photo archive for something to submit. Each one got nixed (No exposed shoulders! No smiling! You're too pretty!) until we Photoshopped her out of a cast photo and put her in front of a white background.

She got the passport the next day.

I made a habit of arriving a day early to every shoot. This gives me time to go over logistics—room assignments, locations to shoot, obstacles—and meet the hotel reps. I'd met Isabelle several times before, and this was our first production together. We had dinner my first night and struck up a friendship that lasts to this day.

Everything was going according to plan—until it wasn't. Mother Nature decided to throw a snit with a huge rain and windstorm in Paris: the day Pauley was due to arrive. I awoke early that morning to find the hotel boarding up one of the entrances. I had no idea it was that serious and had breakfast in the hotel's fancy restaurant, Alain Ducasse au Plaza Athénée. A bowl of cocoa crisps, a Diet Coke, and its signature red brioche muffin with strawberry jam inside cost seventy-eight euros.

As I ate the world's most expensive bowl of kiddie cereal under crystal chandeliers, I got another SOS message: Pauley's flight had been diverted to Belgium, and there were no connections due to the weather. Nor were there trains because Europeans like to strike, and this was one of those times. They often announce such occasions because they happen so often (I'm of the mind they should announce when they *are* working). My only option was a van, for €800, which at that time was $1 million USD. I had five minutes to decide and said do it.

I would have sent the US Coast Guard.

As they made it to Paris, I began making final checks on our schedule and plans. A lot of celebrities require what's known as a "rider"—a list of demands ("No green M&Ms!") you are required to cater to, but Pauley hadn't given us one. This struck me as odd, so I called the show's publicist to confirm. It was true: she had no absurd requests. But maybe, as a gesture of goodwill, it was suggested we leave her favorite beverage—Bud Select in the black glass bottle—to chill out with her friends after an arduous journey.

I was in love with her already. Unfortunately, the hotel did not have Bud Select and didn't even know where to look.

After all she'd done for us already—flying, flying coach, going to the passport office, being diverted to Belgium—I was determined to do one thing nice for her.

The Plaza Athénée concierge was nonplussed with my request.

"Non. Zis iz not poz-ze-bel," the concierge said, befuddled why I was even asking.

Braving torrential wind gusts, I searched myself, walking up and down the Champs until I found several six packs in the grocery side of a Target-like store called Monoprix. I carried them back to the hotel and soon met Pauley, Darren, and Sam, who were incredibly warm and kind considering their journey. I felt an instant bond with all of them.

The last—and most important—part of the next day's shoot was secure, so I turned my concentration to signing off on the schedule, wardrobe, and setting. The Jackal and her trusted sidekick nailed the styling. How they were able to find pieces to recreate wardrobes from the 1800s astounds me to this day.

Everything was set except one thing: I'd slipped a new painting, "The Tea" by Mary Cassatt, into the schedule at the last minute, and it required a child to join Pauley for tea. We wanted everything to match exquisitely, and this meant getting a ten-year-old blonde girl in a white dress and stockings.

Try finding a child model in Paris during a hurricane. On a Sunday.

The situation reached comical levels when we got locked out of our official server because our company flagged "child model" in e-mail requests we sent to agencies. Instead, we used our personal addresses, which only made it look sketchier.

"Bonjour! We are looking for blonde ten-year-olds in white stockings at our hotel tomorrow, and we'll pay you in cash."

This is where the Plaza Athénée could help us. The concierge suddenly got a sense of humor as we asked if they could help us out. We assured him it was legit, and the child model was only for a photo shoot.

"Take her to discotheque, I do not care," he said, jokingly. He contacted a big modeling agency and connected us to the right representatives.

Shoot day turned into something magical. The Jackal had turned Pauley into a painter's muse—tutus, hats, parasols, ballet slippers, ball gowns—and photographer Cliff Lipson brought a classic, rarefied lens to the images.

The entire package still represents one of the proudest pieces I helped create. When an idea comes to life, it's the best feeling in the world. When it fails, it blows up in your face.

I prefer the first kind.

NCIS actress Pauley Perrette poses atop the Hotel Plaza Athénée Paris with author Jeremy Murphy. Photo courtesy of Jeremy Murphy.

Q&A WITH SOPHIA PAULMIER

Sophia: Pauley had no photo ID. What do you mean?

Jeremy: Having misplaced my driver's license many times and not being able to find my Passport, I identified with the predicament. I didn't ask her how; that was none of my business.

S: So Pauley's picture on her passport was a publicity photo from NCIS?

J: Yes! Photoshopped in our office! This was fourteen years ago, so it's by now expired. Personally, I got a Demarchelier photo onto *my* last one, which was flattering. Not so much the new one. I look like a Halloween pumpkin who spent the holiday drinking.

S: Is this how celebrities get their licenses and passports? They don't go to get a picture taken, they have a professional picture sent.

J: I think this was a unique situation, and possibly illegal. Government-issued IDs don't normally invite creative contributions.

S: The concept of reenacting classic paintings is so interesting. You found a different way to capture Pauley.

J: I was surprised she hadn't done a big, glamorous photo shoot already. She's incredibly attractive, has amazing skin, and a dancer's physique. She can wear anything. It gave us license to do something really over-the-top because there were really no restrictions; she was never going to take a bad photo. And I really liked contrasting her character's punk/rocker look with something opposite. That's where the "Goth, Interrupted" cover line came from.

S: *The cover is very clever, but different from the concept.*

J: That came at the last minute. The French impressionist theme needed too much context to explain for a cover, which requires something easily explained and the subject identifiable. We had Pauley stand against a black seamless backdrop, and our crew surrounded her with the beauty tools. One of the hands is mine.

S: *Well, aren't you handy.*

J: It came out better than I thought! Spontaneous ideas don't always work but this one did. It was one of our most successful issues.

S: *You also write affectionally about Pauley's friends, Darren, and Sam.*

J: Yes! They've become lifelong friends. So many gifts came from that experience. We got to shoot at the Hotel Plaza Athénée for the first time. I got to work with Pauley. The concept came together beautifully, and I have incredible relationships with many of the people with us. Darren even did the illustrations in my last book!

CHAPTER 4

······★······

Ink-sanity

The articles were handwritten.

The paper was from a copy machine.

The pages were stapled together on the top left corner.

Fan Club was as low budget as you could get, but its salty prose and curious mix of stories wound harbinger the future.

Mine, at least.

It's a surprise to no one that I became a magazine editor. I've served that role since I was ten years old, writing searing and salty opinions about TV, movies, music, celebrities, and even politics in my own magazines. On days off, I'd go with my mom to her workplace and hog the Xerox machine, making copies I shamelessly hawked at school for a dollar. I even sold advertising, riding my bicycle up and down Sample Road in bland Coral Springs, Florida, looking for businesses to buy space. To my amazement, several did.

Where I got this moxie, I have no clue. I was a fat, middle-class kid in the suburbs, who somehow wrote with an authoritative voice as a teenager. I didn't hide behind "I feel" and "in my opinion"; I jumped in front of them shouting, "Booooo!"

Sinead O'Connor? "Raging lunatic."

Phil Collins? "King of Bland."

Jean-Claude Van Damm? "The versatility of a grasshopper."

Kathy Lee Gifford? "Nauseating and sends me into convulsions whenever I have the misfortune of watching her."

New Kids on the Block? "1991 was the year America gave them the finger. Their ballads are about as valid as an Elvis imposter at the Holiday Inn."

I gradually moved on to a typewriter (Smith Corona) and then an Apple IIc. *Fan Club* became *Entertainment 2000*, and I began interviewing actual celebrities. I'd call networks, film studios, record labels, and publicists from our home line, and then I'd hide the Southern Bell phone bill from my mom. Statements for $300 were not unusual.

I never made money doing the magazine, and why would I? It was a learning experience, and a way to get cozy with my favorite actors from *Santa Barbara*, the NBC soap that became my addiction in middle and high school. I convinced its legendary PR woman, Mary Andersen, that I was fun, and she became a mentor to me at only fifteen years old. She even introduced me to Marcy Walker, the blonde goddess who played long-suffering heroine Eden Capwell Castillo (one half of '80s supercouple Cruz and Eden). I thought I had a crush on Marcy, but I was as gay as Christmas. It wasn't hard to notice; I once called in absent from high school because Cruz and Eden were getting married. Um, hello? National holiday!

High school pretty much sucked because I was bored, and *Santa Barbara* was much more compelling than anything classes could teach me. Also, I had to "work" (i.e., pay my keep), which meant menial jobs bagging groceries at Publix and working the "electronics department" at Target as the "floor manager."

All these jobs were terrible because I was terrible at them. And none were learning experiences; getting four dollars an hour is slave labor. If you didn't tip us bag boys, your bread or eggs were smushed by the heavier milk carton. Oops. At Target, I got fired for getting saucy with a couple from a nearby trailer park. "Can you tell me what the difference between a 2-head and 4-head VCR is?" asked the man in trendy jean shorts, mustache, and chewing tobacco. Not impressed, I responded in my snootiest cadence, "One has two and one has four." The store manager saw it with his own eyes and fired me on the spot.

While attending college at Florida Atlantic University in Boca Raton, Florida, I got a job answering phones at the local Marriott hotel. They stuffed me and a crazy woman in a closet-sized office to answer calls coming through the switchboard, and hundreds came in by the hour, mostly from angry wives looking for their husbands. I worked full time while attending college, including weekends, which really pissed me off. One Sunday, I was put on the morning shift—6:00 a.m. to 3:00 p.m.—and began what I thought would be a leisurely day with my *Times* crossword, bagel, and Diet Coke. Sundays were typically easy, but this day must have been "catch-a-cheating-hubby day" because the switchboard lit up and wouldn't stop.

Color me annoyed. The calls were hostile, and I was not keen to be caught in the middle of divorce court. Instead, I turned the entire phone system off and went back to my crossword puzzle. An hour later, emergency response vehicles arrived because people couldn't get through and thought the worst. I got fired that morning.

Studying at FAU was invaluable, and this was twenty-five years before it became a big-league state university. Still, I had an itch to be a screenwriter and looked west. As in, West Coast. I dropped out after the first semester to move to Los Angeles, except I was overweight, had bad skin, and had never lived away from home.

Hollywood, here I come!

I lived in a quasi-garage in the back of a house rented by two wonderful lesbians in San Pedro, which is very, very far from Los Angeles. One of the women, Kimberley Ferren, became a mentor to me and graciously got me a job with her PR company, which was promoting a record company, including its gangsta rappers. As the whitest person on the planet, I was a natural to join this effort. I remember one of the rappers was shot in a drive-by, which we publicized with a news alert. This just in!

Los Angeles—the city—was a two-hour commute each way, which got very old very soon. This was 1994, and I still know the lyrics to almost any song from that year because I spent so much time in my stylish Ford Tempo; I can still sing Salt-N-Pepa's "Shoop" on cue. The PR thing ended in the summer, and I began doing temp work, including working as a receptionist entering data for a medical insurance company; I'm fairly certain I fucked up their entire system and may have bankrupted a hospital. At an energy company, I manned the switchboards and randomly broke into a heavy Irish accent anytime someone called for Molly Donnelly.

This was the summer of O. J. Simpson decapitating Nicole Brown and Ron Goldman. The city was transfixed, as was I. *Santa Barbara* had recently been cancelled, and I needed a new soap opera fix; boy did we get one.

I became obsessed with the investigation and his upcoming trial, and my father was worried I'd try to get on the jury. He bribed me with a new car to go back to college. I returned to Florida in exchange for a year-old Ford Mustang.

Back at FAU, I immersed myself into the campus newspaper. There, I had a column where I'd bitch about pretty much anything: pop culture, politics, sports, news events. It was opinionated and sassy and got me in doo-doo. I took a swipe at a local weatherman, who I called Bob "No Talent" Weaver. I thought it was funny until learning the editor in chief of our paper was his son. Oops. You'd think that would have taught me my lesson.

I also began doing freelance writing work, including for a new glossy magazine called *Fashion Spectrum*. One of my professors recommended me, and at nineteen years old, I was assigned a big story on the "nexus" between Hollywood and fashion. It sounded easy until I heard "the get"—it needed a quote from a famous designer.

"No problem," I assured the assigning editor, not knowing any. Coincidentally, I'd read Isaac Mizrahi, the brilliant couturier featured in the iconic documentary *Unzipped*, was going to be in Bal Harbour—a ritzy enclave near Miami—to launch a new product line. I stood in line, and when face-to-face pulled out a tape recorder and got the money quote. It made the story and got me my first byline. Twenty-five years later, I met Isaac again and thanked him profusely. He was genuinely touched and gave me a warm hug.

There's no money in college newspapers, which required me to get a "real" job at Blockbuster Video, where I manned the "rewind" desk for tapes that didn't get rewound (sorry), waived fees on videos returned late (you're welcome), and restocked shelves. This necessitated the painful task of reading the cassette and then finding its box to slip behind. I didn't care to do this either, so if you found *Barney* behind *Basic Instinct*, that's on me. But I comped your late fees so let's call it even.

I moved into an apartment with three friends, but in our college days, we were living off Monopoly "winnings" at McDonalds and student loans, which I spent recklessly around the glossy shopping center Mizner Park in Boca Raton. Wagu burgers at Max's Grille were an *entirely* reasonable purchase for someone making fifty dollars a week writing pissy movie reviews. Living with three—sometimes four—other dudes was fun and didn't exactly inspire going to class. I wound up missing most of the 2005-2006 semesters, and it got worse: I became editor in chief of the college newspaper, and also continued my snotty Opinion column "Murphy's Law," which made class attendance even more rare.

How this led to NBC News befuddles me, but I was selected to participate in its Washington, DC, internship program for the 1997 fall semester. I'd be stationed on the third floor in the "Dateline NBC" bureau, which anchor Stone Phillips might describe as a "recipe for disaster." The politics and machinations made *Game of Thrones* look like *Mr. Roger's Neighborhood*.

My first day was a Tuesday—three days after Princess Diana died—and half the bureau was empty. They'd gone to Paris and London to cover the story, and I spent that week logging video tapes with time codes, researching for producers, and thinking of ideas for stories.

I didn't know anyone in DC, and the other interns were total randoms who could bore paint off the walls. Our "boss" was a militant, unfriendly, and way-too-serious Asian woman who was distracted—rightly so—with an investigation into Sears and if they were selling used car batteries. The only person I *did* like was a desk assistant named Jameela Donaldson, who was smart, talented, and funny. We had the same sense of humor and rolled our eyes at the same people. Writing this book reminded me how much I enjoyed *our* laughs, but generally I don't look back at the time there with fondness, and it did nothing to help my career.

The internship was also unpaid, so I worked nights in the Christmas department at Neiman Marcus, where well-coiffed ambassador wives would scowl at me for selling ornaments in October. As if it was my choice. The managers made the mistake of putting delicious peanut butter brittle near my cash register, and as soon as the security camera shifted direction, I ate the entire plate—every night. I also learned how to talk to rich, horrible people. "I know, Deidre, you can never trust the help." Meanwhile, I was behind a register wearing a name tag and making eight dollars an hour. *Helping.*

The irony was I could dress casually at NBC but had to go home, comb my hair, and put on a suit and tie for Neiman Marcus.

When I returned to Boca Raton, I went straight to the *Boca Raton News*, the city's small daily paper owned by Knight Ridder, the most prestigious newspaper owner in America, arguably the world; a small daily paper didn't fit a portfolio that included the *Miami Herald*, *Philadelphia Inquirer*, and the *San Jose Mercury News*, which was a harbinger of what was to come. It was now late 1997, and the managing editor of the *Boca Raton News* had become a tough-but-maternal woman named Phyllis. When I initially applied, I met her at the front desk of the newsroom and handed her what I thought was a well-written cover letter. She took one look, then handed it back.

"Come back when you're ready," she said, dismissively.

I'd spelled her name wrong. And I was applying to be a copy editor. D'oh!

I reapplied and this time got her name correct.

Phyllis had an endearing, though scary, habit of using the word "fool" after sentences.

"Who do you think you are, fool?"

"Why are you so late, fool?"

On Sundays, she wore a black sweater with a graphic of a lightning bolt and the words: "If Phyllis isn't happy, ain't no one happy."

Early in the job, I experienced trial by fire: I worked the night desk—editing copy and designing the A section of the next day's newspaper—and shit was about to get real. The Bill Clinton/Monica Lewinsky story broke, and I was responsible for placing the wire stories. At this point, we had four sources of national and global news: the Associated Press (AP), the *New York Times* (*NYT*), *Los Angeles Times-Washington Post* (what we called LAT-WOP), and Knight Ridder/Tribune (KRT). You had to check all four and choose the best copy.

That day, the biggest story since Watergate was breaking, and so was I. The AP, in particular, took twenty years off my life; they were sending and killing stories throughout the night, each with lurid, farcical accusations that became true. Every time we placed copy in the layout, we'd get a notice it was bad, and a new version was coming. The AP—a consortium of news organizations—is largely looked at as the most fair, reputable news source. Not exactly sexy, but meat and potatoes. When they were hearing crazy shit, and killing said shit, you knew shit was real.

Working the night shift was grueling because you never knew when you could leave. After sending the final proofs to be plated, you had to walk to the presses and stand at the end to inspect the first edition in case you'd gotten anything wrong. This could go to 1:00 a.m., or later.

Weeks later, I got my first writing assignment—a thrilling flower shower in the "Pink Plaza" across the street—and returned to the newsroom, proud to have gotten exhilarating quotes from locals enjoying the petals. But Phyllis saw I'd relied on my tape recorder and chewed me out.

"What if that didn't work, fool?"

She gradually warmed up and began to find something to like about me, but I was a fuckup even back then. I got a few last names wrong in obits—the worst offense—and once made up clues for the Daily Jumble, which is a scrambled word game that "delivers brain-teasing enjoyment." Not when I was doing it. In my defense, we were on deadline, and Netscape, where we downloaded the content, was slow as fuck. So I just made shit up. The next morning, the switchboard lit up with seniors in full rage.

But I met friends I'd keep for life—Kim Rutledge, George Sterling, Jon Boho—and had a lot of fun.

Until I didn't.

Knight Ridder had sold the paper to a circus clown private equity company masquerading as a news organization. Slowly, they began selling off the assets—real estate, printing presses, equipment—which was their entire "raison d'être." The CEO of the company had given his inexperienced brother a plum position as publisher, and he began to milk what was left to live a luxurious life. Our overtime was being cut, but he'd buy $5,000 tables at charity galas to bring his friends. We started calling him Mickey Mouse.

The death knell came when a rotating list of editors in chief got worse and worse. Legendary newsman John Futch had been replaced by a Burl Ives–type clone who hid in his office most of his tenure. I never really had a problem with him because he was in hiding, but every now and then, he would emerge to bless shitty work. "Good idea, good idea," he'd mumble about the worst ideas, including a "redesign" of the paper done by someone who operated the presses. The editor left—or did he? We wouldn't have really noticed—and a new man came to run the newsroom. This guy had a face you just wanted to punch. I can't remember where he came from, but he brought patronizing games and contests, as if we were a newsroom full of country rubes interested in gift cards to Applebee's; Boca Raton didn't even have one of those. His enthusiasm was met with a collective sneer, mainly because he was an idiot. He and Mickey Mouse went on to purchase the paper, which had a dwindling circulation, no assets, and fleeing advertisers.

Once Phyllis and my other friends began to leave, I followed.

I went back to Knight Ridder and its Florida west coast paper, the *Bradenton Herald*, which was in a fierce circulation war with the neighboring *Sarasota Herald-Tribune*, owned by the New York Times Company. Bradenton is a deeply conservative community on the "Gulf Coast," and not at all fake-glamorous like Boca Raton, where disgraced CEOs move after they've raided their employee pensions.

I was hired as a feature writer by a guy named John Bicknell, who was friendly, cerebral, curious, incredibly talented, and fought for his writers. He shielded me from his number two, an assistant editor I'd rather not name. She was friendly, but our styles didn't match. She didn't get my bitchy, urbane humor. I didn't get her perm.

The editor in chief was a whirlwind named Joan Krauter, who was a star in the Knight Ridder firmament. They plucked her out of the *Fort Worth Star-Telegram* to shake up the *Herald*, and that she did. This once-sleepy paper had suddenly become a bustling news organization that covered politics, crime, education, and business aggressively. The only problem was she didn't give a shit about the features section. Joan was a hard-charging news woman, and we were the fluffy-fluff balls.

And then came Mac Tully, another superstar in the Knight Ridder hierarchy. Mac also decamped from Texas, and now as publisher, he gave the *Herald* cojones. He was outgoing, friendly, and smart, but you didn't dare cross him because he'd win. Mac had a deft hand with the community and could glad-hand with the best of them, but he also had big-city smarts and a sophistication that was missing. His wife was one of my favorites because she was very cosmopolitan and not at all pleased to be in cow town. They both noticed my writing had bite—I wasn't afraid to throw in bon mots, thinly veiled insults, and clever word plays.

Mac ordered the features department to create a "People" section that would cover the area's social engagements. But not a society section: a first-person account of the various galas, soirees, and other events throughout the community. To my surprise and horror, I was selected to lead this charge. I would be the voice of this section.

My column, "Scene & Heard," was a bitch-slap to the pretentious nonprofits spending thousands of dollars on their fundraising balls and a cheerleader for scrappy charities trying to raise attention for worthy causes. I created my own "Cosmic Family" with local favorites, including "My New Best Friend" Marie Dietrich, who was number two at the Manatee County Chamber of Commerce. She was joined by "Cosmic Mother" Dottie McCarthy, the town eccentric who lived in a giant mansion in the good part of Bradenton. Dottie kept a dead frog in the glove compartment of her Jaguar that she'd use to get out of traffic tickets. "Officer, it just jumped out and scared me to death!" Joining the clan was an editor who worked the *Herald* features desk, Jana Smedley. I dubbed her the "Cosmic Soul Sister."

My column established local heroes and villains, including Nick Bollettieri. I dubbed the famed tennis coach "No Show" because he had a habit of signing up for community events and not being there. Very classy.

Every weekend, I hopped from event to event with a rotating cast of plus-ones: Jana; Nicole Sneed, a copy editor; Rob Coon, another copy editor; Rod Harmon, the paper's witty music writer, and Roger Moore, the caustic, brilliant movie critic who appreciated my writing. There was also a ditzy woman named Bobbie, who sat next to me. She used to say working with me was like taking your kid to work, and I'd say I'd been "discom-Bobbielated" listening to her.

Joanne Mamenta Bjordahl became editor of the department once John Bicknell left, and she brought her own brand of smarts and sass, as well as heart. The features meetings ran notoriously long, so she made us stand up at the next one; it lasted fifteen minutes. She also had us take the Myers-Briggs test, which identifies different psychological preferences and how people perceive the world. I got that off Google so let me summarize: it's a personality quiz that reveals future leaders, basket cases, and psychos, measuring people using specific criteria. I'm an E (Extravert), N (Intuitive), F (Feeling), and J (Judging). Fortunately, there were no sociopaths on our staff.

While jumping from gala to gala, I also had to write feature stories, which was taxing and a total snore. We had a cheesy section called "Neighbors," which profiled clubs and groups throughout the community. A year in, I exhausted the supply and began to consider profiling AA meetings. I was also assigned an "investigation" to discover which Bradenton pizzeria had the best slices; this was admittedly a low bar, but I went ahead and ordered from five establishments and rated each one. Several of them were shitty, and I said so in my breaking news report. Editor in Chief Joan did not want to upset any local businesses and watered it down so everyone came out greasy.

By day, I was a hard-charging features writer out to expose tea parties and garden clubs; by night, I was a low-rent society columnist with an ill-fitting suit, cherubic face, and clueless gaze. I also still looked twelve, which explains why one guest handed me his car keys thinking I was the valet.

Bradenton was the red-headed stepchild to neighboring Sarasota, which was glossy, glitzy, and glamorous. The truth, though, was that the family wealth in Manatee County—which included Bradenton, Palmetto, Anna Maria Island, and Holmes Beach—could buy and sell Sarasota tenfold. It just didn't look it. And it didn't help that the previous mayor spoke like an extra from *Deliverance*.

Ironic, then, that my time there taught me sophistication. Sean Murphy and Susan Timmins from The Beach Bistro, and now the area's hottest bar, The Doctor's Office, exposed me to Michelin three-star-quality food and wine. Their restaurant was the number one establishment in Florida, and they would invite me to private dinners where Sean insisted I taste everything before telling me what it was. This surprises people to this day because in normal circumstances—when not eating at a three Michelin star restaurant—I tend to eat very basic foods: pasta, steak, burgers, salmon, sandwiches. But throw a tasting menu at me and I'll devour everything.

Jeremy Murphy with Sean Murphy, right, who owns and runs The Beach Bistro on Anna Maria Island. Photo courtesy of the James W. Murphy Photo Collection.

I tried to infuse my column with culture and hit pay dirt when a Sarasota library invited me to a book signing by Dunne, who wowed the crowd with stories, gossip, and his honest, candid history. Dominick was incredibly gracious when I interviewed him and even posed for a picture—this was pre-selfie age—which hangs on my wall today. In the background is a very confused woman wondering why some young fatty is going goo-goo-ga-ga over an old man. Two weeks later, I was in my luxury cubicle when the mail drop came—a personal letter from Dominick thanking me for my wonderful column. A reader had cut out my story about the signing and sent it to him. I could not believe how kind and thoughtful the gesture I was. I also kept the envelope; you'll understand why in a minute.

The "People" section gave me the first taste of being noticed. It became a popular part of the paper and created much buzz about town. But it was Bradenton; it's not like I could use that to get a table at Balthazar. I began to itch for something bigger and fell out of love with the job. Joanne left and the assistant editor I didn't mesh with began to edit my column heavy-handed. And I didn't have the confidence to make it an issue. I just sulked and grew bitter. Getting anything in that was clever became that much harder, but I was not going to settle for just listing who attended tea parties.

I began applying for other positions, to no avail. Until *Mediaweek* magazine in New York came a-calling. I'd added a local TV column to my work at the *Herald* and taught myself how local media worked: TV and radio stations, newspapers, radio, cable. I flew up to New York for the interview and got the job offer at lunch with the editor Bill Gloede and his number two Brian Moran—for $37,000 a year.

Woo-hoo! I thought I'd won the lottery.

On my first day, as I took the elevator, an executive looked at me. I was beaming with excitement.

"First day?" he asked.

Uh-huh.

"Three things, kid. First, it's all about your shoes," he said, looking down at my sad Hush Puppies. "Second and third: lunch in the Grill Room, dinner in the Pool Room."

He was talking about the Four Seasons *restaurant*, not hotel.

My beat was local media. For the *entire country*. I had to teach myself the terrain of every major market, especially the top ten. At that time, it was (1) New York, (2) LA, (3) Chicago, (4) Philadelphia, (5) San Francisco, (6) Dallas, (7) Boston, (8) Washington, DC, (9) Atlanta, and (10) Houston. I found contacts at every entity and called them daily for news and gossip. It was grueling, and the staff was not friendly at first. After all, I was twenty-five and looked twelve, and had a lot of energy and excitement. They were industry veterans not impressed with my eagerness. I learned later they called me "The Beaver." I was also excluded from lunches.

Gradually, I earned their respect (I think). Bill Gloede was a force to be reckoned with. He had a laugh that could disarm Harrison Ford. Bill also was famous for meeting ad buyers on Friday nights at a midtown steakhouse called Ben Benson's, where he got the best scoops. Brian Moran was always kind, and his managing editor, Michael Burgi, began to warm up to me; in truth, he was the friendliest from the get-go, but I still had to prove myself. Burgi showed me tough love and made me a better writer.

John Consoli was *Mediaweek*'s network TV guy and regularly got the big story. He was a throwback to newsrooms of old: cynical, sarcastic, a great BS detector, and had little patience for spin. Alicia Mundy was the DC "bureau chief," covering the machinations of media regulation in the capital for a trade magazine that didn't have a bureau. She got incredible exclusives and had deep contacts in town. At first, I thought she was a snob because she didn't give me the time of day; I came to realize she was just hard to impress. Thankfully, I did eventually. My favorite became Katy Bachman, who was also in DC. Katy knew the ins and outs of Washington and was more industrious; she liked the nitty gritty and turned out copy in record speed. We became buds, and I still saw her after I left. She's now retired and living her best life with her husband, Tom, who I follow on Facebook.

Most endearing was Lisa Granatstein, who covered magazines. Lisa had the cubicle next to me, and I enjoyed hearing her chew out stupid publicists calling when she was on deadline. Her reporting gave *Mediaweek* the best coverage of the publishing business, but she was also very experienced and I felt inferior. My normal disarming humor did not disarm. We were cubicle mates without being mates, which was odd for someone outgoing like me. I wanted to at least be friendly, so I found an opening: she was a fan of The Velvet Underground, the '60s–'70s post-punk/alternative/rock band fronted by Lou Reed. They were championed by Andy Warhol and developed an incredible underground following. It just so happened the drummer, Moe Tucker, is a childhood friend of my mother's. Admittedly, I didn't like or understand the music. Once, backstage at a concert, I was introduced to Lou Reed but looked at the wrong person. He was a fucking asshole about it. I begged my mom to ask Moe for a signed copy of their famous album, *The Velvet Underground & Nico*, made more famous by the illustration of a banana on its cover by Warhol himself. I gifted the autographed album to Lisa, who recognized my attempt to be friendly. Lisa has gone on to become the chief content officer of *Adweek*, which absorbed *Mediaweek*.

Developing contacts in the local media markets was slow going at first, but after a few months, I began to hit my stride. My all-time favorite contact was Kim Sartori (now Kahl), who was a junior publicist at WBZ-TV, the Boston CBS station. Kim was my age and just as wet behind the ears. We were both starting our careers, and when she visited New York, I took her to lunch and brought a bag filled with thoughtful gifts—Zagat guide, New York City map, Yankees hat (I don't think she liked that much). We clicked instantly because we had the same sense of humor, and she became a great resource in understanding the craziness coming out of WBZ, the perennially last-place TV station in Boston even though it had *Survivor*, *CSI*, and other hits as lead-ins.

At the same time, I was beginning to adjust to life in New York and realizing $37,000 a year is near poverty. My take home was $2,000 a month, which sounds like a good sum, but not when your rent is $1,200, student loans are $200, credit cards are $400, subway card is $90, and then there's the cost of, I don't know, *eating*? I was miserable and began wondering why I'd left the lazy life in Bradenton and being a big-shot local. Now, I was "The Beaver on a Budget."

I lived on Cedar Street in downtown Manhattan and shared an apartment with Paul Krasinski, who became a very good friend, although hanging out with him is weird because he is six foot nine and I'm five foot seven. We once walked to the movies to see *How the Grinch Stole Christmas* and looked like the poster from the movie *Twins*. Him, Schwarzenegger; me, DeVito. Not exactly a confidence-builder. Paul's brother is movie star John Krasinski, who'd just graduated from Brown University. He wanted to be an actor then but began bartending and doing odd jobs. He stayed in our apartment more than once, usually sleeping on the couch. John was incredibly nice and funny and had out-sized charisma. *The Office* was on the horizon.

New York was very tough that year, but I found some allowances. I dug up the envelope from Dominick Dunne's letter, which included his home address, and sent him a letter of my own alerting him I was in New York—fatty stalker on the prowl! I had the moxie to invite him to lunch, and to my great astonishment, he accepted the invitation and suggested a restaurant called Aretsky's Patroon in midtown Manhattan.

This was before 9/11, when people were still happy and companies had budgets. Well, it seemed everyone did *but* me. Patroon was not going to be cheap either. It was a "see-and-be-seen" steakhouse in the heart of New York's media sector. My dad let me borrow his credit card; good thing I was not drinking at this point—he would not have gotten it back.

Dominick was exactly as you'd expect: bespectacled, dressed nattily, and talkative. We got the best seat in the house, and numerous "bold-faced names" came to pay homage. He graciously introduced me as his friend and regaled me with stories—one I will never forget because it's very crass and really fucking funny. Something about Bill Clinton and Jesse Jackson had made the news and inspired an eye roll from the cynical author. Being incredibly naïve, I surmised they were friends and that the reverend had provided the former president spiritual counseling during the Monica Lewinsky scandal.

"They weren't talking religion; they were talking pussy!" he said, laughing.

My mouth nearly dropped.

Life changed in an instant on 9/11; our apartment was across the street from the World Trade Center and basically blew up. Paul was leaving when the first plane struck, and he hurriedly caught a cab.

My apartment after 9/11. Photo by Jeremy Murphy.

I had a different experience.

I'd flown to Boston the night before to cover an event being thrown by its NBC affiliate, WHDH, which was adding *Access Hollywood* to its "access hour" (7:00–8:00 p.m., EST). This is the time slot between local news on stations and network TV primetime that location stations fill with syndicated shows. Namely, *Wheel of Fortune, Jeopardy, Entertainment Tonight, Seinfeld* reruns, and *Extra. Access Hollywood* was relatively new. Ed Ansin, the billionaire real-estate titan, owned the rascally station, and he was throwing a big party to celebrate it adding the show to its lineup. Pat O'Brien, pre-voicemail scandal, was invited to come and help schmooze local advertisers and media reporters. Including me. I'd done a feature on Ansin for *Mediaweek* a few months before, which he liked. And he didn't like much. At his behest, the station's PR director, Ro Dooley-Webster, invited me to attend. The party was scheduled for September 11.

I got to Boston late on the 10th. Coincidentally, The Ritz-Carlton Company had opened its new Boston Common hotel a few days before. I'd begun doing travel writing for a glossy Boca Raton magazine and used it as a way to get a free room; hotels will comp accommodations for journalists as a way to get positive coverage. The PR director was an elegant, stylish, and memorable woman named Caron LeBrun, who was straight out of central casting: long platinum hair, chic black or polka-dot dresses (usually Chanel or a high-end brand), brooch, and an animated way about her. I fell in love and we, too, became great friends through the years.

I went to bed on the 10th, ending the night and a way of life. I woke up the next morning none the wiser and took a stroll around Boston Common to start the day, not knowing New York was under attack. My father hadn't heard from me, and now couldn't reach me because I'd forgotten my phone in New York (this was 2001, before iPhones became human limbs). Finally, when I returned to the room, he called me and said three words I'll never forget: "We're at war." I flipped on the TV and saw my neighborhood burn to the ground, literally. How surreal it was to watch this from a luxury hotel room hundreds of miles away.

I got trapped in Boston for the week as planes, trains, and rental cars were not running or available. I had clothes for two days, max, and had only been comped two nights with no money for more. This is when Boston became one of my favorite towns. Caron met me in the lobby of the brand-spanking-new Ritz-Carlton and told me to she'd comp however long I needed to stay, including food and unlimited phone calls. Ro Dooley-Webster brought me a giant bag of sweaters, T-shirts, and windbreakers from her station; we still laugh that I became a walking advertisement for Channel 7 and NBC that entire week. She also took me out to dinner every night and introduced me to her co-workers. And a wonderful Boston PR pro named Chris Lyons invited me to dine at all her restaurant clients.

I still have tremendous guilt about spending that week in luxury as my city burned. But I was broke, and The Ritz-Carlton, of all places, was offering shelter. For ten years, I returned to Boston every 9/11 to see Caron, Ro, and other friends I'd made.

Returning to New York a week after 9/11 began a strange, new life because my old life wasn't there when I returned. My father lived in New Jersey, and I spent the next nine months living with him in Clark, a working-class town in Union County. Spending that much time with this man I barely knew—my parents divorced when I was five, and I only saw him once a year—was incredibly strange but affirming. A US Marine who grew up in poverty in Rockaway Beach, New York, he was opinionated, tough, sarcastic, conservative, and very straight. I was the happy, funny, gay kid who loved pop culture, media, and Abercrombie & Fitch catalogs.

We watched movies together on weekends, TV on weeknights ("What is this, the 'Left Wing'?") and shared the same sense of humor. We especially loved the CBS show *JAG* about military officers serving as attorneys. It was unapologetically patriotic and became a huge hit after 9/11. The storylines were dopey and situations farcical—Mac, the Marine played by Catherine Bell, magically spoke a new language every episode, and Harm, played by David James Elliott, once went to Russia disguised as a Romani traveler to find his dead father. But *my* father never stopped being a Marine and enjoyed *JAG* for its pro-America storytelling; I was more interested seeing Elliott in Navy dress-whites (undressed would have been good too).

I enjoyed staying "home" more than I did going to work, mostly because the commute from New Jersey was two hours each way going to a job I no longer enjoyed. I'd take the train from Cranford to Newark, and then the PATH train to 9th Street in the Village, and return home exhausted. Something had to change.

At the same time, Kim Sartori had accepted a job as an assistant at a major company in New York that owned media assets I'd written about at the magazine. Kim soon got promoted to junior PR rep and, as a joke, suggested I apply for her previous job as an assistant. It was funny until I learned the salary was *double* mine as a reporter. I subtly suggested I'd be open to it, which Kim shared with her bosses. The problem was I was overqualified. The people running her department were familiar with my work, but, fortuitously, a copy editor in the department was retiring and they wanted to fill and expand her position. I interviewed with three executives but did not hear anything for a couple of weeks. Then, when I was sent to Dallas to write a *Mediaweek* cover story, I received a phone call offering me the job at an even bigger salary. I accepted it on the spot. It took several weeks to find an apartment, and hilariously, it was John Krasinski who showed it to me when he was a runner for a rental agency in 2002. I still live there twenty-two years later.

The new job was very boring at first. There was really nothing to do but copy edit press releases, which I could do in an hour. So could the woman I'd replaced, who spent the rest of the day reading romance novels. I know this because she'd left them in the office I now inhabited. I would have preferred an A&F catalog. The job gradually expanded to include writing press releases, pitching stories to the trade media, and playing Andy Sachs to my boss's Miranda Priestly.

Living in Manhattan was great, and so was the money, but the job soon became dull, through no fault of the company. I was just bored and began to look elsewhere. I became the runner-up for a bigger job with

Ritz-Carlton corporate working under PR legend Vivian Deuschl. We'd become buds through my travel writing and hated the same people. She fought for me but was overruled by the chain's flashy marketing head, who wanted someone more glamorous with a PR background in travel. I finally got an offer from Fox to be the communications director of its New York TV station after months of lobbying. The vice president of PR for the station group was an elegant, sharp, and sophisticated woman, and Lachlan Murdoch was her boss. I could learn a lot from her, and I'd have my own turf in New York; even better, the station was four blocks from my apartment on the Upper East Side. I waited all summer for an offer and finally got one in August 2004. To my great disappointment, it was less than I was making. My father and I worked the numbers to see if I could swing it financially, but it wasn't feasible. Declining the job was heartbreaking.

There I was, trapped in non-golden handcuffs and becoming more and more miserable. I always did the job well—admittedly, I was not detail-oriented—but put more effort into outside pursuits, like travel writing. In February 2005, I used a friend's wedding in South Florida as a springboard to take my first solo vacation to St. Thomas, an hour away from Miami. Vivian had arranged a long (and free!) stay, and my friend Mike Flanagan from American Airlines comped a press ticket. The vacation was virtually free.

And it changed my life.

The St. Thomas Ritz-Carlton is a strange bird. It's situated on the opposite end of the island from the airport, and the drive between is not exactly pleasurable. Frightening is a more apt description. The property is spread out unexpectedly, with multiple buildings, hallways, aisles, floors, and walkways. It's hard to navigate. It's also not posh. The construction, at the time, was shoddy, and the buildings were not maintained properly. I had brown water come out of one faucet. Service took forever, paint chips filled the walls, and you needed a golf cart to get anywhere. I heard it has since been renovated/restored.

The on-site PR director was a very glamorous Jamaican woman with a tropical insincerity. As she "listened" to me, she constantly looked over my shoulder for someone more important to kiss and hug.

Traveling solo is boring—Stella can stick her groove up her ass. My suite was spacious but tacky. Nothing seemed to work correctly. And eating by yourself blows, at least it was before iPhones.

I read everything I could to pass time, starting with James Stewart's book *DisneyWar*, about the machinations of Michael Eisner and Jeffrey Katzenberg in the Mouse House. But it's so well-written it became stressful; the "you-are-there" access he got puts you there. In a courtroom with those two divas. I don't want to be in a zip code with either of them.

I was ready to read the mattress tag at one point when I found *The Ritz-Carlton Magazine*, a glossy, tastefully designed publication with beautiful layouts, engaging stories, compelling photography, and a quirky perspective. I was very familiar with The Ritz-Carlton Company and instinctively knew they did not produce this fantastic read. Their PR and marketing are top-notch, but they are not in the publishing business. The masthead confirmed this; the publisher was identified as McMurry, an entity I'd never heard of. I wanted to know more and made a mental note to follow up when I returned. Why? I wasn't sure. Mostly out of curiosity.

The rest of the "vacation" was ho-hum. I got a sunburn after unintentionally leaving an arm exposed in the poolside restaurant, which served meals in a steel baskets. Clearly, life was not working out as well as I'd hoped. I couldn't even find pleasure in a free vacation to the Caribbean.

Coming back to New York in February was anticlimactic. Nothing changed. The job was still there, killing me loudly each time I clocked in. I'd gotten no new prospects. I was perpetually broke and living worse than I did when I made one-third the salary. I was also single and missed hanging out with my dad.

Getting back to my office, I remembered to follow up on McMurry and left a voicemail for its owner Chris McMurry. Within a few hours,

I got a call back from its president Fred Petrovsky, who answered all my questions about custom publishing and *The Ritz-Carlton Magazine*.

I floated the idea of an *Entertainment Weekly*-like magazine but focused on television stars. This was the era of the crime-scene procedural and family situation comedy: shows America watched but glossy magazines like *Vanity Fair* and *Vogue* ignored. *Mad Men* had not premiered yet, and *The Sopranos* and *Sex and the City* were considered novel. It wasn't television, after all. It was HBO.

My concept was a bit novel: give TV personalities the movie-star treatment. Bring them to Paris, make them glamorous, dress them in couture.

Fred, sensing I was onto something, flew to New York from Phoenix the next day and met me and my "work wife," Beth Feldman, for lunch. Beth is one of media's top publicists, now a senior executive at a very smart company that owns TV stations, a national news network, and other assets. Previously, she was a vice president in my department, and the best sounding board one could ask for. I begged her to join us for lunch.

A trick to getting expensive meals for free in New York is to have a vendor bring you; they want your business, and you want the lobster. I "suggested" to Fred we eat at the 21 Club, the vaunted power lunch locale on West 52nd Street housed in a five-story brownstone behind a gate with twenty-one ceramic horse jockeys. It was a speakeasy back in the day and had evolved into a place to see and be seen. It was famous for hosting celebrities, business titans, politicians, media stars, and bold-face names. The ground floor included the "toy room"—the casual dining space whose ceiling was dotted with hanging toy trucks, trains, planes, and other vehicles. The servers had all spent their careers there and had stories. Even the bathroom attendant, "The Rev" (Lorenzo Robinson), added color to the experience. A twenty-three-year-veteran of the restaurant, he was known for telling ribald jokes that would make you blush.

Fred greeted us in the lobby and was friendly and enthusiastic. He, like me, tends to raise his voice when he gets excited, which provided a concert the neighboring table did not appreciate. Fred came with mock-ups of what a cover could look like, as well as ideas for stories. We swam in the possibilities, and then the man next to us handed Fred his Palm Pilot (this was pre-iPhone). Written on the screen: *Please stop talking so loudly.*

I was about to shout. I loved the idea. Not only would it get me back to journalism, but it would also get me away from what I'd been drowning in. I raced back to the office to show the mock-ups to several executives and spent the next few months working myself around the building, trying to convince all the stakeholders—sales, marketing, communications, finance—of the viability.

This was a good time to be in publishing. The shock of the internet bubble bursting had subsided, and September 2008 was still three years away. George W. Bush was president and encouraging janitors and strippers to mortgage multiple homes because money was that plentiful. Condé Nast, the glossy arbiter of taste, fashion, and style, was still king of the hill. Its employee cafeteria was designed by architect Frank Gehry and was said to cost $12 million. *Vogue, Vanity Fair, GQ, Gourmet, Details, Lucky, Glamour,* and *Allure* all flew off the newsstands, as did Hearst's *Cosmopolitan, Bazaar, Esquire,* and *Marie Claire.* Time Inc. was printing money with *People* and *InStyle,* and Jann Wenner had resuscitated *US Weekly* into a sales monster.

Starting a magazine had logic, but we were not a publisher. I wouldn't let it go and found a way to eliminate any risk. McMurry, through Fred, agreed to assume all the upfront costs.

I had to sell it first.

Slowly, I got the sign-off, mainly because no one was risking anything. The big meeting came in June 2005, during a blistering heat wave in Manhattan. I got the green light to pitch the idea to the CEO of our parent company, whose office was in a taller building in Times Square, and I remember arriving in a puddle of sweat. A private elevator flung me up to the floor, only to find myself standing face-to-face with none other than Robert Redford as the doors opened.

Editing the first issue. Photo courtesy of Jeremy Murphy.

There were very few offices on this floor because they were all stadium-sized. I was whisked into the big guy's office, which was an out-of-body experience. For starters, it was the day Michael Jackson was acquitted for the latest child molestation trial, and people in the office wanted to watch. The TV was literally the wall. One of the executives attending the meeting started doing Michael Jackson impressions, which sounded like Mickey Mouse.

Post-verdict, I got a few minutes with the CEO and sold him on the merits and math. I'd prepared a whole presentation with splashy graphics and charts, which he didn't need to see.

"I got it, I got it," he purred. "Don't spend money, don't lose money, and you got a deal."

He had grasped the idea immediately, and its possibilities. But his mandate was going to be tough to reach.

The rest of the summer was a whirlwind. As I built the business model, the editorial team from McMurry came to New York regularly. I got to know and like them, including the director, Beth Tomkiw; we share the same taste in movies, pop culture, and TV (sans reality), and her laugh is infectious. Almost twenty years later, we are still friends. Jeff Ficker was our editor, and I think I aged him with my crazy ideas and inferior content. And Sharon Seidl was the art director. She is as kooky as I am, which is why we got along. She made said content at least look good.

I honestly don't remember much else because at the same time my father was diagnosed with Stage 3B lung cancer. I found out on my thirtieth birthday. He was going to get treatments at Memorial Sloan Kettering, one of the world's most respected cancer treatment centers and three blocks from my apartment; naturally, I insisted my dad live with me while he was being treated. The more likely the magazine became, the less my father's chances to survive.

We lost him on July 10, 2005, five months before the first issue came out. I often wonder what he'd think of it. I was damned proud when I held the first issue, which featured Charlie Sheen (winning!) and Jon Cryer from *Two and a Half Men* on the cover. Beth Feldman got terrific quotes from the actors, which we used for the story.

Lest I leave this chapter on a sad note, I found great humor in a Sloan Kettering follow-up a few weeks after my father's death. They sent a customer satisfaction survey *to him* at my address. Rather than be offended, I laughed heartily and took out a black Sharpie to write a message *from him*.

"I died, so not that great."

I hope whoever received it got as good a laugh as I did.

Q&A WITH SOPHIA PAULMIER:

> *Sophia: As a ten -year-old journalist using your home phone to call celebrities, film studios, and publicists, who was your favorite to call and who was the worst?*
>
> Jeremy: Two favorites: Kimberley Joy Ferren, who became a great mentor to me and taught me by best qualities. Also, Mary Anderson, the *Santa Barbara*

PR rep. When I moved to Los Angeles, they both set up a lunch with the couple who'd created the soap opera. This was nirvana. Over salmon at Jimmy's in Beverly Hills, I amused Bridget and Jerry Dobson with one particular story about my affection for their series. On a field trip to see a Broward Community College orchestra, my fifth-grade teacher Margaret Gorra-Porter called me to the other side of the theater and asked something gravely serious: "Who pulled the plug?" On *Santa Barbara*, the respirator for C. C. Capwell had just been turned off, and his daughter Eden was implicated. But her evil stepmother Gina was the real culprit. She dressed as Eden to fool everyone, then climbed out the window. Bridget and Jerry howled at the story.

S: *Did you ever get into any big trouble or scary situation over the phone?*

J: No, but I did in hiding the phone bill from my mother! It was hundreds of dollars every month because long-distance calls were expensive back then. There were many 212, 310, and 818 area codes listed on the statement, so I couldn't exactly deny it was me.

S: *Did you pick up any special sales terms or skills as a salesperson at Neiman Marcus that you still use today?*

J: I learned the art of insincerity. Feigning interest in what people are saying is a particular skill. There is nothing remotely interesting in $800 Christopher Radko ornaments, but they were objects of fascination with Neiman Marcus shoppers. I also perfected my eavesdropping skills. Behind my register was the make-up department, and hearing the salespeople talk shit about each other was my daily soap opera. They were all such bitches, especially the artists.

S: *What was copy editing like when everyone and everything was not yet Google-able?*

J: I found it easy because I missed everything. I was the world's worst copyeditor, but I was fast with doing layouts, which we designed on a program called QuarkXPress. When you're doing a daily newspaper, deadlines are crucial because delaying the presses costs money. I could whip out pages with record speed. And typos, too.

S: *What was it like getting hired to be a featured writer for* The Bradenton Herald? *Do you have any nostalgic memories?*

J: Oh, so many. Looking back, Bradenton was a golden time in my life. The Oscars of the town was the annual "Snooty Gala" to raise money for The South Florida Museum, home to Snooty the Manatee (who has since passed, sadly). This was the see-and-be-seen event of the year and people took it very seriously. Our coverage was hard-hitting. I also attended the Sarasota Film Festival and stalked Wilford Brimley, the famous actor from *Our House* and *The Firm*. He didn't understand why a fat, pasty-skin man-child was following him throughout the event, and he was traumatized by my insistence we get a photo together.

S: *"I wasn't afraid to throw in bon mots, thinly veiled insults, and clever word plays. Tell me more about the growth you've had since then. Did New York wear on you or was it the weight of the press?*

J: I wouldn't call it growth; I've probably gotten worse. New York gets you jaded. I've lost my faith in most of humanity and generally hate people, which is interesting for someone who does PR.

S: *Scene & Heard but make it upper east side edition.*

J: It'd be called "Scared and Hiding" because New York allows you to be vicious and I'd be public enemy number one with my musings. There are too many characters here to mock; I'd have a field day. And a very short life.

S: *What are your feelings on Perez Hilton?*

J: I have very deep gratitude for Perez Hilton because his site gave me something to read on boring days at work. Copyediting storylines from *Touched by an Angel* is not particularly compelling. Seeing penis doodles on Chace Crawford is.

S: *Any interesting moments from Scene & Heard that stuck with you?*

J: Well, one reader did not appreciate my humor and wished me cancer. I also got in hot water when I wrote the sound at a street fair was so loud it could have woken Sunny von Bülow. "Claus! Turn down that ruckus and bring me more insulin" was the line I used. And I was super pissed the best quote from my interview with *60 Minutes* correspondent Lesley Stahl was edited out. When I asked about her coverage of Watergate, she said, "it was more interesting than getting a little nookie in the Oval Office." The night editor didn't think that was appropriate language.

S: *You're moving to New York, your life's about to change. Describe that lunch when Bill Gloede offered you the job at Mediaweek?*

J: We went to the Knickerbocker, which is a restaurant in the Village and a few blocks from the *Mediaweek* offices. Bill took me to lunch with Brian Moran, and I fell in love with his hearty laugh instantly. I think they felt lucky to get a reporter at such a low salary.

S: *Biggest take back of Mediaweek?*

J: You're not that important. They were very good at popping balloons, and I'd just arrived as the star columnist from the *Bradenton Herald*. I thought I was very important. That lasted a day. They put me through the magazine version of boot camp.

S: *Describe the Krasinski brothers in two words.*

J: Very tall! I don't know what those parents feed their children; all three sons are huge! I remember Paul and John being very different. I'm still very good friends with Paul, and at first, I thought he was too good to be true. He's so outgoing, friendly, warm, and genuinely interested in what people are saying; it's real. He is the true thing. John had charisma even then. He was a bit more skeptical than Paul, but just as friendly. He slept on our couch every time he visited New York, and one day we hung out and had lunch at the Hardrock Cafe.

S: The Office *or* A Quiet Place?

J: *A Quiet Place*, most definitely. As much as I like John—the *Jack Ryan* series is terrific!—I never got into *The Office*.

S: You almost became the communications director of The Ritz-Carlton, where do you think you'd be today had you gotten that job?

J: Unemployed. Almost all my PR colleagues from my travel writing days are either dead, retired, in other jobs, or looking for work.

S: Let's talk about your friend's wedding that brought you to The Ritz-Carlton St. Thomas on your own vacation when you first came up with the idea of the magazine. Did you ever thank that friend and tell them? And are they still married today?

J: Yes, many times. And no, they are not. I want my blender back.

S: "Give TV personalities the movie star treatment" is an interesting concept. How do you feel about today's age with content creators and influencers? Would you consider them today's TV stars?

J: I loathe "content creators" and "influencers," more so the "influencers." It's a paid racket.

S: What's your favorite Dominick Dunne book?

J: He wrote a book called *Another City, Not my Own* in 1997, which blended genres. He created a composite character that was basically him, and he covered and investigated the O. J. case. I found it fascinating. I also enjoyed *A Season in Purgatory*.

S: Did you ever cross paths with him again?

J: No, I was too nervous and shy to ask again. He's an icon and I just felt fortunate to get the time I did.

S: A bittersweet moment having the magazine launch right after you lost your father to lung cancer. It seems similar to 9/11 bringing you two together. Do you feel like New York and your interest in journalism brought you closer to him for a reason?

J: New York, definitely. He was a New Yorker through-and-through. I remember when he died, I went to the funeral home, which strongly recommended placing his obit in the *New York Times* for an outrageous sum. He despised that paper, and I could hear him shout "pinko, communist, bed-wetting rag" in my head the minute it was suggested. We didn't buy the obit.

S: Do you think he would have enjoyed the first issue had he lived to see it?

J: He enjoyed everything I did. When he died, my brother and I cleaned out his apartment and he'd kept all the hand-written articles and newsletters I did as a kid

S: I'd imagine this all to be overwhelming to a kid who grew up in Florida. What kept you going during this time?

J: I wasn't drinking yet, so probably something just as bad but eaten. I gained a lot of weight back that summer.

CHAPTER 5

The Good Life

JULIANNA MARGULIES
PHOTOGRAPHED BY PATRICK DEMARCHELIER
AT THE HÔTEL DU CAP-EDEN-ROC

Julianna Margulies on the coast of the Hotel du Cap-Eden-Roc in Cap
Antibes. Here, she wears a stunning white dress by Versace, styled by
Chris Campbell, and photographed by Patrick Demarchelier.

The Good Wife changed network television.

When it premiered in 2009, the genre was just beginning to materialize into the artists' medium of choice. Studios, which had always held up their noses toward TV, had begun to abandon the creative, risky, and culture-defining movies for safe bets like superheroes and sequels about superheroes. Writers, directors, and actors segued to cable TV—mainly HBO—and then basic cable networks like AMC, which suddenly became their playground. *The Sopranos*, *Sex and the City*, and *Six Feet Under* started this trend, followed by *Mad Men*.

The broadcast networks followed, led by shows like *The Good Wife*.

The series was created by the husband-and-wife team Robert and Michelle King, and it told the story of a woman whose life is nearly destroyed when her politician husband gets caught in a myriad of scandals and is forced to resign. The collateral damage is his family. Alicia Florrick is left near penniless and forced to begin anew with her children, starting with getting a job. A lawyer before she became the dutiful wife, she joins a law firm and begins to rebuild a different life. At the time, the airwaves were filled with procedural crime dramas that dominated the ratings; *The Good Wife* represented a huge risk for its network, as well as the actors who'd play its multi-dimensional characters.

Julianna Margulies became a star in the mid-'90s on the hit show *ER*, and did incredible work after, including an arc on *The Sopranos*. She took on the role of Alicia, which now made the show sellable. Other known actors—Josh Charles, Christine Baranski, Matt Czuchry, Archie Panjabi, Alan Cumming—joined the cast, and the show was given a competitive Tuesday nighttime slot.

To everyone's delight, it became a hit and a critical success. The storylines were sharp and engaging, the dialogue snapped, the characters were complex, and the acting was better than any cast on television.

I became a huge fan, as did everyone else on the magazine. And I suddenly had a smorgasbord of people to put on our pages.

JULIANNA MARGULIES

The hardest to get was Julianna, who greatly valued off-screen time. She was in nearly every scene and had dozens of pages to recite each day of filming. As a new mom, she worked to achieve balance in her family life while headlining a hit series that needed constant promotion. Getting access to her was difficult, and her publicist was a pit bull. We tried everything.

Finally, in 2015, I threw a Hail Mary pass and offered a cover shoot in the South of France at the world's most glamourous destination: the Hotel du Cap-Eden-Roc. Nestled on a bluff in Cap D'Antibes, the property is famous for its picturesque setting, iconic path between its mansion and seaside pool, and its celebrity clientele. They rarely allowed photo shoots, and we certainly were not first in line.

Fortunately, I had Peter Greenberg, the popular travel expert who penned a column for our magazine called "Peter's Passport." To say he is connected is a profound understatement. He lives and breathes the travel industry, but always with a journalist's skepticism and advocacy for his readers, listeners, and viewers. Peter was our secret weapon, and when I could not land a sponsor or hotel as setting myself, I'd call him. More often than not, he came through.

Especially this time. I told him we had a chance to shoot our first cover with Julianna Margulies, but it had to be at the Hotel du Cap. As we ate lunch at the popular midtown restaurant Fresca by Scotto, where Peter is practically mayor, he looked at me with a raised eyebrow and knowing glance.

"You've got some chutzpah," I imagined him saying.

To my great relief, Peter had a relationship with the hotel's owner, the Oetker Collection, and was going to be meeting its CEO, Frank Marrenbach, the next week. He pitched Frank personally and got the green light: the Hotel du Cap agreed to host our entire crew and let us shoot on property. Only Peter Greenberg could have pulled this off.

I knew this had to be off-the-charts spectacular and began to assemble an A-list crew: Demarchelier to shoot, Christopher Campbell for styling, and Bruno Weppe for hair. Julianna's team wanted a makeup artist from London, who turned out to be fantastic.

Before leaving, I presented the concept and details of the shoot to higher-ups, who naturally had questions. One being why we needed five days to do it.

"It's a very elaborate production," I explained, nose growing like Pinocchio. "Pre-production, story boarding, scouting, lighting; so many variables. We'll be lucky if we finish in five days."

With Patrick shooting, we'd be done in five hours

I wasn't sure if they believed the bullshit I was spewing, so I threw in more photography terms ("tethered!", "strobes," "plating!") to make it sound overly complicated ... and get the answer I wanted, which I did.

Julianna and her devastatingly handsome plus one Keith (who media call "The Good Husband") arrived the day before our shoot, and, as customary, I met them in the lobby for check-in. They were incredibly friendly and gracious, and looked resplendent.

That afternoon, Julianna did the wardrobe fitting with Christopher and liked everything. This usually sets the mood for an entire shoot. If the talent don't like the clothes, they're going to sour on the whole experience. This is why we used stylists like Christopher, The Jackal, Fabio Mercurio, Cannon, Sarah Nash, and other top talents we normally hired.

After, our whole team met for drinks in the Hotel du Cap's lobby bar—Julianna and Keith included—and talked about the next day. Julianna was open-minded to everything but wasn''t sure our idea to style her hair would work.

Christopher envisioned a wet, slicked back look, which would look sleek and modern with the dark couture he had pulled from top designers.

Julianna poses in a jumpsuit by Blumarine in Cabana at The Hotel du Cap, styled by Chris Campbell and shot by Patrick Demarchelier.

I approved the concept and left it in his and Bruno's hands to see it through.

Day of shoot, Julianna warned her hair is naturally frizzy and would not stay wet and slick for long.

"No problem," replied Bruno. He'd use "cock grease."

Whatttt?

"Grease of the cock," he repeated.

Julianna was taken aback, as anyone would be, and demanded to see what he was talking about.

Turns out, it was chicken grease. Cock-a-doodle-doo, indeed!

The day turned out to be incredibly stress-free, and the photos were among the best I'd ever seen. Patrick shot Julianna at the famous Eden Roc pool, on the bluff, running across the legendary pathway of the Hotel du Cap, and even in the elevator. Most breathtaking was one of her sitting on a rock in a white Versace dress with the water and sky behind her.

Jeremy, *Good Wife* star Julianna Margulies, and Patrick Demarchelier at The Hotel du Cap in the South of France.

A month after it came out, Julianna was on *The Tonight Show with Jimmy Fallon* and shared her experience doing the shoot, including one story I didn't know. When she returned to her suite after the shoot, she told Keith she'd be ready for their dinner but "had to get the cock grease out of my hair."

Jimmy Fallon nearly fell off his chair he laughed so hard.

Seeing the images back home was the first time, after nine years, I truly felt we'd made it. They were on par with anything *Vogue* or *Vanity Fair* were doing.

I knew instantly the image with Julianna sitting on the rock would be the cover. An editor on our team suggested cropping it very tightly so you'd only see her face, which is standard for many magazines, but I thought it would rob the cover of a sense of place. With the rock, ocean, sky, and Julianna front and center, Patrick had captured the easy elegance of the Côte d'Azur.

The next problem were the cover lines. The issue had lots of other great stories we'd normally promote with a headline, but I felt the photo said everything it needed. Text would take *away* from the image and rob it of its simplicity and grace. I decided we'd run the image as is.

But to allay fears, we did a small second run with cover lines. The image was still stunning, but the typography distracted you from its serenity.

The au naturel edition proved to be a big hit and our finest ever. Julianna loved it, as did her publicist, who hated everything (and most everyone). Patrick put copies of the issue on tables in his studio, and we even got word Donatella Versace saw the cover and liked it. When Julianna went on *The Tonight Show*, she and Jimmy Fallon talked about the shoot, and he showed the cover.

What made the issue even sweeter was when Christian Dior took the opening ad spread, and not just for fragrance. My good friend Charlie Siem, a celebrated violinist you'll read about in the following pages, was going to be the face of Dior's 2015-2016 fall/ winter men's line, photographed by Karl Lagerfeld, and as a favor he told the marketing team at Dior to include *our magazine* in their ad campaign rollout.

Christopher Campbell and I talk about this experience often. It was ethereal, and we wondered if we could ever top what we'd created.

I lost touch with Julianna until 2021 when, during the height of pandemic shutdown, I read her book *Sunshine Girl*: an autobiography of her life growing up between two parents in different countries and lifestyles. I found it riveting, and celebrity bios are never such. I wanted to tell her myself, but how? Determined, I went to IMDbPro and found an email for her agent to whom I expressed my sentiments, hoping he'd pass them along.

The next day I got the nicest email from Julianna thanking me for reading. She also recalled the photo shoot with warm memories. A year later, I saw her speak at an event for her book's paperback release, and we had a short reunion. I shared that I had just written my first book and offered to give her a copy.

She wouldn't accept it for one reason: she wanted to buy it herself, and purchased it on Amazon.

JOSH CHARLES

An actor since his teen years, Josh Charles was mostly known for his role in the 1989 superhit *Dead Poets Society*, starring Robin Williams as a schoolteacher who inspires his students to defy convention. Josh played Knox Overstreet, who comes of age as he pursues the girl of his dreams but gets rejected.

The gifted actor went on to work on many big projects and was a get for *The Good Wife*, on which he played the law firm's partner, Will Gardner. He showed an incredible gravitas in the role.

Josh agreed to do a shoot for us but asked if his photographer friend, Randall Slavin, could do it. I looked at his work and approved it happily. His celebrity portraits are compelling and tell a story without text.

For reasons I just can't remember—I think it was his schedule—we decided to shoot this locally in New York, but I was running out of settings. We'd already used most of the exclusive hotels, which were always preferred because it was a controlled setting.

Barbara Bahny to the rescue! She was a friend of thirteen years and had just added the Barclay Hotel in midtown to her PR portfolio of InterContinental Hotels. I met her on a press trip to Washington, DC, where she handled its most famous property, the Willard. She knew me well enough to offer the Barclay as our setting.

For the wardrobe, I envisioned something cool, masculine, and classic. Christopher Campbell, who normally did our shoots, was not available. It presented an opportunity to use a quirky, creative talent anyway: Brendan Cannon, whose professional name is just Cannon. Redheaded, kind, and reserved, he's hard to get to know, but his taste is exquisite, and his ideas are inspired. Every time he pitched me on a concept, I was surprised by its audacity and sense of wonder.

Finding *where* to shoot was a problem. The Barclay—pre-renovation—didn't leave many options, so we settled on a piano in a suite, bar, elevator, and several outdoor shots.

One particular setup got awkward. We desperately wanted Josh for a cover, but this shoot was slated for just a feature in our men's issue later that year. It was not relayed to either Josh or Randall, and they began picking out images that would work best on the face of our magazine. I didn't have the heart to say otherwise at that moment.

Turns out I didn't have to. The images were fantastic, and Josh looked great. We did a double run on the December issue.

It sold and was received well, and I was already imagining where we could bring Josh next. But I didn't have the chance to overthink it because his character got killed off the show the following year.

ARCHIE PANJABI

Archie was a complete surprise to American TV viewers. She came out of nowhere and just burst off the screen, which is ironic because she's very soft-spoken, demure, and almost shy. She grew up in the UK and has an impeccable British accent that makes you want to serve tea and eat scones.

On *The Good Wife*, Archie played the firm's private investigator, Kalinda, whose petite frame belies her badass techniques. Wearing a leather jacket and kickass boots, she was fierce. I wanted to shoot her for a cover, but we weren't sure it would sell. Kalinda was not a main character, but when she won the Emmy for Supporting Actress in 2010, I was able to sell the idea.

We hadn't shot in Chicago, but word had gotten through the PR reps at Peninsula Hotels that our features were an effective promotional tool for their publicity efforts. I wasn't surprised when the rep for its Chicago hotel called and offered us an opportunity to shoot on its property, which is the fanciest and arguably the best in the Windy City. I knew its classic Asian-flavored accents would photograph beautifully.

To shoot, we chose Jeff Lipsky, who had worked for us twice by now, and The Jackal for styling. Archie arrived, and though hard to hear at times, was friendly, collaborative, and beautiful. She fit the whole wardrobe easily.

Jeff photographed her throughout the hotel, but the roof shot made me incredibly nervous. The wind was especially harsh that day, and I was deathly afraid a strong gust would knock Archie off the building. It didn't, thankfully.

The cover wound up being one we hadn't even considered. Behind the concierge desk hangs a fifteen-by-seven-foot mural by French artist Gerard Coltat featuring Chicago personalities and landmarks. The style is French Art Deco–meets–Art Nouveau using textured oil and sparkling gold, silver, and copper leaf elements. Jeff had Archie stand on top of the desk to get the full perspective, which turned out to be a rich, supple background for a cover.

Afterward, our staff celebrated the incredible day at The Bar at The Peninsula, where I had one too many Dark and Stormy cocktails.

The drink lived up to its name, especially after too many.

Tall, thin, blond, good-looking, and charming, you want to hate Matt Czuchry until you meet him. Then you want to be his best friend. He is exceedingly gracious, modest, and kind. If I looked like him, I would be anything but; when you're that hot, talented, and famous, life requires you be a douchebag. Matt is the exception.

On *The Good Wife*, he played Cary Agos, a junior associate who vies with Julianna's character, Alicia, for the firm's one permanent position. He doesn't get it, and instead becomes a prosecutor who works against the firm. Matt brought a quiet intensity to the role. "Still waters run deep" is how I described it to him. Having come from playing the teen heartthrob on *Gilmore Girls*, he wowed audiences with this new character.

MATT CZUCHRY

Jeremy with *Good Wife* star Matt Czuchry at The Kensington Hotel in London.

We'd already worked with him and costar Archie for a 2012 cover (see chapter 19) but in 2013, I felt he deserved one solo. We flew him to London to shoot at The Kensington, a hotel so boring its own website doesn't tell its history. They didn't need to. There's nothing interesting to write about anyway. Or shoot against. Good thing we had Matt, who provided all the visuals we'd need.

I hired Keiron O'Connor to shoot. Tall, British, bald, and offbeat, Kieron brought a different eye to every assignment. We had an easy chemistry, and his ideas were always out of left field. On a previous shoot, we photographed *Blue Bloods* star Bridget Moynahan as a modern-day superwoman. For Matt, we both agreed to play off his gracious, aw-shucks vibe. Each setting would be a somewhat animated "good guy" experience, from helping an older woman down a staircase to fixing a car outside. Matt was game, and stylist Christopher got the British label Dunhill to provide the wardrobe.

Matt does not take a bad photo. The concept worked well and reflected what we already knew: he's a class act in *any* setting.

CHRISTINE BARANSKI

Jeremy with *Good Wife* actress Christine Baranski at Castiglion del Bosco, a resort-winery high atop Montalcino in Tuscany. Photo courtesy of Jeremy Murphy.

"Barcelona...Bora Bora...Argentina," Christine purred as she sat being photographed in British Airways's (BA) iconic Concorde Room lounge in JFK.

She was joking about all the places we *should* be shooting instead of an airport. But it was lighthearted and fun. Here's the backstory.

Peter Greenberg, our Hotel du Cap hero, had introduced me to BA's New York PR rep Michele Kropf, who was friendly but has a poker face that makes her hard to read. She doesn't suffer fools, which makes her a brilliant and effective PR rep for any airline.

Peter convinced Michele to meet with me, and we had dinner inside BA's Concorde lounge. The cuisine was surprisingly haute for an airport, and as our meal progressed we got on fabulously. Michele and I liked the same TV shows and actors, shared the same opinions about *almost* everything, and knew the same people. We struck up a friendship that continues to this day.

On a later drink date, she pitched me something unique: a photo shoot with a star inside the Concorde Room. I liked the idea because it was unorthodox. Who expects to see an airport as a setting for a celebrity magazine spread? But getting an actor we'd both agree on would be a stretch when you'd already brought their costars to Paris and London. Christine Baranski was on our list of gets, and this was outlandish enough to get her attention. She'd also sell covers because America loves her.

A Juilliard graduate, the actress has won two Tonys, an Emmy, and countless other awards for her work. She gained instant recognizability in the sitcom *Cybill*, in which she played Cybill Shepherd's divorced bestie, and in *The Bird Cage*. I remember her most fondly from the 1994 comedy *The Ref*, where she was the obnoxious sister-in-law in a family taken hostage by Denis Leary. The dialogue is hysterical. In *Cruel Intentions*, she tried to dispel her character's perceived bigotry with the line, "Oh, don't give me any of that racist crap! My husband and I gave money to Colin Powell!" She's gone on to gain more fame and notoriety in movies like *Reversal of Fortune*, *How the Grinch Stole Christmas*, *Chicago*, and *Mamma Mia!*

On *The Good Wife*, Christine was cast as Diane Lockhart, a poised but tough litigator who swam successfully with the sharks and could crunch with sharper teeth. She was a fan favorite from the start, including among our staff.

Day of shoot, Michele organized us into groups of four and guided each one through TSA with military precision. She even got an ironing board, hair spray, and numerous other products through the detectors, which was great (and comical) for us but doesn't bode well for the future of airport security.

Pavel Havlicek, a photographer from Prague, undertook the challenge to shoot, and he worked with the team seamlessly. Christopher Campbell's wardrobe was so strong, Christine bought several of the pieces and took him shopping later.

Michele was right: the Concorde Room turned out to be a great setting. It had an adult élan, still classy but virile. We photographed her in numerous settings throughout the space, including at the table where Christine jokingly suggested alternative locations she'd rather be photographed.

Michele watched the clock closely because we had a hard out at 5:00 p.m. The lounge was still in use for BA's first-class passengers, and they wouldn't appreciate a photo shoot disturbing the tranquil setting.

To no one's surprise, the shoot hit all the right notes and was perfect for our July travel issue. The photos were so strong, I commissioned a split cover run with Christine gracing half our circulation.

Michele Kropf became our hero, and we worked with BA for many years.

I promised Christine I'd find a new opportunity that involved flying and not just posing on airplanes, and I did. A well-known, highly respected PR pro in the travel world, Geoffrey Weill, took my team to lunch soon after, and over crab cakes pitched me somewhere we had trouble believing existed: Castiglion del Bosco, a resort-winery high atop Montalcino in Tuscany. The nine-hundred-year-old estate is a postcard come true, complete with a hotel that has forty-two suites, eleven villas, two restaurants, a cooking school, and spa. Who doesn't want to shoot at a resort that served as the setting for da Vinci's "Lady with an Ermine" painting? I was more excited that its vines grow my favorite Italian wine, Brunello. The Ferragamo family bought the property in 2003 and restored its glory, including the San Michele church that sits on its land and the ruins of a medieval castle that dates back to 1100 AD.

Christine loved everything about it and agreed to be our subject after *The Good Wife* wrapped its fourth season. I took a small crew with me, and we hired Milan stylist Fabio Mercurio for the wardrobe.

Christine remembered me fondly from the Concorde lounge shoot and thanked me profusely for living up to my word. She was again gracious, self-deprecating, and eager to enjoy the experience.

Every setting was better than the last. Christine has the body of a cheerleader and can wear anything elegantly. Fabio had gotten incredible dresses—many from Ferragamo—that glistened on camera. Our cover subject was having a great time, which is exactly what you want during a production like this.

In one setup, Christine stood high atop steps near the castle ruins. Standing below, I started shouting her best lines from *The Ref*, including, "The spirit of Christmas is either you're good or you're punished, and you burn in hell," "Shut up, we're celebrating the birth of Christmas," and my all-time favorite, "Slipper socks, medium!" She laughed heartily, but responded, "Jeremy, you forgot the last one. "Get the Jew (-ish lawyer)." It's from *Reversal of Fortune*, in which she played the girlfriend of Claus von Bülow, who was convicted for the attempted murder of his wife, Sunny. Upon hearing unsettling legal news, he considers hiring famed lawyer Alan Dershowitz (said Jew), who wound up freeing him on appeal.

It was a surreal experience, as was the rest of the trip: wine tasting, tour of the property, leisure time in our rooms, and a gourmet dinner in one of the suites.

Christine returned to Castiglion del Bosco later that year on a personal trip, and I've recommended it to many friends who wound up staying.

ALAN CUMMING

Jeremy with *Good Wife* star Alan Cumming in Edinburgh,
Scotland. Photo courtesy of Jeremy Murphy.

I had no idea Alan Cumming's Scottish brogue was so thick until I met him. On *The Good Wife*, he played the brilliant Machiavellian political consultant Eli Gold, who gets Alicia's husband reelected after he's released from prison. Alan made what could have been a smarmy character likable. In several scenes, I rooted for him and his schemes.

The PR agency representing Scottish tourism offered to have us shoot a star in Edinburgh, which was not a hard sell. Nearly every part of the city would add reverence to any photo—except the crappy hotel they put us in. I'll get to that in a minute.

Alan agreed as soon as we made the offer, and I knew exactly which photographer to hire: Mark Mann, a Scottish native with a less heavy accent. Mark had done many covers for us, including *The Big Bang Theory* cast, Jennifer Love Hewitt in Hawaii, *Elementary* star Jonny Lee Miller in London, and several others. For wardrobe, we used Sarah Nash, the London-based stylist, who was eight months pregnant but still as energetic as always. She pulled traditional Scottish items, including kilts, jackets, trousers, hats, and the like.

By the time I got to Scotland, I was exhausted. We combined five photo shoots in one trip, and this was my fourth week on the road. I know, it sounds like a white people problem for sure. I was hoping to stay at a grand hotel like The Balmoral, but instead, we got The Glasshouse, an incredibly odd place to set up shop. A 170-year-old property, it was originally built as a church but was converted into a hotel in 2003. They shouldn't have bothered. The elevator didn't go to the lobby; it stopped on a different floor, which necessitated a trip on the staircase while carrying your own luggage. The ambiance was "contemporary" (read: cheap and uninspired), the rooms bland, and there was virtually no service. Instead of a bar, the hotel set up a mini fridge they rebranded the "honor bar"; you listed the items you'd taken on a clipboard. We renamed it the "dishonor bar" because we stole nearly everything.

Alan arrived and was witty, friendly, and a bit mischievous. After dinner one night, he dared our crew to compete him doing handstands. One of our team took on the challenge. They both stood upside down to uproarious laughter from the crew. Though at times I couldn't understand him, I found Alan to be incredibly fun and easy to photograph.

Mark got him in all the classic settings—churches, castle, streets of Edinburgh—before we moved the setting to Gleneagles, a five-star resort in Auchterarder, Scotland. With 232 rooms, six restaurants, four bars, and surrounding lane bathed in warm shades of green, it was a welcome contrast from The Glasshouse.

A shoot with no drama—what a perfect way to end a month-long schedule that saw us shoot in the South of France, Ischia (an island off the coast of Naples, Italy), Jerusalem, London, and now Scotland.

Did I say no drama? Spoke too soon! Our pregnant stylist Sarah suddenly went into labor while steam-pressing the clothing. Stupid me, I started Googling "how to deliver a baby" as if that was going to happen. Sarah was brought to a nearby hospital, where she gave birth that night.

Q&A WITH SOPHIA PAULMIER

Sophia: The Good Wife *had an all-star cast with multi-dimensional characters. Who was your personal favorite actor and character on the show?*

Jeremy: Julianna. From the first episode, when she slaps Chris Noth after his Eliot Spitzer mea culpa, to the last episode, when Christine Baranski slaps her, she was Alicia Florrick. Her performance was so real—she captured the fragility of the character but also the strength she didn't know she had.

S: You had the pleasure of working with all of the leads. Who was the most like their character and who surprised you the most?

J: All the actors were completely different from who they played. That's what makes them good actors. But Alan surprised me most. Eli was the operator who did anything to win, and he was always scheming. Alan was like a little kid, full of mischief. But fun.

S: The Hotel du Cap is one of the most exclusive resorts in the French Riviera. Some of the biggest prolific creatives have stayed there. It's the hot spot during the Cannes

Film Festival. And most recently, it was the backdrop to Sofia Richie's wedding. How would you summarize your stay there?

J: I don't think I could do it justice. A year before our shoot, we were covering the Monte-Carlo Television Festival in Monaco when Prince Albert II brings all the stars to Monte Carlo. We were there for several nights on a photo shoot, but the du Cap was only an hour away by car. How could you not take advantage of this opportunity? My colleagues and I visited the hotel for a site inspection, dreaming of one day working there, and its PR director invited us (read: free) to stay the night. I rarely feel truly at ease; I'm always worried, stressed, or distracted with a mind that doesn't sleep. Not here. The knots in my shoulders, pains in my back, and thoughts of impending doom magically went away. Of course, it's a five-star resort on the Cote de Azur; I wouldn't be human to feel anything less.

S: How'd you come to meet Peter Greenberg?

J: Peter is the most known and powerful travel journalist, and he is very good friends with Ritz Carlton savior Vivian Deuschl, who introduced us. Peter and I met for lunch at Fresco by Scotto, which is the midtown restaurant media people want to be seen at. Peter was the mayor. I might as well have been the busboy. He was gregarious, smart, friendly, and curious. Getting him to do a travel column would put a feather in our cap because he's a name. Over pasta, we created his regular spread "Peter's Passport."

S: After spending five nights in the beautiful Hotel de Cap, what can you recommend to someone on their first visit?

J: First, be thankful you are there. Breathe it in. I'm a middle-class kid from a broken family who had no business being there.

S: *What does chicken grease smell like, and were you curious to try it on your hair?*

J: No idea and no, that has not piqued my curiosity. Ever.

S: *The photos of Julianna are some of the magazine's best work. I particularly like the shots of her by the infinity pool and the French elevator. Did you have any trouble shooting these locations with guests during peak summer season?*

J: No, the hotel has a wonderful woman named Valerie Muller, who arranged everything. No guest experience was affected.

S: *Let's talk about this wordless cover. The photo of her is so captivating it, words would ruin it. Was this a popular trend when you suggested to not include any cover lines?*

J: Not at all. It was very uncommon, especially when you are buried on newsstands. We were never a top seller anyway, so I didn't worry about sales. Most of our readers were getting it in the mail anyway.

S: *When did this trend start and who started it?*

J: Certainly not us. It wasn't common, but I did remember Annie Leibovitz's iconic cover of *Rolling Stone* with John Lennon and Yoko Ono in bed. I think Jann Wenner, who started that magazine, set that precedent. It can't be a trend, though, because it loses impact if you do it every time. It has to denote something special. To our magazine, this actress and that photo were.

S: *The cover photo is powerful. I can see why you think the wordless version worked better; "Julianna Marvelous" in big text feels too hungry and competes the image. Do you think part of your team couldn't understand the art of Demarchelier's vision?*

J: I wouldn't call it Demarchelier's "vision." He took a beautiful photo created by an incredible team of talents, but that's what he does every time. And my team was well aware it was a powerful image. Some of them were just not prepared to run it without text; I'd never asked.

S: *This is by far your best issue. You should be proud!*

J: Trust me, there are a lot not to be proud of! I cringe at the earlier ones. This is very special issue to me because it's the first time I truly felt we'd made it to the club.

S: *Josh Charles asked to bring on his friend as the photographer. What a bold move!*

J: He would not have if Randall had not been qualified. His photography was very strong, so it was not a hard choice. Josh was smart.

S: *How lucky were you when you discovered his friend was the talented Randall Slavin?*

J: We did our homework. And yes, I felt fortunate to have a new eye shooting for the magazine.

S: *Josh sounds like a cool man. Did you miss working with him after his character was killed off the show?*

J: I was confident we'd have the chance again.

S: *Describe Archie in a few words.*

J: Elegant intensity.

S: *Did she make a playlist for this shoot?*

J: No, I didn't know her at that point.

S: *Favorite place to dine out in Chicago?*

J: I should say Rosebud's steakhouse or somewhere fancy, but the truth is The Cheesecake Factory in the lobby of the Hancock Building.

S: *Which Peninsula was your personal favorite: Beverly Hills, New York, or Chicago?*

J: Chicago! Beverly Hill was great, but the Weinstein stench is still there. And the New York hotel is on the wrong corner of 55th and 5th. There are homeless people and hot dog stands on the street—not what you want to see when paying $1,200 for a room. Not that I ever did; I only stayed when it was free or someone else paid.

S: *Did you ever spot Harvey Weinstein at any of their locations?*

J: No, thankfully!

S: *Matt Czuchry in London: Did you guys have tea and did he FaceTime Rory Gilmore?*

J: Neither. But we did drink and go out a lot. He's very modest and quiet, so takes a bit to get comfortable, but once he does, he couldn't be more charming.

S: *Give me some underrated spots in London to grab a drink.*

J: It's been so long, I don't know what's there anymore! We always stayed in the hotel, so my recommendations are limited. I liked Bar Boulud. The Rivoli Bar inside The Ritz London is really cozy. The Bar inside the Dorchester is very posh, as is 45 Park Lane. Scott's in Mayfair has a 1920s London elan. And Cecconi's, also in Mayfair, is fun to chill out with a martini. I got lucky and was admitted to a club called 5 Hertford Street, so I tend to go there when in London. All of these places I experienced while editing the magazine, so I never worried about the bill. Today, I'm not likely to be seen.

S: *Favorite Christine Baranski movie?*

J: *The Ref.*

S: *Is she as funny and sweet in person as she plays on screen?*

J: Yes, more so. She's incredibly warm and self-deprecating once you realize she's not the Upper East Side haughty socialite she tends to play on screen.

S: *Christine is that scene stealer. Name another actor who does this?*

J: There is no one that does what Christine does.

S: *Were you nervous doing a photoshoot in an airport?*

J: Yes, incredibly. It's a tightly controlled setting that you don't control. Getting through TSA without having tickets to fly somewhere is not an easy thing to pull off.

S: *Tuscany with Christine Baranski sounds like a dream. What was your favorite meal while you were there?*

J: Pizza!

S: *Alan Cumming has been in everything. Did he tell you which of all his projects was his favorite to work on?*

J: No, I didn't ask that. I knew of his work but not like I did Christine's.

S: *But I have to know: Did you happen to ask him what it was like working with Kubrick on his last film and just what his desk character really meant?*

J: We didn't have that kind of time with Alan. It was a pretty quick shoot, and I don't think he was staying in the hotels with us.

S: *"One night he dared our crew to compete against him doing handstands." Alan Cumming's energy is my new philosophy.*

J: He is like a kid. Incredible energy!

S: *"I started Googling 'how to deliver a baby' as if that was going to happen." This is hilarious, but more importantly, what did Google suggest you do?*

J: Go to medical school.

CHAPTER 6

"I Have Patrick!"

Jeremy with Patrick Demarchelier. Photo courtesy of Jeremy Murphy.

"Get me Demarchelier," hissed Meryl Streep as the ice-cold Miranda Priestly in the 2006 hit movie *The Devil Wears Prada*.

She was referring to fashion photographer Patrick Demarchelier, famous for his stunning pictorials in the world's glossiest magazines. I remember the name because it was one from my childhood; in my grandparents' apartment were copies of fashion magazines I spent much of my youth reading. On trips to their home in Tamarac, Florida, I'd often sit in the TV room and pretend to watch cartoons when I was really flipping through pages looking at all the beautiful images. I remember reading Demarchelier because, at a precocious twelve, I had no idea if it was a name or garnish.

You've probably seen Patrick and not even known. In addition to being named in *The Devil Wears Prada*, he is featured in *The September Issue* documentary and the *Sex And The City* movie. He passed in March 2022 after a glorious career in fashion and photography; his images of Princess Diana sitting and wearing her crown have been seen by billions, as have portraits of Angelina Jolie, Nicole Kidman, Madonna, Gisele, SJP, and every other screen goddess.

Hearing his name in *The Devil Wears Prada* was kismet; I'd recently become a magazine editor myself and could maybe finally meet him professionally. The only problem? We were not yet glossy and had pennies to spend.

Our magazine had produced two issues at this point: sixty pages, paper-thin as tissue, and held together by stapler. In publishing, they call this "saddle-stitched"—the cheapest way to make magazines. Even if we *could* pay his rate, he'd never shoot for our level of quality. But I'm a dreamer and never gave up. Except *every* day was some kind of setback, hurdle, obstacle, or bullshit before we could even get to the point where we could consider Patrick.

It's amazing, looking back, how much people did *not* want us to succeed, mostly inside the company. Some even on our "team" who we called termites. I'd take Super P and The Jackal to the King Cole to fret about this often; we knew *who* they were but could never understand *why*. It seemed stupid, and it still does. But then again, these were not the smartest people.

Those run-up years were very, very hard. I do not recall them fondly, even with a stiff Macallan.

In 2009, I got a signed edition of a new coffee table book the photographer was releasing that celebrated his work. Someone at his New

York agency must have read my mind because I was starting to imagine the impossible. We survived 2008 and the aftereffects when others— *Portfolio*, *Gourmet*, *Men's Vogue*, *CosmoGirl*—did not. After a year of contraction, people were starting to spend again, and it was still a buyer's market. I met his agent, a soft-spoken Black man with an impeccable British accent, and began the dance.

I worked all fall and winter of 2009 and 2010 to sell hiring Patrick, but I needed buy-in from sales and our edit partners. Super P was smarter than me in this area: Patrick's name was gold with advertisers. It says you're serious, and it opens their checkbooks. Our custom publisher in Phoenix also loved the idea. Its editorial director Beth Tomkiw thought it was bold, and she told me later that she was proud I followed my conviction.

Beth and I locked horns earlier because the magazine's footprint was growing bigger than our feet, and we were not ready to lace up. We'd been placed on newsstands across the country, but the product was not sellable.

"If you really want to go for it, I'll back you," she'd said. "But you have to go for it."

I did, and she backed me, starting with Patrick.

I remember meeting the legendary photographer like it was yesterday, and with great irony: it was St. Patrick's Day 2010, a day most people like me don't remember after 10:00 a.m. Patrick had a studio in Chelsea on West 21st Street, and a small group of us braved a cab that wove through streets of drunken revelers. His studio was on the top floor of a six-story loft building. Its elevator was hospital-size and had an operator who filled it with furniture, candles, and a stack of shelves holding religious figurines. It opened to Patrick's workplace, which included sets, makeup and hair stations, wardrobe racks, piles of equipment, and walls dotted with priceless art and prints. Your eye did not know where to go; it was chaotic brilliance.

Patrick was tall, thin, older than I expected, and very casual. He was wearing a button-down shirt, old jeans, scuffed sneakers, and a backwards baseball hat. The man was sixty-seven years old and dressed younger than the small group of thirty-year-olds in his studio. I could not understand a word the photographer uttered; it was a garbled mishmash of English and French only he and few others understood.

The idea I'd come up with was simple: *Big Bang Theory*'s Kaley Cuoco, reenacting scenes from the iconic "Justify My Love" video by Madonna. Directed by Jean-Baptiste Mondino in 1990, it featured the singer in various forms of provocation throughout Paris's Le Royal Monceau hotel. It's most known for the grainy footage of the popstar stumbling, gyrating, sliding, slithering, crawling, and however else one can find pleasure in a dark, empty Parisian hallway. I love celebrating iconic moments in pop culture with clever twists, and "Justify My Love" was about to turn twenty. Patrick also had a connection to the song: he shot the album cover.

Jeremy with *Big Bang Theory* star Kaley Cuoco, center, and Patrick Demarchelier. Photo courtesy of Jeremy Murphy.

I showed him portraits of Kaley and reference images from the video but could not comprehend anything he said.

Except one sentence.

"I play with ze hair; I make her sex-zy," he said, animatedly.

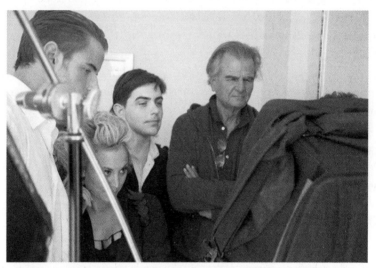

Looking over photos from the Kaley Cuoco shoot. (Left to right) Brandon Stoughton, Kaley, Jeremy, and Patrick Demarchelier. Photo courtesy of Jeremy Murphy.

We did the shoot at the Peninsula Hotel on 5th Avenue and 55th in April 2010, and it was one of the easiest days of my career. When you hire Patrick, you get the whole shebang: him, the best crew, digital tech, equipment, producers, hair, makeup, and assistants.

There were two "suggestions" he approved. The first and most important was using our stylist, The Jackal. Using her was a must, and once Patrick saw her book, he understood why.

Our other demand was that the male model be Kaley's co-provocateur and chew toy: Brandon Stoughton, the ripped, chiseled pretty boy from Britney Spears's "Womanizer" video. Everyone wanted chew time with him by the end. Brandon was a charmer and became a good friend.

Patrick's team handled everything else, and on shoot day they began quietly setting up and pre-lighting the locations around the hotel. The ease everyone brought was refreshing. Not a hint of drama, which was highly unusual…and welcome. Patrick arrived like clockwork at 9:00 a.m. and wanted to start shooting immediately. We were more than ready, and he began doing portraits of Kaley against a white seamless backdrop in a suite. The actress looked spectacular: tousled, toned, tan, tantalizing. Patrick's crew aimed a fan as she shook her head, blonde locks flying in the wind.

"*Magnifique!*" he shouted as he took frames with his camera.

One of Patrick's incredible images of Kaley, shot at The Peninsula
New York hotel. Photo by Patrick Demarchelier.

I could see early images pop on a screen nearby almost instanta-neously. They were electric. I'd never seen anything like it. Patrick is known for shooting sparingly; he takes, maybe, twenty frames for each setup. This is very rare; most shooters do hundreds, living in the shot for up to an hour.

After minimal clicks, he pointed to the screen.

"Boss, boss," he said to me. "You like?"

I stared and could not believe my eyes. We were fifteen minutes into our first setup, and he nailed the cover. Also, Patrick was asking *me* what I thought. Twenty years ago, I was admiring his work from a dowdy TV room in Tamarac, Florida. And now he's looking for my approval?

I smiled and he gave me a high five.

Patrick was working faster than we were and starting to enjoy the day.

"I shoot black dress," he announced after the first setup.

We didn't plan to use a black dress for the shoot, but The Jackal was prepared anyway. Patrick did more portraits of Kaley against the white backdrop but with a different look, more doe-eyed and vulnerable.

We coasted the rest of the day; everything was so light, relaxed, fun. People were practically giddy. That never happens. I even accompanied Patrick to lunch, where we ate steak and pommes frites in the Peninsula lobby restaurant. I had not yet developed an ear for his unique dialect, so I nodded, smiled, and responded in mocked French outrage to whatever the fuck he was saying in my shitty French accent. "*Non!*" (no), "*C'est fou!*" (that's crazy!), and "*Tu ne peux pas être sérieux!*" (you cannot be serious) are the only phrases I know to fake French "quelle horreur."

It was one of the proudest days of my professional career, and a great decision in retrospect. With Patrick shooting our magazine, we began to get traction with beauty and fashion advertisers. We used his work to herald a big redesign of the magazine Super P, Beth Tomkiw, and I envisioned, as well as our upgrade to perfect binding—no more stapled pages!—and a slicker stock of paper. The issue—with "Big Bang Baby" screaming from the cover lines—was our 2.0 moment.

During our next shoot with the cast of "Blue Bloods," Patrick worked at his typical "voilà!" speed. So much so, he was faster than anyone else and used timing between shoots for cat naps in the middle of the studio.

Our relationship with Patrick continued over the next six years, including shooting Pauley Perrette from *NCIS* as Babe Paley in New York, *2 Broke Girls* actress Beth Behrs at the George V Hotel in Paris, *The Good Wife*'s Julianna Margulies at the Hotel du Cap in the South of France, and *Mom* stars Anna Faris and Allison Janey at the Hôtel Plaza

Athénée. Most of these experiences are detailed in-depth throughout these pages.

In time, I got to understand most everything he said, and I enjoyed talking to him about his work, family, dog, sailboat, art, fashion, and life. He had a childlike exuberance for life, and he loved showing whatever new video game or app he downloaded to his iPhone. Patrick was also very kind; he took my headshot several times, one of which I got on my passport. He also took a portrait of my friend Charlie Siem, as well as my cat Champers, who I snuck into his studio.

His last shoot with the magazine, the one with *Mom* stars Allison Janey and Anna Faris, was mine as well. I was out, and he was most associated with my editorial vision. They would not use him again.

But I would. When I started my company, 360bespoke, he and his international agent Angela de Bona asked me to help bring his successful 2006 photo exhibit, Images et Mode, from the Petit Palais in Paris to a comparable museum in New York. For weeks, I sent books to all the curators at the Met, MoMA, Whitney, Frick, Guggenheim, and a few other top locations, showing the exhibits, as well as presenting ideas for funding, sponsors, and times. I was making headway with the Met and the Costume Institute until February 2018, when Patrick retired.

Patrick spent the next four years of his life sailing, enjoying his life with his family in St. Barts, and enjoying the spoils of his amazing legacy. I am so thankful to have worked with him at the tail end of that career.

Q&A WITH SOPHIA PAULMIER

Sophia: What's your all-time favorite work by Demarchelier?

Jeremy: Princess Diana sitting casually wearing a tiara. It's a historic photo and one of the few images that captured her joy in the moment, but that's the magic of Patrick. He finds it. Patrick also convinced her to cut and slick back her hair, which was shocking. It showed how she had evolved and became her own person.

S: *Before working with Demarchelier, who was your most expensive photographer?*

J: Yikes! That was fourteen years ago. I have no idea. Certainly not that much. We paid it because Patrick's name opened doors for us with talent and advertisers.

S: *Was this Kaley's first time working with Demarchelier?*

J: Yes, but he shot her for *Allure* right after us.

S: *How did she react to meeting Demarchelier on set?*

J: Everyone was in awe. He was an industry legend. But it was hard to talk to him because he talked in garbled French/English.

S: *Did Brandon Stoughton get some good shots on his own?*

J: Yes! We did solos of him undressing in the elevator. It got as far as his shirt. I would have kept going!

S: *How did he like working with Demarchelier? Had they worked together prior?*

J: Everyone did. It was a bucket list moment for the whole team.

S: *This was a defining time in your career that propelled the magazine to a higher status. How did you feel? Were you scared at all or surprised?*

J: I felt anxious; I wanted to impress him, even though we were the client. We were very deferential, but so was he. It was a love fest. I have a problem living in the moment, so I did not afford myself time to really soak it in. That came later. I'm glad to have worked with him five additional times.

S: *After first working with Demarchelier, who were some of the advertisers that undoubtedly signed on to buy spreads in your magazine?*

J: You can't attribute it all to him; I had a publisher who was a fierce advocate, and Patrick was a selling point for sure. But we had great writers, editors, designers.

S: *Did Demarchelier teach you anything about photography in the time you worked with him?*

J: Very much. Simplicity. Also, lighting. He made everything beautiful without a bag of tricks. And his work transcends time. I look at some of the images he'd shot for us, and they are not dated. They're timeless.

S: *What was your favorite memory of Demarchelier?*

J: So many, but during the first shoot he'd come up to me and say, "Boss! Boss! You like?" and point at the screen. He was asking me what *I* thought. That was a pinch yourself moment.

S: *Was there ever a shoot in which you wanted Demarchelier or wish he shot?*

J: I was very thankful and satisfied with what he did for us. But we had such great shooters—Ian Derry, Mark Mann, Jeff Lipsky, Keiron O'Connor, Gilles-Marie Zimmermann, Cliff Lipson—that I rarely regretted our choices.

S: Last thing you wish you'd said to him?

J: I was very effusive with praise and gratitude and expressed it every time. But he heard that from everyone so I'm not sure how meaningful it was to him. I do know that he really enjoyed working with us because we were fun and had great ideas, and but for one shoot we always used beautiful settings. We were "on-brand" for his work.

CHAPTER 7

······★······

Spilling Over

"Your life is going to change drastically," said the urologist, somberly. No worries, I thought. I'm going to end it anyway.

It was a frigid January day in 2014, and I had just gotten news that a painful condition I'd developed would only get worse.

Just what you want to hear when you're thirty-eight and in the prime of your life. As I stood outside his office, the wind chilling me straight to my bones, I contemplated the unthinkable. A bus was hurling down 5th Avenue, and I was ready to jump in front of it. I'd lived with three years of writhing pain that I'd kept hidden, and it would only get more excruciating. There are many people who live with worse, but I was not prepared for that eventuality. Thankfully, the bad angel on my right shoulder was on break, and the dullard sitting opposite had a captive audience.

I don't share this often because it's not exactly a campfire kind of story. My bladder was not contracting, and any liquid I'd drink would spill over and try to force itself out. Many times a day. I tried to hide it, but coming back to a table puffy faced because I'd just been crying was getting harder to hide. The nights were even worse. Midnight nature callings became nightmares. The loud, wailing shrieks of pain convinced my neighbor something was very wrong, and she knocked furiously on my door at 2:00 a.m. to see if I was OK. I'd gotten good at disarming people and made some stupid joke about it being a reaction to the end of *Mad Men*, which was bad enough to illicit such torment.

To ease the pain I'd been experiencing, I began drinking more, which only made the cycle more vicious. Macallan had to get out too, even from me: the best host imaginable. Being the fun, tipsy raconteur helped convince publicists, writers, photographers, and talent to work with us because we were fun. I'd take people out to the Polo Bar, King Cole, Bar Pleiades, wherever, and wine and dine them with jokes, laughs, war stories, singing, whatever. Anything to make the sale.

I also began acting more spontaneously, unpredictably, and irrationally, all made worse by constantly hosting booze-soaked drinks dates, dinners, and soirees.

On a night in 2014, I inadvertently started a bar fight at a pub on the Upper East Side. I'd joined a small group of women standing near the counter when one used a homophobic insult, which I flagged. She turned her venom toward me at that point, which I felt warranted "cunt" because she was being one. She did not share this sentiment and splashed her drink in my face.

Hell hath no fury like a gay publicly embarrassed.

I returned the gesture, and her boyfriend nearby came charging my way. Thankfully, a friend blocked him, and we hightailed it out.

These incidents became more frequent as my condition got worse.

A friend suggested it could be neurological, so I booked an appointment with a specialist at a nearby hospital. His tests were less invasive—no need to call Stabler and Benson at *SVU!*—but included an MRI. I'm highly claustrophobic and feared being slid into a coffin-sized space enclosed in a very loud machine. I had a full-on panic attack, which ended the test. The next time, I came with an arsenal: three Xanax, Jamaican music, and an eye mask. It felt like I was poolside at a beach resort listening to steel drums and sipping piña coladas. Bob Marley might as well have been doing the procedure.

The neurologist found nothing. Another heartbreak. He surmised it may be psychological and suggested I see a psychiatrist.

Here we go again. Nine months in and still no clue how to fix this condition. A colleague recommended his doctor, Shane Spicer, who got his training at Columbia University and Northwestern University. He has extensive clinical experience in adult psychiatry, psychotherapy, and addiction medicine. He's extremely hard to book an appointment with—he's high in demand—but my colleague convinced him to see me, and I liked him from the start.

Before we began treatment, he advised me to get a second opinion from a urologist. Except I needed a new primary doctor to make the referral.

Being incredibly lazy, I wound up finding the closest one—three blocks away—and she turned out to be one of the best: Dr. Danielle Nicolo, not just a primary care physician but a cardiologist at Weill Cornell as well. She earned a PhD in immunology and microbiology at Temple University, then an MD from Temple University.

I liked her too and gave her my history, including the "issue." Instantly, she advised I see Dr. Bilal Chughtai, a urologist who sees patients at Weill Cornell and New York-Presbyterian Hospital. He was serious, and surprised at my Irish black humor at first, but he grew to appreciate it. Again, I was put through torture as they performed tests, but it was easier than the alternative. I came back for the results, ready to hear there was no solution. Instead, I cried—and not from pain.

"I know exactly what's wrong with you," he explained.

Dr. Chughtai had found what was preventing the bladder from contracting, but more importantly how to fix it. Doing this would require surgery, and I'd never be able to have kids.

"Where are the scissors? I'll do it myself!" I joked.

Now he was beginning to like me.

The procedure was more than successful: it saved my life. But it affected it too, just in an unexpected way.

Two days after the procedure, I began to feel euphoric, which is a natural sensation after being cured of writhing pain every day. But this was different. I checked into the St. Regis Hotel for several days, even though I lived twelve blocks away, and I began to act more reckless and outrageous than before, including buying an entire bar drinks, shopping furiously (and expensively), dancing and singing when I shouldn't, and other shenanigans.

I also got weird bursts of creativity, far more than I'd ever experienced. I suggested our magazine use a pet as a mascot and impulsively bought a kitten, even though I'm allergic. I named him Champers and gave him a column in the magazine, using writer/comedian Frank DeCaro as his voice.

I began writing my own column too, but under the guise of Fritz van der Flagen, a made-up dilettante who traveled the world on someone else's dime (sound familiar?), getting in trouble in all the right circles. Fritz traveled with his own entourage, including Fran Lebowitz, Buster Poindexter, Champers, and a teddy bear named Smuggle. I'm surprised Dr. Shane let me leave his office.

A musical score for our print magazine was an insane but successful idea, as was turning images of LL Cool J in Paris into van Gogh paintings.

I even cold-emailed David Lauren—son of Ralph—to do a *Polo* magazine. I envisioned a glossy, *Vogue*-like publication about lifestyle, fashion, travel, and pursuits but seeped into the RL world of timeless glamour. To my great surprise, David responded he loved the idea and invited me to pitch it at their headquarters. Which was great, but I had nothing to show. I found an art director through colleagues and hired him to create templates of layouts, all in the RL aesthetic. A few weeks later, I went to their headquarters on Madison Avenue and showed the idea and the possibilities to their top media executive, and she loved it instantly. To make a long story short, the idea was hot until it ran into corporate hopscotch. There were a lot of internal changes at Ralph Lauren, and my idea fell victim.

Weeks later, while watching *Homeland*, the Showtime spy series starring Claire Danes, my curiosity was piqued. On the spy thriller, she plays Carrie Mathison, a CIA agent who's bipolar. Inadvertently, the condition helps her see things others don't, but it also makes her life a mess.

Could this be what's affecting me?

I went back to Dr. Shane, and he diagnosed it easily and has been treating me to this day. It took several medications to achieve balance, and it has. Life is less reckless these days. I still enjoy Macallan without swinging from chandeliers. I left the magazine, started a PR company called 360bespoke, and wrote my first book. I also dusted off old screenplays during the pandemic, getting them to the point where I could circulate them without embarrassment.

I owe a lot of this to the incredibly talented people—Dr. Bilal Chughtai, Dr. Danielle Nicolo, Dr. Shane Spicer—who saved my life, as well as people at the magazine, most especially my publisher Super P, who put up with my antics.

Q&A WITH SOPHIA PAULMIER

Sophia: This is a very personal, intimate chapter that a reader might identify with. What would you say to them?

Jeremy: For starters, thank you for reading! Writing about yourself is tough when you've spent your career writing about *other* people. A lot of this stuff I haven't shared before. I'm still a fuck up with a messy life. I certainly haven't done anything to give people comfort. But if you are finding it hard to pee, definitely see a urologist.

S: "The fun part of this is the creativity I experienced. I began to see more vividly and started getting crazy ideas." This is a very interesting and positive take on your way of dealing with the situation. Do you feel like you survived a near-death experience and began making creative decisions like never before because you felt free to live again?

J: There was a moment I wanted to end it, but that was the only time death ever entered my mind. I feel grateful to have had an incredible experience, and I've learned how being bipolar has helped and hindered my life. It certainly explains many of the unexpected things we did at the magazine.

S: "I even cold emailed David Lauren—son of Ralph—to do a Polo magazine. I envisioned a glossy, Vogue-like publication about lifestyle, fashion, travel, and pursuits but seeped into the RL world of timeless glamour." I would have loved this magazine, and many more would agree. If the opportunity came back, would you jump at it in today's post print, internet-obsessed world?

J: Yes, absolutely. But it would have to embrace all those mediums, which is the only way magazine brands can survive these days. Ralph Lauren has such a deep collection of categories we could explore—fashion, beauty, home, style. It would have been fun, but a friend in the industry warned me Ralph is very particular and changes his mind frequently. So maybe not as much fun.

S: Any crazy creative thoughts or ideas in your recent days?

J: Not really. One of the disadvantages of being on medications is a loss of vivid color in your imagination. I take a mood stabilizer called Lamotrigine, which ended the extremes, but any anticonvulsant will dull sensations. I am still able to think creatively, but coming up with the idea to create a musical score for a magazine would not happen today. At least not for me.

S: Do you find it interesting how all your biggest challenges have played into your best memories? Examples: 9/11, reconnecting with your dad, pitching the magazine to your boss' boss, losing your dad to cancer, urological surgery, creating a new cover for LL and pitching a new magazine to RL.

J: Perfect people are boring. Adversity, pain, loss, and obstacles all make you a wiser and I'd even say a better person. Going through those experiences may not be fun at the time, but they make you who you are.

S: *Lastly and most importantly, who are your least favorite doctors?*

J: Dr. Drive Thru! He was a psychiatrist on the Upper East Side when I first moved to New York and realized I had attention deficit disorder. He put me on Wellbutrin, which I still take, but was very uninterested in hearing how I was doing. I'd go once a month to get a new prescription and we'd talk for maybe ten minutes. Once, when I told him my father had passed, he responded, "What else is new?" He also had the world's nastiest receptionist.

S: *What would Fritz van der Flagen's bio be if he were around today?*

J: Bios for Fritz changed for every column. Among some of my favorites: he once served as Hillary Clinton's e-mail administrator; had a column in Vogue North Korea; was the world's reigning champion of Kerplunk!; authored bestselling memoir *Hold that Door, I'm Late for my Colonoscopy!* and *Tuesday's with Scotch*; DJ'd at Coachella; sold used cars; was a fifth member of Ace-of-Base; and rightful heir to the Romanov Dynasty.

CHAPTER 8

★

Pressing Start

With the incomparable Vivian Deuschl, who oversaw all PR for The Ritz-Carlton Company. She was one of the first supporters of our magazine. Photo by Jeremy Murphy.

In late 2007-2008, the old writer's strike was still in full force, and we had no stars to shoot because they had nothing to promote. Luckily, the Grammys were in February, which opened our door to music talents who were nominated or scheduled to perform. Or just good for ratings. On a lark, I reached out to Celine Dion's publicist; the megastar had something to do with the awards show, but I don't remember the details—I doubt anyone else does either. It didn't matter: Celine was a huge get. Her voice is said to be one of the "four" (her, Barbra, Whitney, and Mariah), and she has a string of number one hits and top-selling albums. Celine is also said to have flawlessly recorded "My Heart Will Go On" from *Titanic* in one take. The song was better than the movie. Give *her* the life raft.

Unbelievably, her publicist was receptive as long as we used already taken stock photos for the cover and feature, which was an easy yes. Photo agencies like Getty have thousands of images to "license" (i.e., pay to run), and we used a warm, light, and friendly image *Good Housekeeping* would consider, which is satirical considering I don't clean or do anything else related to household duties.

Securing an interview was also a question. We were not a priority, which was understandable. In that case, we could use existing quotes and do a "write around." It was a bit *US Weekly* of us, but it worked.

On a cold November afternoon, as I ate my very nutritious Big Mac for lunch at my desk, the phone rang. It was Celine's husband, René Angélil, calling from a limousine. He handed the phone to the legendary chanteuse, who talked to me for what seemed to be an hour. She was friendlier than I expected, as well as modest, self-deprecating, and grateful for her success.

"I feel fortunate to be able to still have the passion about singing, and I have to say that I enjoy my work and my singing much more today than ever before," she said in her Quebecois accent, which reflects her French-Canadian heritage. "Before I needed to prove myself in the industry—that I could do it. It was like I was in a Jacuzzi where the water was hot, and I was not even questioning myself. I took some time away for a little bit—even though I kept myself quite busy. Now that I'm back, it feels like a fresh new start and a brand-new career for me. I recognize the fortunate years we've had."

I was surprised about her candor and the fact that she used the word "Jacuzzi." Never in my life did I think: (a) I'd get to interview Celine, (b) she'd call me at my desk without any warning, and (c) she'd mention a hot tub.

Flying home from Sydney in December 2009, I got bumped up to first class and sat across from movie star Hugh Grant. He was perfectly kind, but less so in Los Angeles, where he learned Qantas had lost his luggage.

"This inept airline!" he snipped after a sixteen-hour journey back home.

I didn't stay to hear how it ended—the gate agent was wise to my eavesdropping and scowled me off.

A decade later, I saw Hugh again in Bemelmans, the lounge inside The Carlyle Hotel. He was in New York filming the miniseries *The Undoing* with Nicole Kidman and was ending the night with two female friends in the jazz bar.

I relayed my story to my friend Stephanie, and she dared me to see if he'd remember. You don't have to ask me twice. I bravely walked up to his table and introduced myself.

"Mr. Grant, I doubt you'll remember this, but we were on the same flight ten years ago from Sydney, and they lost your luggage."

Deadpan, he replied, "Was I a (bad word)?"

I responded, humorously, he was, and we had a great laugh.

When we started the magazine in 2006, people thought it was a joke. We were not ready for primetime, and it showed. Supporters were few and naysayers were many. Luckily, the right people cheered for us to succeed, inside and outside of the company.

Our most ardent fan was Vivian Deuschl, the head of all PR at The Ritz-Carlton Company, which at that point owned the country's most exclusive (and expensive) hotels. They were natural settings for our magazine. But were we classy enough for them?

I'd met Vivian a couple of years before as a travel writer, and there must have been something she liked about me (I wish she'd shared; it would have made therapy much less expensive). She is a legend in the industry, including when she served as top PR person as the old Ritz-Carlton in DC where Nancy Reagan used to come for burgers in its Jockey Club. Vivian has instincts, intuition, and a bullshit detector unique to the profession. When word got out that bed bugs had infested a big US city, attention naturally turned to local hotels. "Bed bugs can't afford to stay at The Ritz-Carlton," Vivian quipped, ending the "controversy" dead in its tracks.

I reached out to tell her about the magazine weeks after starting, and she pledged her support.

In the years since, we photographed stars at its hotels in New York; Los Angeles; Boston; Washington, DC; Miami; Palm Beach; Laguna Beach; Lake Tahoe; Beaver Creek, Colorado; Tysons Corner, Virginia; the Sonoran Desert near Tucson; St. Thomas; and Berlin.

When she received a Lifetime Achievement Award from the Hospitality Sales and Marketing Association International—a very prestigious organization in the travel industry—I put her photo on a poster-sized mock cover of our magazine. That's when I met her daughter Lisa, who was battling cancer. Tragically she passed, and I lit a candle for her at Notre Dame Cathedral in Paris. We also celebrated Vivian's birthday a few years later at the Four Seasons restaurant in New York.

Vivian is one in a million, and you will read her name often throughout this book. There are not many true supporters in your life. When you find one, count your blessings. And be there when they need you.

Jeremy with Robert ("Bobby") Konjic, one of fashion's top super models. Photo courtesy of Jeremy Murphy.

Shooting fashion/cover spreads requires more than the celebrity. There's the photographer, stylist, groomer, producer, and models often used as extras. One became my best friend: Robert ("Bobby") Konjic, a tall, striking Swede with a smile that could light Times Square. He was introduced to me by our mutual friend, Joanna Della-Ragione, in 2013, and I cast him twice. First, when we imagined fashion makeovers of beloved TV characters: Bobby posed as "Leonard," the engineering-scientist-mathematician nerd played by Johnny Galecki on *The Big Bang Theory*, shot by the brilliant Kim Myers. A year later, I hired him to pose with actress Allison Janney from the sitcom *Mom* for a photo shoot in Paris.

Bobby steals the lens. Croatian by birth, he was raised in Sweden and later discovered by photographer Mario Testino. Within months, he was the face of a global Gucci campaign, including on a giant billboard gracing Sunset Boulevard. Bobby is most famous for the Nautica ad shot by Peter Lindbergh, which featured the shirtless, smiling model sitting on a seaside cliff (had I even attempted to remove my shirt, someone would have pushed me *off* the cliff). When we met, I was surprised to find conversation easy and natural. It was like meeting your best friend for the first time. That was a decade ago, and I can honestly say Bobby is someone I will know and love the rest of my life.

Chuck Lorre is the most brilliant mind in situation comedy. I write that with full conviction because it's true. From *Roseanne* to *Cybill*, *Grace Under Fire* and *Dharma & Greg* to *Two and a Half Men* and *The Big Bang Theory*, there is no sharper, funnier person writing and creating TV comedies. Chuck had written a first-person essay about creating comedies for a bigger glossy magazine (I think it was *GQ*) but insisted it be published word-for-word—no editing. Of course, it had a few f-bombs, which made it a bit sensitive to print. Magazines are sold on newsstands and, just like network TV, there are things you can't do (at least, that was the case back then). A PR rep for *Two and a Half Men* had shown me the essay, and I couldn't believe any magazine turned it down. It was brilliant and accurately summarized the Hollywood experience selling a TV comedy script: drinking, self-hatred, doubt, more drinking, false hope, network bullshit, talent bullshit, you get the picture. I had to have this for *our* magazine. And, being completely out of my league, I convinced myself that I could get Chuck to let us run his essay *with* edits. We couldn't print the expletives either, but surely me with my two and a half years of experience running a magazine had the charm to convince him where others had not. I could not, but to his credit he was extraordinarily gracious. As I sat at my desk eating my "power lunch"—Big Mac value meal with McFlurry—he called from his car and explained his stance, which I appreciated then and still do now. The McFlurry didn't taste so great when I hung up though.

For several years, as our fashion and luxury profile began to grow, Super P and I would sneak away to Paris for meetings: he got us in to see top luxury advertisers, who are all based there, and I set up lunches, dinners, and drinks with PR contacts, writers, photographers, and agents. Of course we had no budget for these excursions, which necessitated favors. As an editor of a celebrity magazine with a heavy travel angle, I had a lot of chips to cash in.

On our first trip, after an overnight flight at 7:00 a.m., we took a car to the George V hotel, which was hosting us, and got dressed while the car idled below. Super P and I then went to the headquarters of L'Oréal, where he sold them on advertising Yves Saint Laurent fragrances. We then went to luxury powerhouse Richemont and landed Van Cleef & Arpels. Others followed, but my favorite stop was Christian Dior, where we met their top PR people in the designers' original atelier on Avenue Montaigne. There, I pitched them a cover shoot with a star showcasing their fall/winter 2012 collection. They showed us the wardrobe in a private showroom, which was another pinch-me moment.

No trip to Paris—at least for me—misses a comical interlude, and mine was a doozy. I'd taken a nasty fall before coming and fractured my tailbone. It hurt like a motherfucker. The hotel concierge arranged an appointment with the house doctor, who wasn't in-house. I took an hour-long cab ride to a hospital, where I found a bored physician more attentive to the clock on the wall than to my dilemma.

Surely, there had to be something he could do, right?

Completely unsympathetic, the doctor sneered in full Parisian snit, "Would you like me to put a cast on your ass?"

Our last night there, Super P and I had dinner in our hotel's lounge, and as we ate overpriced finger sandwiches, we saw former French president Jacques Chirac sitting across from us, with his wife and the notorious dog who took antidepressants. We were in a celebratory mood after our successful meetings, and I decided it was prudent to approach President Chirac after a bottle of bubbly. I thanked him for standing up to President George W. Bush during the US buildup to war with Iraq. Without skipping a beat, he mumbled the equivalent of "fucking retard" in reply.

I hope he wasn't talking about me.

By 2012 we finally began to hit our stride. *WWD*, the *Wall Street Journal* for fashion/beauty, did a half-page feature on our magazine, and the result was immediate; suddenly, design houses were calling *us*! The communications director for Salvatore Ferragamo reached out and invited me to Bergdorf Goodman for lunch, and we discussed ideas on how we could work together.

A couple of weeks later, she called with an idea: shoot an actor in the designer's 2013 spring/summer men's collection. I was flattered to be asked until I saw the clothes: bold, bright, fluorescent colors. It looked like the wardrobe for a Wham! video.

Who the fuck am I going to get for this?

Pickings were slim. At the same time, the CW Network had premiered the superhero/drama *Arrow* and was looking for PR to spread the word. The lead, Stephen Amell, was a teen dream: blond, gorgeous, ripped—right out of an Abercrombie & Fitch catalog. I inquired about his availability, and he had a small window between filming.

Stephen was perfect. Ferragamo loved him too and suggested we use as a stylist Christopher Campbell, who I only knew by reputation. He'd done work for the *New York Times*, *Departures*, *Time's Style & Design*, *Black Book*, etc. I looked at his work and booked him instantly.

Off to Toronto we went.

My producer and I arrived at the hotel and had a boys' night out with an actor friend who was filming a hit series in Toronto. We all met in the lounge, caught up, and had fun.

It didn't end.

Back in my room, we emptied the mini bar, talked, laughed, and...I don't remember. The next morning, I awoke to find my actor friend sleeping on the floor and the other guy passed out in the hallway.

I readied myself for a planned breakfast with our new stylist in the lobby restaurant. Christopher was excited because we were a magazine on the rise, and this was a great opportunity.

I came to the table, introduced myself, and sat down.

"What happened to you?" he asked.

I had a black eye from the night before. No idea or memory of why or how.

And that's how I met Christopher, who went on to style thirty shoots for us. He tells this story often.

The photos came out better than I thought, but Stephen Amell was standoffish. He was also ripped, and some of the sample-sized clothes were very tight.

"No problem," said Christopher, who tailored the suits and jackets on-site, taking them apart with a seam adjuster and then stitching them back together.

That's a professional.

The most shocking—and hilarious—thing I've ever seen is penis puppetry. Wow, that's quite an opener. This was a phenom in New York years ago—artists on stage making puppets with their junk—but it was new to me until a trip to Europe, where a writer I contracted demonstrated the technique after a photo shoot. Literally. He took down his pants in front of our crew and made several shapes with his penis, including a burger, the Eiffel Tower, and a signature move by gymnast Mary Lou Retton. Our jaws dropped seeing this, especially in a secluded setting at the bar. I may have cried with laughter.

He did it again after another shoot, and this time one of the photo assistants joined in. We were sitting in the corner of a famous Parisian bar—secluded—and two of my guests were entertaining people with their cocks.

We eventually left—by choice, thank you—and as we walked away, the server chased after us and shouted, "Sir, you forgot your belt!"

Phil Keoghan, the popular host from the reality series *The Amazing Race*, was a favorite of mine, and over the years did shoots for us around the world, as you'll read. In our early days, I'd gotten wind he was doing a cross-country drive with his father to promote the show and his book *No Opportunity Wasted*. Mercedes Benz sponsored the campaign, but they needed a hotel sponsor. Enter Beth Feldman, PR extraordinaire. Beth knew I had connections through my travel writing and reached out to see if I could help. I enlisted our Ritz-Carlton friend Vivian, who informed me the brand didn't work with reality or soap opera stars. I didn't know any of the other companies well enough to ask, so I gave up. A few days later, Vivian called again: a top executive at Ritz-Carlton was a huge fan and loved the idea. They'd put Phil and his father up at their hotels in New York, Philadelphia, Dearborn (Michigan), St. Louis, Phoenix, and Los Angeles. For some strange reason, we could not book him at The Ritz-Carlton, Chicago so we paid it ourselves. Afterward, he appeared on *The Late Late Show with Craig Ferguson* to talk about the drive and show photos from the trip, including his father and him relaxing in their robes at the *Chicago* Ritz-Carlton. The problem? The hotel robes have *the Four Seasons*' leaf logo—the competitor to The Ritz-Carlton. Chicago is the one city in America where The Ritz-Carlton didn't manage the branded hotel, but Four Seasons did, which explained why it wasn't comped. No one knew this, but fortunately people in Ritz-Carlton corporate understood. One even laughed.

We brought the incredibly sexy, vivacious, kind, and beautiful Rachelle Lefevre from *Under the Dome* to Hampshire, England, for a cover shoot by photographer Ian Derry. He's a British shooter with a rock star edge; everything about him is cool, including his work. As was customary, we brought Rachelle, Ian, and his crew to dinner at the hotel's bar/restaurant the night before the shoot. Rachelle is as gorgeous in person as she is on-screen.

The morning of the shoot, I awoke in my room and prepared for the day, mindless to what had happened the previous night. A writer friend from London had visited, and we apparently hosted a lively after-party that may have damaged furniture. I didn't see anything as I left for set, but in between the photography, the hotel's PR rep pulled me aside with a "we have to have a difficult conversation" opener.

That is among the statements that never work well for me, along with the question, "That was you?"

Typically, yes.

She showed me images of a slightly damaged carpet and table that they'd need to repair. Which meant that they'd have to take the room out of service, a cost that would be passed to me.

Fuck.

Fortunately, any damage costs were rolled into normal wear-and-tear fees.

No word on my liver.

It was time to go home after a long trip to London, where we photographed two big TV stars. As I stood in the lobby of the posh hotel directing the departure, a publicist approached me and said one of the stars forgot to tip "Snuffie," the concierge.

I guaranteed her there is no concierge in history with this name, but she insisted we check. You haven't witnessed sneering like the kind I got asking the perfectly groomed staff at the desk this question.

She wouldn't let it go, and I was curious. I did more digging and finally discovered "Snuffie" is the neighborhood coke dealer.

Carmine Giovinazzo and Eddie Cahill, who starred on *CSI: NY*, were cool as fuck. Crime dramas were all the rage in 2007, and these guys were the show's man candy. It helped that they are both terrific actors.

I wanted to do something nature-y with them, but upscale nature because I hate the whole concept. The Ritz-Carlton had a resort in Beaver Creek, Colorado, high atop the mountains and wilderness, and they extended an invitation to bring two stars to promote their summer offerings. RC Vivian put me in touch with Steven Holt, the property's in-house PR director who had something very special to sell: in the winter, the log-cabin resort is covered by pristine white snow; in summer, it's bathed in sun peeking over the mountain tops.

Carmine and Eddie loved the idea of a free trip to the mountains, where they could play golf, whitewater raft, eat and drink by a firepit, and just hang casually.

Casual it was not, but damn did we have fun. Steven and I arranged several setups, including the aforementioned rafting and golf, as well as a hot-air balloon ride, gourmet dinner, and roasting s'mores. Of course, we added trouble.

I brought The Jackal as my plus-one because there is no one more entertaining. Steven put us in a very large cabin of our own and warned us to keep the doors shut because of roaming bears. After drinks the first night, we returned to the cabin and heard grunting.

"The bears!" we said in unison before calling the hotel's version of 9-1-1.

"Ritz-Carlton emergency. Does your duvet have a thread count less than one thousand?"

Turned out I left the TV on, and a *National Geographic* special about the wilderness was playing loudly.

The next day, after shooting the nature setups, we returned to the resort and began drinking by the firepit when a spontaneous rap song emerged; everyone was supposed to add rhymes to an ongoing beatbox sound by Eddie. I am not the person to ask of this, and my suggestions were lame. Carmine also played guitar; he was better than a lot of famous musicians.

Late into the night, some of us pretended to sword fight with fire pokers. We also had a drinking contest with Johnny Walker Blue...and an obligatory visit from hotel security.

The next morning, Steven met me for breakfast.

"So...last night," he began.

I said I did not have much memory except for it being fun.

"I can tell by the security report," Steven responded. "I was going to comp the entire night for you but can't now with this on record."

Oops.

Steven went on to host us at their hotel in Lake Tahoe. When I started my company, 360bespoke, years later, he became a partner.

One of the biggest stars on TV was suddenly available, and we arranged a quick shoot in London at a fancy hotel. The actor was nicer than I expected and highly literate. He also brought his girlfriend, who was beautiful and petite. The night before, we took both to the bar, per usual, and had a lively gathering—not as rowdy, but not entirely sober either.

The next morning, as we photographed him in the hotel's bistro, his girlfriend walked in still wearing a white bath robe and slippers. Her face was red and angry, and you can tell she'd been crying. She pointed at him dramatically, and then walked away without saying a word. This was in front of our crew and other patrons.

Allegedly, their night had not been eventful because he didn't return to the room and instead spent the evening drinking and getting into other hijinks.

Astonishingly, they broke up later.

Jeremy with cast of *The Big Bang Theory* (left to right): Simon Helberg, Johnny Galecki, Kaley Cuoco, Jim Parsons, and Kunal Nayyar. Photo courtesy of Jeremy Murphy.

In 2009, *The Big Bang Theory* was getting ready to make its name literal. The show had popped in its Monday nighttime slot and was moving to Thursdays—the holy grail in network television. This is the last opportunity advertisers have before the weekend to sell you cars, movies, food, groceries, whatever. I knew *Big Bang* was going to crush it, and I raced to get the cast on a cover while I could. I had the perfect location too: The Pierre, a majestic five-star hotel on 5th Avenue that had been renovated by the Taj Hotel company, which spent hundreds of millions on a full-gut makeover. It was due to open within a few weeks, and its marketing team loved the idea of hosting a big shoot with the entire cast.

The cast was game too: Jim Parsons, Johnny Galecki, Kaley Cuoco, Simon Helberg, and Kunal Nayyar all agreed to come to New York for the cover shot.

Booking travel for celebrities is always an interesting experience because many don't want to give their real age or name. Prying this information from their publicists is difficult. I had no problem with this cast because they were young, fresh-faced, and not yet famous. AA put all five in business class from Los Angeles.

As the plane was flying to New York, a colleague raced into my office.

"You put them *all* on the same plane?" she shouted.

Yeah, the magic carpet wasn't available.

I seemed to have forgotten or not realized the "heir and the spare" rule. There's a reason Princes William and Harry never travel together.

"If that flight goes down, you've killed a billion-dollar franchise" were the last words I heard before grabbing a bottle of wine and hiding under my desk, praying they arrived safely.

(Obviously, they did.)

One of our more elaborate productions was shooting the cast of *Blue Bloods* in a New York studio in Chelsea Piers, a hideous collection of tennis courts, a golf range, restaurants, and other activity spaces on the West Side. The TV series had emerged a surprise hit, and the cast wielded enough star power—Tom Selleck, Bridget Moynahan, Donnie Wahlberg—to warrant a cover.

Shooting one big talent is stressful enough, but five...at the same time? That's masochism. But by this time, we'd gotten good at it, and I took up the challenge.

I needed a space big enough to not just shoot the five cast members but also create sets to photograph against. Chelsea Piers was big enough but did not offer great scenery: it was an empty studio we were expected to fill. Also, we were going to use Demarchelier again, and he'd expect something interesting. His office suggested we use famed set designer Marla Weinhoff, a legend in the industry, who made her name creating photographer Richard Avedon's backgrounds.

Marla had her own studio in the Meatpacking District, and I brought "The Jackal," with me to meet and go over the concept. My idea was simple enough: classic family settings. I envisioned a backyard barbecue, dinner, packing up a Winnebago, and so on. Marla jumped at the chance and began showing us swatches of wallpaper, carpeting, even furniture chips. She also had suggestions for the Winnebago.

What the fuck had I gotten into?

Shoot day turned into a madhouse. There had to be fifty-plus people setting up the sets, scenes, equipment, and hair and makeup stations. The Jackal and her team had clothing racks for all five stars. Actually, four.

Donnie had a last-minute conflict and couldn't do shoot day but offered to go to Patrick's studio the next week for fill-ins. This is when you use an extra to play him and then Photoshop the real person in later.

The sets were impeccable. Marla not only found the station wagon, which came up a very big freight elevator, but a classic police car circa the 1950s: the Eisenhower era, which was the tone I wanted to hit.

The whole cast was friendly except for one: Len Cariou, who played the grandfather. He was surly and not happy to be there.

Chelsea Piers had a commissary for lunch, and Super P and I retreated for a bite. As I ate lukewarm pasta, a publicist on Tom's team approached me with an issue. In the backyard setting, I wanted the family to fire guns at objects instead of barbecuing because they played a family in law enforcement, and I thought that was a clever spin.

"Tom doesn't want to hold a gun," she advised.

Umm, he was on the board of directors at the NRA. As in, the National Rifle Association.

I expressed my incredulity, but Tom was a big star, and I did not have the power to overrule him.

Marla found a barbecue.

Q&A WITH SOPHIA PAULMIER

Sophia: Name one advertiser you fought to get. What changed and how long did you have to wait before you got them?

Jeremy: Dior. It was our Moby Dick. I tried since 2006 when we started the magazine, and Michael and I did *everything*. Finally, we went to Paris to visit their atelier on Avenue Montaigne, and we applied our mutual charm. That's a whole chapter! (See Page 237)

S: You can only pick one, Plaza Athénée or Ritz-Carlton.

J: Plaza Athénée, hands down.

S: London, Paris, or New York?

J: Impossible choice! They all offer something unique, especially as an editor of a magazine. I have such fond memories of each, and a few scandals I caused that are too saucy even for this book!

S: Robert ("Bobby") Konjic became a close friend. What would you say you learned is the biggest cliché about a model?

J: The Zoolander myth. Many of the models I've met are very smart, especially the veterans. It takes a lot of grit and discipline to survive that profession.

S: If you could cast Rachelle LeFevre in any new show, movie, or remake, what would it be?

J: Something where she's the president. I'm actually selling a scripted series—James Brolin is a producer!— and there are a number of roles I can see her in. She just has the presence, voice, hair, skin—perfection!

S: *Be honest, is Hugh Grant a zaddy IRL or an old coot?*

J: I'm forty-nine. I don't know what the fuck that means.

S: *Was he difficult on that flight?*

J: No, he was snoring the entire time, and very loudly! He was directly across from me, and I did everything I could to block it out, to no avail. Finally, I summoned the flight attendant to ask if there was anything they could do. She knelt down beside me and basically said I'd been upgraded and should be fortunate for just being there.

S: *Your blind item story about the photo shoot of an A-list TV star breakup has me nostalgic for "Crazy Days and Nights." Have you ever read their posts, more so in the early days of that website?*

J: No, but I've heard people like that site. I don't follow any celebrity news.

S: *What was your favorite blind item of all time read?*

J: No idea. I remember reading them a lot when I was in my twenties.

S: *Has there ever been a whole cast that died in a plane crash?*

J: Not that I know of. Just that soccer team in South America. But they didn't die, they just ate each other. There's a movie about it.

S: *Marla Weinhoff seems like a dream to work with. I see her influence time and time again on so many campaigns and online platforms. Did she give you a new appreciation for set design and art direction?*

J: Oh my God, did she ever!!!! I had no idea the details and effort that goes into set design, especially at that level. We were looking at paint swatches! And carpet samples!

S: *Best Celine Dion song of all time?*

J: "All By Myself." She hits that crazy note towards the end that would have burst anyone else's lungs.

S: *Did you ever see or talk to Celine again?*

J: No, that was a one-time experience.

S: *I heard Salvatore Ferragamo makes the best leather shoes. Did the communicators director gift you a pair?*

J: Not leather, but I got a great pair of suede rider shoes!

S: *Did you ever find out how you got the black eye?*

J: Still don't know. There's a lot about that night I still don't know, lol.

S: *As a huge Proenza Schouler fan I have to know, what's Lazaro like?*

J: He was very sweet but shy. And handsome!

CHAPTER 9

········★········

If You Remember It, You Weren't There

I've always had a mischievous streak, and as a kid growing up in sleepy unpleasantville, I lived vicariously through MTV and its Top 20 Countdown. In the late '80s, glam rock bands like Mötley Crüe, Guns N'Roses, Def Leppard, and Bon Jovi dominated the charts, and I became a closet fan (and case; go figure). The hedonistic, party-all-night lives of Tommy Lee and Nikki Sixx were infinitely more interesting than mine; my Dante's *Inferno* had become a wildfire of suburban monotony. After my 3:00 p.m. viewings of Santa Barbara, I would check in with Alan Hunter to see what videos had made the list, and for what seemed like a year, it was Mötley Crüe's "Home Sweet Home."

I assure you: they were not writing about Coral Springs.

Never did I imagine I'd reach that level of riotous rebellion.

Until I woke up in London to see my hotel room trashed, strangers passed out the floor, clothes hanging from doors and ceiling fan, mini bar (and many refills) emptied, and the drapes burnt.

My guests and I had somehow set the room on fire.

With no memory of how or why.

I visited in August 2013 to scout locations for our next shoots and got to stay in several fabulous places, one of which I will keep to myself and the police report. There, I was given a very glamorous suite named after a royal, which was huge and totally uncalled for: I was unworthy. After checking in and settling into my new "home," I went down to the lobby to meet a colleague for drinks in the bar, but fate took a different turn that day when we were refused entry—he was wearing shorts and a T-shirt, which exposed his tattoos. This was a no-no at the luxe hotel.

Instead, my friend suggested we go to the Groucho Club, an ultra-exclusive private gathering space for cool people: actors, musicians, artists, writers, people famous for nothing, and the like. Everyone but me. There, you could expose body ink; collared shirt and khakis, not so much.

It was late afternoon, and we started on the rooftop. There I sat with my colleague, as well as other known names. There was also a long wait to bump rails in the bathroom. With the world's worst bladder, that made an uncomfortable thirty minutes.

As the night progressed, I began to feel terribly insecure and befriended a group of people just like me—no-names who shouldn't have been there either.

Several Scotches in, I invited my new friends—and several quasi-celebrities—back to my giant suite at the famous hotel.

The gathering turned more festive than I imagined.

The next morning, I awoke on one of the couches completely hungover and confused. The room looked like Mötley Crüe and Guns N' Roses had a party-off.

I had no recollection of what happened and began cleaning furiously. Thinking irrationally, I also tied the curtains back, hiding the charred portions. (Housekeeping won't notice!) I filled many garbage bags and placed the refuse in the rubbish bin, destroying evidence as any criminal would.

Hotels have an option of virtual checkout, which I used out of embarrassment. I thought I'd done a decent job of tidying up and snuck out like a schoolboy just caught doing something he shouldn't.

On the way to my next hotel, I got a call from the last one. The damage was considerable. I've just finished paying that bill (thank you, Citibank).

This was not my finest moment. In fact, I was mortally embarrassed and left a £300 tip for the housecleaners, which was all I had left in my wallet; I would have given more.

Friends still tease me about this night and what happened. What thirty-something editor behaves like this? It took a lot of soul-searching, as well as putting the (kind of) breaks on these shenanigans. I haven't done it again, that's for sure.

I hoped it would be a dirty secret kept to a few, and was horrified when Bobby Konjic, my Swedish model friend, informed me the story had made its round throughout London. He and another friend met at a party and compared notes about what they'd heard.

By now, I was horrified, mitigated only slightly by the experience being kinda cool.

"The Stones. Zeppelin. Ozzy. Depp. Murphy," Bobby joked.

All known for their wild ways and bans from establishments around the globe.

I joined them. And to this day, there is a lifetime ban on me at that London hotel.

Q&A WITH SOPHIA PAULMIER

> *Sophia: This story sounds like you relived the movie The Hangover in this hotel suite in London.*
>
> Jeremy: Everything except the tiger, missing tooth, and Tyson!
>
> *S: Any regrets from that night?*
>
> J: Aside from setting it on fire? Hard to top that! But it was a famous suite named after a famous person and I never enjoyed it "properly."
>
> *S: The Groucho Club sounds extraordinary. Was there a part of you that just wanted to network with all these famous faces surrounding you?*
>
> J: I'm terribly insecure around that level of cool people, so no. And I don't smoke. Most of the networking seemed to be going on outside.

S: *Is the Groucho still the hot spot of London today?*

J: I assume. I haven't been in ages. I'm fortunate to have gotten a membership to 5 Hertford Street, which is more...dignified.

S: *Have you ever been back to that hotel or the Groucho Club again?*

J: Yes to Groucho. No to the hotel. As you might have read, I'm banned. I tried to get in years later for drinks and the doorman turned me right around.

S: *Would you do it again, had you been around the same situation today?*

J: I'd be in bed watching Netflix by 9.

CHAPTER 10

★

Bonding with the Bow

Violinist Charlie Siem performing at The Carlyle in New
York City. Photo courtesy of Jeremy Murphy.

I never considered myself especially cultured. I like *pop* culture and can
to this day sing many songs from the eighties word-for-word: Wham!,
Madonna, The Police, Thompson Twins, Crowded House, even Run
DMC. Occasionally, though, I'd hear opera performances my mom
watched on our local PBS station. "Madam Butterfly" was particularly

haunting. I also enjoyed hearing classical music but had no understanding of its significance or origin.

Moving to New York in my mid-twenties reinformed my startling lack of culture, and I began to immerse myself in books, music, and theater—off the radar; I didn't want to expose my naivete.

And then violinist Charlie Siem came into my life. To understand his talent you must listen to him perform, especially Paganini or Vivaldi. He is known for passionate expression and technical precision, with interpretations of classics that bring to the listener emotional depth and a dynamic range. On a snowy day in January, as I ate breakfast at a local diner, I read about him in an obscure British arts magazine, and then YouTubed his work. It is captivating, charismatic, and modern. His background is equally impressive: he attended Cambridge and studied with master violinists Itzhak Rashkovsky and Shlomo Mintz.

Charlie Siem recording "Canopy" with the English Chamber Orchestra.

Our magazine had just launched a culture section called Muse, which featured profiles of writers, painters, sculptors, musicians, chefs, fashion designers, luminaries, and even the guy who creates perfumes for Yves Saint Laurent. We got to write about Fran Lebowitz, Thomas Keller, Michael Kors, Thierry Despont, Jeff Leatham, Tomas Maier, even Naomi Campbell. Rebecca Ascher-Walsh brought incredible taste, discernment, and style to the section. Her choices always grew my mind.

Muse became a great source of pride for the magazine and a candy store of sorts for me. I lived for this kind of knowledge and sophistication. Not everyone else did though. There was one particular executive who hated the section and was constantly trying to kill it. He didn't think it fit into our mandate.

I didn't care what he thought, but I did Super P, who was of the same mind as me: Muse provided a refined environment that advertisers—luxury automobiles and financial services, especially—savored.

I regularly sent Rebecca ideas on who to feature. She was diplomatic in responding to my suggestions, especially when rejecting them. I gave her this power because I believed in her. She also knew much better than I did. But we both agreed Charlie would make a terrific profile. Rebecca found him in a couple of hours—on a Saturday!—and assigned the story to Wickham Boyle, whose writing was wonderful, full of color and great quotes. Charlie told her his violin—a $15-million 1735 Guarneri del Gesù violin once owned by the King of Prussia—was his "intense mistress. My life is consumed by playing the violin. It requires unending attention from me, and I so happily give it. Day in and day out, for now it is the most rewarding relationship in my life."

Charlie appreciated the feature, and when he came to New York for a performance, he agreed to be the guest of honor at a cocktail reception we threw for advertisers at The Carlyle Hotel. Its PR director Jennifer Cooke worked with us in planning this event, which took place high above its tower in a suite with a view of New York's skyline. Everything about the night was memorable for all the right reasons. *Good Wife* star Matt Czuchry attended, as did actress Sami Gale from *Blue Bloods*. Super P invited top clients, who loved the night and inspired us to do more "salon"-like events. I was also very happy my Tom Ford tuxedo fit perfectly; it does not anymore.

Charlie Siem, Jeremy Murphy, and Matt Czuchry from *The Good Wife* at The Carlyle.

Charlie and I struck up an email kinship, and when I went to London the following September, he invited me to hear him perform at Wigmore Hall, one of the city's most prestigious theaters. Afterwards, we went to lunch at a popular restaurant called Cecconi's in the Mayfair neighborhood and found surprising camaraderie between us. Charlie was raised in aristocratic London, attended Eton between Princes William and Harry, and travels in circles I don't even know exist. I'm from the suburbs of South Florida and dreamed of being a Capwell on *Santa Barbara*. Over lunch, though, the conversation between us was effortless. James Bond with a violin was interested in what I was saying.

At the same time, our culture section Muse began to thrive. Interviews became easier to get, and advertisers continued to sign on. Incredibly proud of what we created, I wanted to produce a video to celebrate the section that we could use for marketing purposes, and enlisted an agency called Team One to produce a "sizzle reel" highlighting all the great content we were producing. The company is the luxury division of Saatchi & Saatchi, one of the biggest and most prestigious advertising agencies in the business. We worked with their incredible team—which included Nick Teare, Jamie Kerr, and James Hendry—to capture the magic of Muse. They came back with an inspired idea: take the visuals from the layouts, add in sound bites from the talents featured, and score it to music.

I knew just who to call. We happened to be doing back-to-back photo shoots in London, which gave us a window to film Charlie's performance of Bach's "Violin Partita No. 3," shot by Mark Mann. The final product—hearing the words from Fran Lebowitz, Thomas Keller, Patrick Demarchelier, and others over Charlie's music—was stupefying. It did everything we wanted and more.

Including a new idea: create a musical score of our own to highlight the *entire* magazine and our brand. With so many eyes going to YouTube, social media, streaming channels, and websites, why not use those platforms to promote what we were doing in its entirety?

It sounded absurd at the time, and it probably was. We barely had a website, and our Facebook following was a joke. But I felt there was something to this.

Back in London the next spring, I took Charlie to lunch at 5 Hertford Street, a posh private-members club in Mayfair, and proposed the idea.

"My primary reaction was to recoil," recalled Charlie. "I'm not a composer."

I wouldn't give up and continued to lobby him throughout the summer until he finally broke.

"They came back to me several months later, and I thought maybe I should really give this a go," Siem said later. "Perhaps I should venture into the uncharted territory of writing an original composition. I'm a big believer in getting out of your comfort zone and seeing what happens."

He just had one condition: it had to be rooted in art.

"To just commission a jingle or theme tune would undermine the entire concept," he told a music critic later. "What I loved was the idea of getting a young artist to write something original and use it as a calling card for the brand. I was playing with an idea in my head, and this style and inspiration gave me the conviction that I could do something that would be meaningful to me as a person and a musician."

Throughout the next few months, he began developing a hook, and in the fall sent me an MP3 of a rough rendition. I loved in instantly and instructed him to keep developing. In the meantime, I'd work with his manager and Team One to figure out how the fuck I was going to pull this off.

Hiring a musician of his caliber to write an original piece of music is expensive. So is recording and filming it, then turning it into a slick sizzle reel. Just as I did selling the magazine idea, I had to use ingenuity to get this through. It was worth the risk.

Once we figured out the details, the real work began. Charlie would finish the composition and record it with the English Chamber Orchestra in London in December, when we'd be there again. He chose Saint Silas the Martyr, an Edwardian church in a leafy northern suburb, for its acoustics, and I worked with Team One and his record company, Sony, on the logistics. It was getting more elaborate and expensive.

I arrived at the church on a frigid late December day to find what looked like a movie production in the works. Cameras, lights, cranes, a sound booth, thirty-two chairs for the orchestra, and me having a heart attack. Leading the charge was Phil Rowlands, a Grammy-winning producer.

This was going to get me fired. Charlie had written "Canopy," a composition with five distinct melodies, and I was risking my career to film it.

I have no regrets.

Charlie Siem with Jeremy Murphy at the London debut of Charlie's composition "Canopy."

"The opening pizzicato section stemmed from a simple four-chord sequence that I was messing around with on my violin," Charlie said, describing "Canopy." "The middle section is a rhapsodic melody from the solo violin in an almost folkish style, somewhat inspired by the romantic lyricism of Vaughan Williams. The final section brings back the rhythmic semi-quavers to a climactic buildup toward the end of the piece."

Charlie, wearing a light sweater and jeans, performed the song with the orchestra—including one very nasty, frizzy-haired woman who gave me the stink eye—several times for the camera, each time better than the last.

I'd never done anything like this before, so I didn't know if it had gone well or not, but I loved what I had witnessed. Once Charlie, James, and the people from Sony expressed enthusiasm, I knew we'd crossed the first hurdle. Now we had to do something with it that was just as worthy.

Returning home, we sent B-roll video from all our photo shoots to Team One and enlisted Pauley Perrette to do the voiceover.

The final result blew my mind. Executives, colleagues, and even my coworkers who had been cool to the idea were surprised by its uniqueness. So was Stuart Elliot, the columnist for the *New York Times* who covered the marketing industry. Stuart was the most powerful reporter on the beat, and his columns could make or break your career. He was also very hard to impress.

"The idea was so unusual, so unexpected, that it struck me as an appropriate subject for an article," he recalled later. "I felt others in publishing, and allied fields, would be interested in seeing how they could use original, artistic content to promote their brands along with, or instead of, traditional promotions or ads."

He wrote a glowing feature on the campaign in the *Times*, and we premiered it the next day across all our promotional channels, as well as those of our parent company.

To my great relief and gratitude, the coverage we got was effusive. In addition to the *Times*, Adweek and numerous others wrote about it. Even *Vogue Arabia*! I got the green light to keep promoting the campaign, so we took Charlie to Los Angeles for a week to do interviews with *Entertainment Tonight*, *Extra*, *Access Hollywood*, the *Hollywood Reporter*, and others.

We ended the launch campaign with a private reception in London. My very good friend Sarah Cairns was the director of communications for the Mandarin Oriental Hyde Park, London and agreed to host the event honoring Charlie. They and Sony covered the expense. That evening, Charlie spoke and performed, and we played the sizzle reel on giant flat screens. I was highly amused that my guest list included virtually no one, and his had Simon Le Bon, Boy George, and other celebrities.

Our magazine used the song for video for two more years, featuring voiceovers from Michael Weatherly and Julianna Margulies. Team One incorporated new video into each one beautifully.

To this day, it's my proudest accomplishment.

"The way I see it, [Jeremy] is using me to create a real piece of art, and that in itself signifies the groundbreaking direction that the brand is veering toward," Charlie said at the time. "It's a huge statement to do something like this."

Charlie helped promote this as hard as I did. After the premiere in London and the media tour, we thought we were done. But the good press continued, and I wanted to keep the momentum going. I asked Charlie if he'd come back to LA and do another private concert, as well as more media. He accepted my invitation without asking more.

Once there, we put together another schedule of interviews, as well as an appearance on a daytime show called *The Talk*, which was challenging *The View* in ratings, making Joy Behar less joyful. We booked Charlie to talk about our campaign and his new album, "Beneath the Stars," but upon arriving at the studio, we received surprising news.

Because of Screen Actors Guild (SAG) bylaws, Charlie could not speak on camera, only perform.

"Jeremy," Charlie quipped with unmistakable British wit, "there's no talking on *The Talk*."

Who needs dialogue when you have Charlie Siem?

Q&A WITH SOPHIA PAULMIER

> *Sophia: Muse profiled up-and-coming creatives as well as people at the top. Did you carry any of these relationships with you when you started your own PR company?*
>
> Jeremy: Yes! Charlie was my first client. I also represent Jeff Leatham (celebrity florist) and Iestyn Davies (opera singer).

S: After discovering Charlie Siem in an art magazine, when did you first hear his music and how did it make you feel?

J: I have trouble putting it into words. Every great artist affects you differently. Hearing him, I closed my eyes and saw myself somewhere else.

S: Charlie sounds like a pretty gifted man with impeccable taste. Did you ever feel insecure being around such talent?

J: Him, always. He is incredibly kind and thoughtful but corrects my mispronunciations. He taught me you don't sound the G in Gstaad, and you replace the Z in Ibiza with "th." Also, the champagne Taittinger is not pronounced as spelled. It is "tat-tar-j." He's really the one I felt insecure being around.

S: How did you get introduced to 5 Hertford Street? I heard it's very hard to become a member.

J: One of my first trips to London after meeting Charlie, I wanted to go somewhere posh as a way to impress him. *Vanity Fair* had just profiled 5 Hertford Street, a private members' club that sounded perfect. Good luck trying. There was no phone number, email, or even address. I mentioned this to Charlie, and he told me his family was involved in the opening. He'd not only got me in but got me a membership. But first, I had to meet people somehow connected to the club, and they were visiting New York. We arranged drinks at the St. Regis, but I planned ahead. I pulled a Clooney and told the waiters to serve me water when I ordered vodka. I tend to get animated and loud when drinking but needed to impress this group. They came and got smashed. I got in. There's a 30,000-person waiting list. I have no business being there and stick out like a rube.

S: *There is nothing better than an original composition.*

J: It was beautiful. I still get chills when I hear it, and I play it often. And show everyone. It's really my proudest accomplishment.

S: *Charlie stated, "to just commission a jingle or theme tune would undermine the entire concept." I couldn't agree more. It seems that popular musicians and even current-day composers are sampling and copying scores from older movies. They put their spin on it but it's not original.*

J: That is so right, although Max Richter's version of "Four Seasons" by Vivaldi is wistful. I listen to the "Spring" part of it often. There are composers who can do it respectfully. However, I'm of the mind that Hans Zimmer's compositions don't need to be remade; they're already perfect.

S: *With a hefty price, a big production, and orchestra, did you worry about the risk?*

J: Constantly. It was a runaway train. But I don't regret a thing. It's a piece of music that will transcend time.

S: *You said you'd never done something like this before, but the song and video proved to be a success. Have you considered doing another original score with Charlie?*

J: We were going to do a new one before I left. We had established such a rhythm to our working relationship and wanted it to continue.

S: What was it like watching the premiere of your sizzle reel?

J: We saw it in a conference room, and I just beamed with pride. Almost everyone in the room was moved, but there was one woman who looked angry it worked. Some people want you to fail, and I didn't. I had many, many times before. Not this time.

S: How was that moment for Charlie? What did he think of it?

J: He's intensely private and doesn't show his feelings. Almost never. But this is a point of pride for him, deservedly so.

S: You're proudest accomplishment. Describe why this particular video and song spoke so much to you.

J: I'd never done something like this before. It was such a crazy idea, and I was so out of my league. Knowing you had a role in creating something this special is exhilarating. The song is incredible, but what's more—to me—is that it got made. We did it. Against all odds.

CHAPTER 11

⭐

Sun, Snow, and Stalking

The Mentalist star Simon Baker on Bondi Beach in Sydney, reading for surfing and sunnies. Photo by Mark Mann.

Everyone wanted Simon Baker, the chiseled, blond, impossibly gorgeous Aussie who was starring on *The Mentalist*, on which he played a hyper-observant consultant helping authorities solve crime. Simon had incredible buzz from *The Devil Wears Prada*, and his new show had become one of the few hits from the 2008–09 TV season.

We tried everything to get him to do our cover, but, as usual, we were last in line. Like NPH before him, I needed something that no one else could offer.

Enter Terry Gegesi, who was marketing and promotion manager for Qantas Airlines in their LA office. Simon is an Aussie, so I cold-called Terry to ask about the possibility of them sponsoring a trip to Sydney. To my great relief, Qantas already had a relationship with Simon and loved the idea. I just had to get *him*.

Getting a major star of a network TV show to fly thousands of miles away for a photo shoot is a tall ask, especially for a magazine no one had heard of at the time. But he wanted to go back with his family for the Christmas holidays and said he'd do it if we could also fly his wife *and* three kids. This was not an unusual request, and I was game, as was Terry. She arranged ten business-class tickets—fully comped—in exchange for shooting Simon in the Qantas First Lounge. I agreed without even asking him.

Everything was locked until one of Simon's reps insisted he and his family fly *first* class. To this day, I don't think the request came from Simon but some eager beaver on his team looking to take credit for getting the upgrades.

Qantas said no: they don't comp first-class tickets, which are more than $20,000—each. We had nowhere near that to spend, so I begged Terry to find a solution. She came back with a huge discount, but it was still a significant hit to our budget.

Whatevs. Just do it. For *them*. Our team would have to slum it in business class. I write this having never flown in this cabin until I was thirty.

Business class on international flights is a raised experience. Sure, you get the flat beds but also a toiletry case with designer skin creams and pajamas. On Qantas, the sleepwear consists of cotton drawstring pants and a gray T-shirt with a giant koala bear on its front, which sounds cute until you wake up in the middle of the night and see an entire cabin of people laying asleep with eye masks and giant feral animals drawn on their chests. It was positively Kubrickian.

The flight was torture. It felt like two days, and with the time change—sixteen hours ahead—it was.

For this shoot, I used Mark Mann to photograph, Hud Morgan to write, and a local stylist named Maia Liakos to do the wardrobe. An A-team, for sure. Finding settings in the hotel to shoot against was an issue, but we found a few vantages, then spent an entire day in a Sprinter van shuttling our crew from location to location, including the Sydney Opera House, Harbour Bridge, Centennial Park, the Qantas lounge, and Bondi Beach. We had the foresight to rent a BMW for Simon, where he did the interview with Hud.

Simon was a tough read. At first, he was skeptical about the concept we'd come up with. It was admittedly stupid, but shot right, it could be interesting. I wanted to simulate a scavenger hunt throughout Sydney, where one clue leads to the next. He teased me about this several times ("What's the next clue, Jeremy?") and I couldn't tell if he was being sarcastic or snotty.

The shoot ended on Bondi Beach. Maia had somehow convinced Louis Vuitton to lend a blue tuxedo, which he wore running on the sand with a surfboard under his arm. It was a great setup but attracted crowds that became hard to manage. After fifteen minutes, we called it a day and raced him back to the wardrobe van.

I thought we'd finished, but Simon graciously invited the crew to a bar on Bondi Beach called The Icebergs. He bought everyone drinks and chilled out, revealing a wit and curiosity I hadn't expected. Back at the hotel, I asked him to autograph a map of Sydney we'd used as a clue, and he did so enthusiastically.

"Jeremy! You did it!" he scribbled. The map hangs on my wall, along with many other tokens.

Returning home was a journey. In the Qantas lounge, I joined my crew in choosing which sleep/anxiety meds to take for the flight. Sixteen hours later, we landed in LA, but with the time difference, earlier than when we took off.

As we prepared the issue, the photo of Simon with the surfboard popped. It was exceptional. Though not intended for a cover, we couldn't deny it was worthy and scrapped the previous choice.

While developing the magazine, a colleague called with a favor. He knew I was not afraid of mischief, which is not necessarily a good reputation to have in corporate America. But I got shit done; don't ask how. This particular person was a heavyweight in our business, and I was not keen on disappointing him.

There was someone working in our industry he did not like, and he asked if I would scoop up dog shit and send it anonymously in the mail. Literally.

You know your rank in life when someone asks you to do this kind of task. I'd swallowed my pride numerous times, but this was a big ask.

"I think that's illegal," I said, trying to get out of it.

It was; you cannot send feces through the post office.

When advised of this, he quickly responded, "Then send it FedEx."

I don't know the law on that one, but I do know my limits; admittedly, they are low, but this crossed the line. Even though the would-be recipient so deserved it.

Our third issue in 2006 almost became our last after a Photoshopping scandal of a huge person in the media. We were doing a big story on her and needed photography for the cover and feature. A photo editor we'd worked with found great images, but one did not reflect this person's size. She is naturally petite and healthy but wore an unflattering suit that made her look much bigger. The editor retouched the image to reflect her natural size.

That is common in magazines, but some go too far. We did not, but I was unaware the photo we used had already been distributed... before retouching. Someone she was working with noticed and leaked "before and after" images to the media.

The issue came out and looked good to me, but I started getting calls from newspaper and TV people after websites picked up the story, including FuckedTV.com, the most popular, and NewsBlues, which named me as the culprit. It did not take long for Page Six to call. Then the *NY Daily News*. Then Fox News. My phone did not stop ringing.

At first, people in our company were amused. One even thought it was great for buzz. "See who we slim down next week!" was his suggestion.

But it turned into a PR nightmare. The *NY Post* called again with the news that it would be on next day's cover. Same for the *New York Daily News*.

A funny anecdote became a national topic of conversation, including on *The View*. Surprisingly, Rosie O'Donnell added some sanity to the "controversy" by explaining this happens all the time. It's not a scandal.

Naturally, the cover girl was extremely upset and embarrassed. Who wants their weight to be a subject of media scrutiny? Especially when you're not weighty. I wrote a heartfelt apology email to her, but never got a response. I'm not sure I would have replied either.

Taraji Henson is one of the most talented, beautiful, and kind actresses in Hollywood. I remember her from *The Curious Case of Benjamin Button*, in which she played Brad Pitt's mom as he aged backward, and certainly from the TV series *Empire*. That show, about an African American family who built a dynasty off a record label, became a huge hit. Taraji played "Cookie," the matriarch who went to prison to save her husband. Everyone loves this incredibly gifted actress.

On *Person of Interest*, Taraji played a detective trying to uncover an unintelligible plot about a machine that predicts peoples' deaths through their Social Security numbers, or something like that. I couldn't make sense of any of it, but viewers did. It became a quasi-hit.

Michael Emerson—famous for being "Ben" on *Lost*—and Jim Caviezel, who played the savior in Mel Gibson's *The Passion of the Christ*—were the leads on the series and put our staff to sleep. Taraji was the one we wanted for a cover. I got Jet Blue and the Montage Deer Valley in Utah to sponsor a winter-themed shoot with lots of snow, skiing, fireplaces, and other cozy settings.

Taraji was *amazing*, and she loved the wardrobe Christopher Campbell pulled: lots of Brunello Cucinelli, Kiton, Dolce & Gabbana, and other top brands. Keiron O'Connor, who was new to us at the time, was hired to do the photography.

Everything about this shoot was easy, fun, and fulfilling. The images jumped off the screen: Taraji in cashmere, silk, ski suits, and even a bathing suit coming out of the pool, surrounded by steam. Not only were the photos strong, but it also felt good to highlight a diverse actor.

Of course, when something goes too well, you know you have a problem. We returned to New York eager to start planning the cover but soon heard Taraji's character was being killed off the series.

Face, meet slap.

First, I could not believe what I was hearing. How stupid was this? My next thought got me incredibly angry: someone knew this was happening but let us do the shoot anyway.

I had incredible photography I could no longer use. A rep from the studio that produced the show called and insisted we run the images anyway.

Ummm, no? "Let's promote an actress who won't be on the show!"

I was heartbroken, and telling her reps the cover was a no-go was painful. But I made it up to them: I gave her team the rights to all the images to use however they wanted.

It was the least I could do.

Actors, especially the big ones, often get photo approval on anything media publishes. Majors like *Vogue*, *Vanity Fair*, and certainly the *New York Times* refuse, but everyone else kowtows to the talent publicist, who also demands approval on the photographer and retouching. Some take this way too seriously, like an actress on an ensemble show who demands Photoshopping—on her costars. And not the good kind. She tried to make them uglier.

I was sick of seeing gorgeous actors and actresses in lab coats and crime scene jumpsuits and proposed an idea: three of the most beautiful women starring on these shows doing a glam shoot in Laguna Beach, California. We chose Cote de Pablo from *NCIS*, Eva LaRue from *CSI: Miami*, and Lauren Lee Smith, who was on *CSI*. The Jackal did all the styling, and Cliff Lipson was the shooter. In one setup, we had the ladies posing on a pathway to the beach when a seagull dropped a big pile of shit on one of the actresses. Good luck?

I'm not traditionally a stalker—at least I hope not—but when I get an idea in my mind, I see it through no matter what. Sometimes that rubs people the wrong way because "no" to me means "find another way to do it." I don't give up.

Hud Morgan, who I mentioned earlier, is a writer I desperately wanted to work with. I tried for months to get him, and did!. As well as Chris Rovzar, an incredible writer and editor who had co-written a cover story in *New York Magazine* about *Gossip Girl*; its cover line is one of my favorites: "Best.Show.Ever." Chris and I met, and I sold him on a regular spread on lifestyle themes, including bringing 90210 stars to five different night clubs. Chris went on to become a top editor at *Vanity Fair* and *Bloomberg*.

Crissy Poorman, who you'll read about later (if you dare!) was the top PR person for The Ritz-Carlton in Palm Beach, and we'd become friends. When I returned to Boca Raton to see family, we met for lunch, and out popped an idea for a lifestyle/fashion/luxury section in our magazine. Crissy is the ultimate Palm Beach girl and has incredible taste and discernment. She's also an incredible journalist and served as a producer for CNN. Over truffle fries, we envisioned a section called "Gilt" that captured everything that was missing. I hired an incredible editor, Loren Chidoni Naylor, to edit the section, and it became one of our most popular.

Rebecca Ascher-Walsh is also one of my proudest finds. She was recommended by Beth Tomkiw, from our custom publisher McMurry, and turned in lively content with a unique, authoritative voice. When we launched a culture section in the magazine, she was the only editor I considered. Rebecca brought us two incredible writers: Michael Musto, who covered the social/nightclub scene for the *Village Voice* and gave its coverage bite, and Wickham Boyle, an incredibly offbeat but brilliant writer, who, like me, does not give up. We gave her a hard task: land an interview with Fran Lebowitz, the acerbic social commentator. Not only did she do it, she and Fran pulled a stunt: Wickham got Fran to sign several copies of her book, and put them back on the shelf in a book store.

Fashion was becoming important to the magazine, and I admittedly know little about styling. We'd need someone to dress all the actors we planned to shoot, and I hit the jackpot when a friend mentioned her daughter was in the business. That's how I met The Jackal. Soon, *everyone* came to rely on her judgement and always asked for critiques. She found a way of being honest without insulting, and it became comedy. On one shoot, a publicist showed her a hideous new purse and asked for her blessing.

"It's like nothing I've seen before," was The Jackal's response.

Truman Capote would have been proud.

Frank DeCaro and Jim Colucci are incredibly endearing finds to me. Jim I couldn't miss; he approached me at a network TV event with confidence, as if he knew I would hire him on the spot. I did. Jim is a walking encyclopedia for TV knowledge, as well as an author whose books on *Will & Grace* and *The Golden Girls* were big sellers. At the time we began working together, I had no idea he was dating—and would soon marry—Frank DeCaro, one of the funniest, wittiest, and most clever writer/entertainers in the business. I invited Jim for drinks to The Ritz-Carlton, Central Park, and my mouth nearly dropped when I saw he brought Frank. Both of them became voices to the magazine, and good friends.

Kate Betts is a vaunted figure in fashion, and I had to have a "name" as our profile began to grow. After graduating from Princeton, Kate moved to Paris and climbed the ranks to become one of *Women's Wear Daily*'s top writers. Legend has it the curmudgeonly owner, John Fairchild, had read a story of hers about boar hunting in Britany and hired her on the spot. Kate went on to *Vogue*, where she became Anna Wintour's second in command and then became the youngest editor in chief of *Harper's Bazaar* history. Later, she was named top editor at *Time*'s *Style & Design* magazine. Everyone in fashion admires—and sometimes fears—her clever honesty and prose.

I wanted to become one of them. It took me months to get her email address, but once I did I pitched her a story I knew she'd hit out of the ballpark: profiles of top women journalists in Washington, DC. Kate expressed interest, but she was at the top of her field, and we were at the bottom. Her fee was considerable, but I found the budget and brought her to DC to interview the women after our photo shoot.

Kate, at first, was guarded and professional. It was our first time meeting, and I was admittedly nervous. I wanted to show a gesture of appreciation and bought her an Hermès scarf, which surprised her, delightfully so. She sent the most gracious thank-you letter, and we continued to work together throughout my time as editor.

Kate's copy was flawless, and I soon sold her on a regular column—"Best Betts"—that became a spread on whatever trend was going on in fashion. Advertisers couldn't believe how spot-on her insight was, and the diversity of items she chose to feature.

I came to really like her too and appreciated her blunt, witty humor. She understood fashion was not brain surgery and could laugh at the absurdity.

Super P was my master stroke. After our first issue, I instinctively knew we needed a top publisher to not only sell ads but to increase our awareness with print buyers. A colleague suggested an account executive at *Entertainment Weekly*, which was then the Bible for pop culture lovers. I reached out and arranged a meeting, and he charmed me the moment he walked in. Handsome, confident, charismatic, and kind, Super P had a sense of humor I did not expect, and a spot-on Christopher Walken impression. Afterward, I offered him the position. After some negotiating, he accepted. It was the best decision I ever made. He joined the next month.

Losing an editor or writer is a tough experience. One of my biggest mistakes, and hardest learning lesson, was Sarah Rose. She is a brilliant, confident, and opinionated writer with the goods to back it up: Harvard degree, reporter for *Reuters*, *Miami Herald*, and *Wall Street Journal*, and author. Her recent book, *D-Day Girls: The Spies who Sabotaged the Nazis, Armed the Resistance, and Helped Win World War II* was critically acclaimed and sold many copies. I met Sarah four years before at a PR function for a hotel brand and we clicked instantly. So much so, we escaped the reception and went to a local bar where we talked media, politics, current events. Her mind and wit fascinated me. And she is one of the few Harvard graduates who doesn't announce so upon meeting.

Over drinks, I shared details about the magazine and what I wanted to accomplish. Our Gilt section had grown too large: it was now filled with lifestyle, luxury, fashion, and beauty. Weeks before, Kate Betts had suggested separating beauty into its own section. Now, sitting across from me, was the person to do it. I just didn't know if she'd *want* to. Sarah is cerebral, honest, substantive; beauty is not. This was definitely a reach. Fortunately, she jumped at the chance. Many cocktails in, we created Glam, which would include make-up, hair, skin care, grooming, and other self-care topics.

The section started successful. Sarah's coverage was fun, frothy, and informative. She even offered herself as a test subject, getting a full day of beauty at Rita Hazan's boutique on 5th Avenue. A few issues in, however, friction with one of our editors reached my ears. It was a personality conflict that had become a distraction, then open warfare. I assembled the two in my office hoping to reach an armistice, but that lasted a week. The situation was untenable, and soon unmanageable. I had to make a decision. Sarah was a freelance editor with many prospects, and I knew I could give her other assignments to soften the blow. Delivering the news was heartbreaking because we both had come to love what we'd created. She took it professionally, and I assigned her several bigger stories more in-line with her hard news chops.

Come 2017, I reached out to Sarah unexpectedly, and apologized. I made the wrong choice and should have found a way to keep both editors. I took the easy, cowardly way out, and it pained me all this time. Sarah accepted my apology and we've become friends; I even helped promote *D-Day Girls*—for free. It was the least I could do.

Joel Stein is one of the funniest in journalism, and he became *Time* magazine's youngest columnist. I made contact and sold him on a column about the Grammy Awards. We were getting full access, but the producers had to bless everything before publication. Joel's copy was hilarious, witty, deadpan, and smart. Of course, the Grammy people removed the funniest parts. What ran is still hilarious, but the original copy was much better. I tried again with a cover story on late-night talk show host Craig Ferguson, who had a thin skin. He took offense to everything, and I had to kill the entire feature. I stopped pitching Joel because I was frankly embarrassed.

The weirdest pursuit was Glenn O'Brien, who wrote "The Style Guy" column for *GQ*. This *was* the best men's magazine in journalism, and Glenn's writing taught me how to dress. It was a must-read for any man, especially when you're growing up in the suburbs. Nowadays, it's hyper metrosexual, which is fine, but I'm not. It no longer relates to me. Nor Glenn, whose tenure ended after many years.

I'd been eyeing a men's section, and he was the perfect persona to lead it. We went to lunch at Le Bilboquet, an incredibly popular restaurant on the Upper East Side, and he brought his agent. That's the first time a writer had done so. He also did not look well and died a few years later. I would have been happy with any time with him, but his representative was delusional: he wanted $20,000 an issue to do a column.

Pass.

Also, pursuing an idea and not being able to see it through is heartbreaking. I had two that I never saw to fruition, and that still gnaws at me.

The first was Versailles. I wanted to bring the entire cast of *How I Met Your Mother* to the historic French palace for a big splashy cover shoot, and even met with its representatives on a trip to Paris I'd taken with three friends over Thanksgiving break. The only problem was we'd spent the previous night drinking, and I arrived for the meeting completely hungover and incoherent. My friends basically played interpreter. That didn't faze the Versailles reps, who smelled money; they gave us a tour of the property and a ridiculous fee for shooting on its premises. Six figures.

The other idea was far more reasonable, cost-wise, but technically very difficult. I wanted to somehow photograph an actor coming out of liquidized paintings. Imagine a person ascending from the Mona Lisa, dripping in its paint. I don't know where this idea came from, but I shared it with photographer, John Messinger, and he knew exactly who to call: Trina Merry, a quirky body-painter who puts people *into* paintings. This is a fine art often confused with tattoos; it's not. It's a very delicate process that takes hours and requires precision, discipline, and an eye for detail. Also, talent. Trina drips of all of it, pardon the pun. A former production assistant in Hollywood, she worked for studios and talents until her car was struck by lightning one night, sending volts through her body. As part of her healing process, she took up painting and discovered she had this very unique gift. John arranged a dinner, and I was smitten. Short, sassy, often with vibrantly colored hair, she is a firecracker and someone I wanted to work with. My idea never came to light, but we did wind up working together on several other projects.

An actress on a big crime procedural wanted a cover, and I was game. She was beautiful, on the rise, and a lead on her show, and we were new to newsstands. This might move copies; at this point, we were bombing in retail. We needed juice.

I arranged to shoot the actress in LA and brought The Jackal to style the wardrobe. We used a photographer from the network her show aired on and shot in a studio.

Day of shoot: The Jackal steamed, pressed, and hung stunning dresses, skirts, jackets, blouses, and accessories in the styling suite. The pulls were fantastic—to everyone except the actress. Unbeknownst to us, her female costar had just done an over-the-top sexy shoot for a laddie magazine, wearing nothing but a man's white dress shirt. And now that's what she wanted.

The Jackal's stylist raced to Nordstrom to find a shirt, and we photographed her as such.

Hawaii Five-o was a huge hit when it got rebooted in 2010. The show was filming in Honolulu, and the cast was game to do a magazine cover. Me, less so. I didn't like anything about it, but almost fifteen million viewers watched every week. And I couldn't deny a *Hawaii Five-o* cover would be great for summer. The cast was also attractive: Alex O'Loughlin, Scott Caan, Grace Park, and Daniel Dae Kim—young, hot, talented.

But I had an issue: We'd have to shoot in December, and I had no budget. American Airlines couldn't fly us either. Like us, they had end-of-year issues.

I couldn't find sponsors to underwrite the shoot until a really great dude, Brad Packer, came to the rescue. He has the best job ever: doing PR for Four Seasons hotels in Kona, Bora-Bora, and a few other tropical locales. The Hawaiian property, in Hualalai, would be perfect, he surmised, and he offered to sponsor our hotel rooms. He also introduced us to a rep for Hawaiian Airlines, who also bought into the idea.

That's usually the hard part. It turned out to be the easiest. The first obstacle was getting the cast from Honolulu to Kona, which required puddle jumpers without first class. This became an issue for one of the actors. Then, Grace Park went into diva-mode with constant changes, questions, demands. We were sick of her before she arrived.

A huge tropical storm hit the day before the shoot, which prevented us from scouting the hotel grounds. Everything was gray and depressing and put us in a sour mood. The cast didn't help. The night before photography, Four Seasons Brad took us for dinner and drinks in one of the hotel bars, and we amused ourselves singing "On My Own," the classic '80s ballad by Patti LaBelle and Michael McDonald. Its video is iconic—both sing separately, him in Malibu and her in Chicago, and they lament their affair has ended. I can do a mean Michael McDonald impression, especially that song, and it does not take much to inspire a performance. Years later, I saw Patti in the lobby of a posh hotel and introduced myself; I'm admittedly a huge fan. She was touched, and then I asked if she'd join me in singing "On My Own" together—in the lobby. For a second she considered, but then looked at her watch and said, "Not now, baby."

Back to soggy Hawaii. That night, we were barraged with flight changes and various questions, and no one was happy. Thankfully, the skies cleared the next day, and the actors arrived on time. Alex was cool as fuck—chill, friendly, eager. Scott Caan started off fun but turned out to be a temperamental dick. Grace Park? By this point I delegated her dramas to two producers. But Daniel was my favorite: grounded, reasonable, inquisitive, and smart. He also had my sense of humor, and the looks on his face—"Do you believe this fucking shit?"—won my heart.

The photographer we used was new to us, and the night before she'd broken her toe and was in writhing pain. We also used a new stylist, Zoe Glassner, who was awesome; I felt terrible to ply four actors on her, two of whom were difficult.

We got what we needed. The photos are good and served their purpose, but a photographer with a broken toe, difficult actors, and a soggy setting does not a cover shoot make.

Q&A WITH SOPHIA PAULMIER

> *Sophia: Simon Baker comes off as the kind of guy who screws over an assistant to get to their boss, is that how you'd describe him or am I just thinking of his character in* The Devil Wears Prada?

> Jeremy: You're thinking the movie. He's actually shy but warmed up eventually. We only had a day with him in Sydney and put him through the ringer. He was

a trooper. After we wrapped the last shot, he took us to a bar on Bondi Beach and let his guard down.

S: *Did you ask him for the unpublished manuscript for the new* Harry Potter?

J: It was too early to gage someone's sense of humor. After a full day with him, I think he would have laughed. But with talent, you never risk offending them. My humor can be dark and cutting so I have to watch my tongue.

S: *That's the first thing I'd ask him if I ever met him.*

J: I had eight set ups to finish throughout Sydney, including the hotel, Opera House, Qantas lounge at the airport, and Bondi Beach. There was no time for chit-chat.

S: *Was this your first trip to Australia? And what was your impression of it?*

J: It was, and I wasn't impressed. I looooove Australians; Australia, not so much. It felt like two days to get to a big city with a few monuments and tall buildings. It was the people who made the difference.

S: *Did you ever cross paths with Simon Baker again?*

J: No, but he did donate a signed surfboard to an auction I staged for a non-profit, which I found incredibly generous. Living in LA and not being on "the scene," I have rare opportunities to cross paths with actors. Hollywood is a business; there is no glamour. And after a decade running the magazine, there is nowhere less I want to be.

Sophia: *On the "Photoshopping scandal of a huge person in media." Do you feel if the "she" had been a "he," it would have still become necessary to photoshop their size?*

Jeremy: It wasn't about gender. It was about an unflattering image that did not reflect the person's true size. Almost everyone takes a bad photo.

S: *"A funny anecdote became a national topic of conversation." Do you feel this was your first encounter with what would have been described today as cancel culture?*

J: No, it had nothing to do with cancel culture. No one was judging you personally or making aspirations about your character. It was more about a farcical situation and embarrassing the person.

S: *If this issue had come out today, do you think with the new gravity of social media your magazine would have still survived this moment?*

J: Good question! Probably, yeah. I retouched my own images, and someone would have done the same to me after I was named as the culprit. We are in a very vicious, retaliatory moment in our culture where everything is personal and certain people like canceling.

S: *Photoshopping is new norm on social media, even going as far as Facetune -- an app that automatically alters the face and body in a picture or video. Do you find yourself shocked that many huge media personalities use it and does it bother you that the same type of thing almost cost you your job?*

J: I find no issue with this; making someone look better is not a bad thing as long as it reflects who they are and their essence. I think it's great that media want people to shine and look their best.

S: *Did you ever come face to face with the journalist who leaked the photo?*

J: No, aside from learning her name, I never saw or talked to the person. It would not have gone well if I had. Not only did they embarrass me, but it also subjected the media personality to intense scrutiny, humiliation, and embarrassment. It was cruel and cowardly.

S: *Had Taraji P. Henson's character not been killed off the show, what over covers would you have used her for and what photographers and location settings?*

J: We had an incredible image of her climbing out of a pool surrounded by steam that was slated for the cover. It would have gotten huge buzz, and showed her as a sexy, strong, beautiful woman.

S: *Did you ever feel bad for the maids that had to spend hours cleaning up these post party messes?*

J: I pre-cleaned! But, yeah, we were reckless and insensitive. Not my best moments.

S: *Did the actress book anything big after the seagull incident?*

J: Yes, many! We used her several times after. It was more of a funny, whimsical moment than anything else. And in some cultures, it's good luck.

S: *Describe Michael Musto in a few words.*

J: Offbeat. He's also very shy, which belies his writing which is witty, engaging, snappy, and sarcastic.

S: *If you could start a magazine or project today with Kate Betts, what would it be?*

J: I don't think I'd be qualified. She's an industry legend; I edited an entertainment magazine.

S: *Did Kate Betts give you any critique, compliments, or advice on your magazine?*

J: Once she began doing her "Best Betts" column, we established a very positive and friendly working relationship. So much so, I asked her to critique every issue before publication. I'd bring the layouts to a chosen restaurant for lunch, and she'd offer suggestions on how to improve every page. For some reason, I remember doing this at Locanda Verde, Robert De Niro's restaurant in TriBeCa. Kate's insight was invaluable. She was constructive in her feedback, but also kind and funny. I miss working with her.

S: *Would you work with Super P again?*

J: In a heartbeat. I always looked at us as equals, and we have a good rhythm. He can think like an editor, and I can think like a publisher, so we understand each other. I'm not sure he can do what I do, and I know I cannot do what he does.

S: *What was the biggest ask from a writer for a column?*

J: Glenn O'Brien, who wanted $25,000 an issue. That was unrealistic.

S: *This* Hawaii Five-o *shoot that turned sour a when a tropical storm hit sounds like movie script—from a rocky start to a chaotic weather nightmare to a night of karaoke followed by a beautiful day for the cover shoot.*

J: Yeah, a horror movie. It was a miserable experience. The only thing I enjoyed was Brad Packer, the Four Seasons PR rep who made everything work.

S: *Did you ever do another photoshoot in Hawaii or with this cast again?*

J: Hell no.

S: *Favorite show or movie made in Hawaii?*

J: *Snakes on a Plane*, because the plane *left* Hawaii.

CHAPTER 12

·············★·············

(Un)Cool J(eremy)

Jeremy with LL Cool J at the Mandarin Hotel in Paris. Photo by Gilles-Marie Zimmermann.

I'd gotten used to being editor in chief, a job that allows you to choose who to put on the cover, where to shoot, what crew to hire, and lots of other decisions that bring your ideas and creativity to the page. Being able to orchestrate great content is an experience second to none. And knowing the people who play great music makes it sweeter. What's sour is when someone *else* tries to conduct.

I'd begun having issues with a higher-up who saw himself as editor, even though I created and ran the magazine. Our meetings grew tense. It got to the point where I'd hide content knowing this person had the memory of a goldfish and wouldn't recall *not* seeing it.

Everyone wanted LL Cool J, including me...*in the right circumstance.* Given his star power, a cover with him would need to be cinematic and highly produced, capturing his natural magnetism. Word had gone down that the actor/musician wanted to go to Paris, and my nemesis insisted *this* was the right opportunity. It wasn't. I would have thought of something much more compelling and, frankly, worthy of LL's presence. My gut told me someone on his team was pushing this. I'd had some exposure to the star, and though he's particular he's not a diva.

I had many problems with this idea, including an inability to make it happen. The well was dry at this point—I'd exhausted all our favors and sponsorships after shooting so far in advance. Without an airline or hotel partner, this would break a bank that had no bank. But I was now locked in.

Desperation is a street I know well; hell, by now I live there...in a cardboard box. In such circumstances, you learn how to survive. I scurried to find sponsors, knowing I'd be lucky to get scraps. If I could pull this off, it would be with huge limitations. I did manage to get an airline but could only extend three seats to LL and his team; to his credit, he accepted.

Finding the hotel also required work. We'd shot covers everywhere at this point, and our usual go-tos were booked: it was July, the height of tourist season in Paris. I finally reached out to the Mandarin Oriental, where we had photographed "Blue Bloods" star Bridget Moynahan several years prior, and they expressed interest. Several of the staff were huge fans, and the hotel was still earning its luxe cred in Paris; they had rooms to spare. We were lucky because it's on one of the most fashionable streets, Rue Saint-Honoré, and very au courant. The hotel's parent company was said to have spent $1 billion to construct the hotel, which has nearly one hundred rooms, four restaurants, and a garden courtyard in the center.

The two main obstacles had now been crossed, but many remained. Every shoot requires a narrative, and I was coming up empty, which was made harder by the restrictions. The star wanted to use his own stylist, who insisted on a dark-colored aesthetic with coats, hats, suits, and lots of grays and blacks. Understandably, LL is not a skinny male model who can wear haute couture—the guy is jacked!—so styling options were limited. His team had a relationship with Giorgio Armani—whew!—but the tone made no sense.

My enthusiasm had waned, and I needed a photographer to fill the gap; someone who could connect with LL's natural positivity and drive and bring their own personality and smile. In Paris, this is called a unicorn, a mythical creature that does not exist. One exception is Gilles-Marie Zimmerman, who is off-the-charts buoyant and brings incredible radiance to every shoot. I'd used him five times at this point, and talent always responded enthusiastically. It helped that he's based in Paris and has a portfolio of top editorial and marketing campaigns, including Hugh Jackman for Mont Blanc.

Gilles-Marie Zimmermann, one of the best photographers in Paris, with Jeremy.

By now you know there's always a plot twist. I liken it to *Law & Order*; just around the forty-five-minute mark when there's new evidence, a shocking confession, a surprise witness. Great for storytelling, but I realized they're shitty prosecutors: the wrong person is on trial every week.

Plot twists are not good for photo shoots either. I'd taken Ritz-Carlton Vivian to dinner for her birthday and began getting SOS messages during our meal. Four days before we were due to leave, I got word LL needed his *entire* team with him.

It would be six more seats/rooms.

It was too late to turn back now, so we took money out of the following year's budget and purchased the extra tickets, as well as additional rooms at the Mandarin; thankfully, they extended an incredible media rate.

As usual, I flew a day earlier and had extra work on my hands. Someone on LL's team wanted to see *which* room he'd be assigned. I know this request didn't come from him, but it was a good exercise in preparation. A manager from the Mandarin took me from room to room, and I took photos/video of each. We wound up touring eight options, one better than the next. LL's rep finally chose the last.

The next morning, I woke up early to greet the star and his rep in the lobby; they'd be arriving after an all-night flight, and I wanted to make their check-in seamless. I did it myself and held the keys, preparing to escort them to their rooms without interruption. I expected them to be tired, weary, and not ready for pleasantries. Instead, LL arrived in full LL mode; impeccably dressed, energetic, and kind.

What fucking airline was he flying?

The rest of the crew arrived later, and pre-production for the next day's shoot went smoothly. Gilles-Marie and I sketched out a shot list, but we both had misgivings about the wardrobe.

We shot LL around the hotel—presidential suite, bar, restaurant, lobby—and then Gilles-Marie brought him throughout the city to shoot in front of the monuments.

By this time, I was exhausted. As LL and the crew walked through the lobby to begin photography outdoors, starting at the Fontaines de la Concorde in the heart of Place de la Concorde, I had a sense of dread.

I approached him to get his temperature; it had been a long day already, and I wanted to make sure he was still good.

LL gave the customary "V is for Victory" gesture, kissing two fingers before flashing a peace sign. It was a made-for-ET moment, but I was in a surly, ungrateful mood.

"Just take the fucking photos," I thought to myself.

I let Gilles-Marie do his thing and stayed behind; I had nothing to add at this point and hung out in the lobby with the writer we brought to pen the cover story.

Back in New York, I looked at the photography: technically, the images were perfectly shot, lit, framed, colored. But they fell flat. The wardrobe conflicted with the setting and time of day and made LL look out of place.

Normally, an editor would kill the entire package, or at least make it an inside feature. But this was LL Cool J, and the interview writer Hud Morgan got was compelling in its raw honesty. "Follow the mantra my grandmother gave me," he said when asked how he keeps going. "If a task is once begun, never leave until it's done. Be thy great or small, do it well or not at all."

I *had* to save this cover story.

And then it hit me: walking to the office, I imagined the photos as Van Gogh paintings. What if we could take Gilles-Marie's portraits and accentuate them with "impasto," a technique the painter used in which thick layers of paint are applied to the canvas with a palette knife or brush, creating a textured and three-dimensional effect.

Several people on the staff questioned the idea, others rolled their eyes. But the art director and editor at our custom publisher, McMurry, pursued the concept and found an artist who took the challenge and added visible brushwork, depth, and movement to the images.

When I saw the result, I beamed with pride. We'd taken images of one of the world's biggest stars and turned them into pieces of art themselves.

Despite all the obstacles, the issue remains one of my favorites.

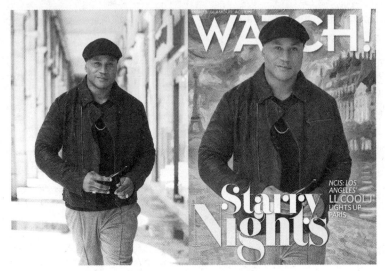

The final cover with LL Cool J in Paris, with a tough of Van Gogh. Photo by Gilles-Marie Zimmermann.

Q&A WITH SOPHIA PAULMIER

Sophia: Prior to meeting LL Cool J, were you a fan of his music?

Jeremy: I wouldn't say I was a fan, but there were several songs I remember liking from the '80s. You cannot deny the man has incredible charisma.

S: Or a fan of NCIS?

J: When it first came on, I enjoyed it, and I really liked the actors. But it became repetitive. And I still had no idea there was so much crime in the Navy!

S: Do you feel like modern architecture in the heart of Paris should be a crime?

J: There are cultural restrictions that keep this minimum. More than any country, the French respect their history, aesthetics, and art. Paris is a piece of art. Most of the modern buildings are segregated to their own districts or specific streets like the Champs-Élysées.

S: *Did you buy extra tickets and hotel rooms for LL's crew at your own expense?*

J: We worked out a deal with the hotel to get highly discounted rooms at the last minute.

S: *As you were showing the rooms on Facetime, did you attempt to lose the FaceTime connection?*

J: The reception was very strong. Also, it was LL so that would not have gone over well. But it was a chance to see all the signature suites in the Mandarin-Oriental, which I savored. It was my lifestyles of the rich and famous moment!

S: *LL had a previous relationship with the sought-out designer Dapper Dan, who would later go onto work exclusively with Gucci, making gorgeous colorful suits in many patterns and prints. Did you know of this?*

J: No, but it would not have made a difference. His team wanted who they wanted. We could not argue with a star at that level.

S: *Looking back, aside from the limiting wardrobe, what would you have changed about this shoot?*

J: I wouldn't have shot it.

S: *Being on a first name basis with LL, do you keep in touch today?*

J: First name? Hardly. He'd never recognize me. LL is a global star who meets 1,000 people a day. I'm no more special.

S: *What was your ideal vision for a location for the LL Cover?*

J: I didn't have time to think! We were glued to shooting in Paris, which is not a controlled environment. Given how expensive it can be to do something on a bigger scale, we didn't have a lot of options. Ideally, I'd like to do something really off-the-charts and whimsical with built sets, color, shapes.

CHAPTER 13

............★............

Lucy Poo

I'm not a fan of Lucy Liu. There, I said it. I used to be, when she played Ling Woo on *Ally McBeal* ("soft L, soft G... *Liiinng*"). But I came to find the character's cold, icy stare was not exactly acting.

I hadn't seen much of her since *Ally*. I know she did the *Charlie's Angels* remake, which I never saw, and not by accident. The only lasting memory I have of it is Demi Moore upstaging all three actresses at the red-carpet premiere with boy toy Ashton Kutcher, who is even less charming than Lucy. Demi had a bit part in the 120th sequel, but if there's anything we know about the sexy siren, she can upstage the Pope. They should have known better.

In 2012, Lucy dove back into TV with *Elementary*, a surprisingly smart spin on Sherlock Holmes with unintelligible Jonny Lee Miller as the celebrated sleuth, younger and more badass. Tweed went the way of tattoos, and a hushed English accent requiring subtitles. He's lucky he's hot. Lucy played Jonny's sobriety coach, a new concept because new Sherlock didn't just talk smack, he did it. That usually gives one a rock star edge when they're tall, hot, and their words don't matter because your attention is elsewhere. Jonny did not disappoint.

Elementary popped because it had a good time slot and clever storylines. The actors had an unexpected chemistry, and I was highly amused Aidan Quinn was again cast as the grumpy squad captain who's "not having it today" but winds up having it every day. Sherlock solved the hardest mysteries, along with sober-watching Lucy, who magically became Jessica Fletcher. Beware the next AA meeting, someone may discover you didn't floss.

Lucy's publicist insisted on photographer and stylist approval; I thought I'd outgrown that when I began hiring Demarchelier. But the

PR woman put two new people on my radar: photographer Ruven Afanador and stylist Jocelyn Goldstein.

Editors storyboard the shoot, then time each setting. Each backdrop gets forty-five minutes, tops. For Demarchelier, fifteen. My team spent time plotting this out over several visits at The Carlyle, a New York institution that agreed to host our shoot, and we considered the settings, aesthetic, size, and relevance to the storyline we envisioned. The Carlyle had so many possibilities that we had trouble choosing. But we did.

Every shoot demands a "walk-through" with the photographer, magazine, and PR rep for where you are shooting. I was told by one of Ruven's reps he didn't need (read: want) us on this obligation. Besides, we'd already timed the schedule with pre-selected settings.

Which his team thought was optional. "They were not feeling" many of our "suggestions" (read: take the fucking photos here) and told us what they'd be shooting, including a shot of Lucy walking an alligator down Madison Avenue.

Read that sentence again. I'll wait for your palm to slap your forehead, like mine did.

We explained why this was impossible but "settled" on a *ceramic* alligator Lucy would pretend to walk, which never happened. By this time, even they recognized it was ridiculous.

The styling, thankfully, was spot on. The wardrobe was exquisite and was accentuated by every backdrop. I'd found a pro in Jocelyn.

The day of this shoot started off frigid: I met Lucy in the lobby of The Carlyle, and she was not warm and fuzzy. That's never a good sign. I brought her to the styling suite and left her in the hands of Jocelyn and the glam crew.

Our schedule by this time was in tatters. Lucy had to leave by 5:00 p.m., and Ruven was doing whatever the fuck he wanted anyway.

It's very important for the editor and photographer to connect. They are bringing your vision to life, but through their eye. You need to trust your shooter, but they need to communicate with you. I never knew if it was shyness, indifference, anxiety, or boredom, but Ruven and I just did not connect. I felt extraneous.

The day continued to get farcical, and I gave up. No one was listening to me anyway. In one shot, Lucy is playing the flute in a suite with a great skyline of New York; I get the city landscape, but what the fuck did the flute have anything to do with our shoot? Do sober buddies spend their time rehearsing James Galway? In another setup, the actress poses in front of a painting of cabaret singer and pianist Bobby Short. Because when you think of legendary Black musicians you think of Lucy Liu.

The breaking point came with a setup of her drinking tea in bed. That'll put readers right there with her...asleep. The space in the room was admittedly tight, and both Ruven and Lucy demanded it be cleared.

Starting with me.

Lucy's hostile gaze could have ended global warming. But at this point, I didn't give a shit. I certainly wasn't going to start an argument this late in the day. I retreated to the downstairs lounge, and gradually, the rest of the crew followed; we'd become "fringe" at our own shoot.

A week or two later, I got the photos, and I had to admit they were good. Some photos were even great. The package was slotted to be the cover of our September/October fashion issue, normally our biggest of the year when design houses unveil their fall collections in glossy advertisements. We had many. The tradition we created was to celebrate with a big party at The Monkey Bar, a posh, retro bar/lounge/old-world "supper club" in midtown. *Vanity Fair* editor Graydon Carter had become a restaurateur of late, and he and a group of investors took it over and added a cosmopolitan sheen. It finally brought glamour to midtown.

We did a buyout in 2011 to celebrate a cover story with *NCIS* actress Pauley Perrette. The following year, we toasted her costar Cote de Pablo, who modeled Christian Dior's fall/winter collection at the Hôtel Plaza Athénée Paris.

We'd built such anticipation for these annual parties that 2013 was a given. It wasn't. No one wanted to celebrate this experience.

Q&A WITH SOPHIA PAULMIER

Sophia: The interaction with Lucy is fascinating. Do you feel maybe that added to her uncomfortable interaction with you?

Jeremy: Sometimes personalities just don't mesh. I'm social, gregarious, happy, fun. That can rub people the wrong way. Who knows?

S: If you were asked to work with Lucy again, what would you do differently going in that might shift the experience?

J: That's a fair question. I would have met with her before to establish familiarity and trust. Shoot day was our first meeting, and being in front of a camera is an intimate, vulnerable experience. In hindsight, I could have done more to create some kind of chemistry. But she struck me as all business/ let's get this over.

S: Who of the crew joined you at Bemelmans?

J: Our whole crew. Lucy had to leave at 5pm, and Ruven and his crew left soon after.

S: You said the photos came out better than expected, would you work with Ruven again with a lesser-known star?

J: No, we did not have chemistry. There are so many shooters who are more collaborative.

S: Aside from McG's Charlie's Angels, *have you seen the newest remake by Elizabeth Banks? Or the original show? And if so, which do you prefer?*

J: I was never a fan of any of it. The original predated me—I'm not that old!—and the movies seemed so contrived.

S: Preferred Demi Moore movie?

J: I'm a big fan of Demi. I love her look, voice, talent. *Disclosure* was incredible. *Ghost* was amazing. I even liked *GI Jane.*

S: Name a movie you wish would stop being remade?

J: Superhero movies. Enough.

S: A movie that needs to be remade?

J: A good movie does not need to be remade.

S: Has there ever been a reboot or remake that worked for you?

J: What Christopher Nolan did with the Batman reboot was nothing short of amazing. He created the blueprint in how to relaunch a franchise. All three films he did were brilliant.

S: Arthur Conan Doyle's Sherlock Holmes or Agatha Christie's Poirot?

J: Agatha Christie, hands down.

S: Lucy Liu in Elementary *or* Kill Bill?

J: Neither.

S: Aside from Harrison Ford and Lucy Liu, have you filmed any other A-list actors with more of the movie star resume?

J: Yes, many. There's no longer a wall between TV and film, they go back and forth. Every actor on TV has done some kind of movie.

S: Did you have a disappointing experience shooting them?

J: Good question. I always said to my crew, leave with what you need. If you get what you want, that's a bonus.

S: *I'd imagine much like saying yes to small roles or working lesser-known filmmakers, that A-list actors feel that it will tarnish their status quo and chances of staying A-list by agreeing to smaller entertainment magazines.*

J: I think it was magazines that covered TV in general, but we never had that bias. Actors knew they'd get the royal treatment—great location, photographer, styling. For many, it was a free vacation.

S: *To what do you attribute the disconnect with the photographer?*

J: He just had his own ideas. Sometimes shooters do that, but they at least communicate with you. Ruven is an incredible talent, but I might as well have been invisible.

S: *Jocelyn Goldstein styled it. You wrote some really good things about her.*

J: I was nervous because we hadn't worked with her before, but she exceeded expectations. Everything was meticulous and caught your eye, from the color to the texture to the fit.

S: *It's incredible. How did she get on that? Was she recommended by Liu?*

J: She was recommended by Lucy's team, and I liked her from the get-go. We hired her again, she was that good.

CHAPTER 14

⋯⋯⋯⋯★⋯⋯⋯⋯

Morning, Today, Tonight, and Whatever Time It Is Now

Jeremy, right, walking with *Good Morning America* anchor Lara Spencer and the staff of The Breakers Hotel in Palm Beach. Photo courtesy of Jeremy Murphy.

Lara Spencer was a home run when she joined *Good Morning America*. Beauty, intelligence, sass, glamour, and a solid journalism background. We discovered this ourselves a year prior when we did a big fashion shoot to celebrate her as cohost of *The Insider*, an entertainment news-magazine akin to *Entertainment Tonight*. It was originally created to give more "in-depth" coverage of stories, but in reality, it was just to sell with *ET* because local stations need something similar to fill an hour of airtime; both were thirty minutes.

The content was atrocious; Lara was the only reason to watch, and how she kept from eye-rolling or barfing was a portrait of courage in and of itself.

Our staff loved her but were not "in the loop" to the backstage machinations of Hollywood. She was about to leave for *GMA*. The only rumor we'd heard was she was a shoo-in to replace Mary Hart as cohost of *ET*. In retrospect, Lara made the right decision. She and her manager were smarter than the studios.

Getting her to do a shoot for our magazine was not easy; she was a hot prospect, and still is. But we aligned with a world-famous resort in Palm Beach called The Breakers and with Continental Airlines to sponsor. *TV Guide* was not offering this.

The Breakers is a world of its own. Its Italian Renaissance–style tower, with two giant turrets at each end, is akin to a pink castle crowning the Palm Beach skyline. A long driveway is graced with a giant Boboli-style fountain, and surrounding the property are restaurants, a golf course, a pool, cabanas, and the beach. It is where the have and have-mores come for the winter.

A dynamo named Bonnie Reuben has done its PR for years. Its in-house PR rep was Margee Morris, who we adored—and still do. Together, they were big supporters of our magazine when they didn't have to be.

Palm Beach is a natural destination when you are selling glamour. It is the US Côte d'Azur, dotted with $100-million mansions, five-star hotels, restaurants, and top designer boutiques. Worth Avenue, its famous shopping district, is on par with Rodeo Drive and Madison Avenue. In the winter ("the season"), it's a billionaire's playground. The summer is sweltering hot and when people less wealthy can afford to enjoy it.

I spent a lot of time on the island as a child but did not live there. My mom worked for First National Bank of Palm Beach, and when school was closed, I'd go with her and run free throughout the town. I remember having lunch at its local greasy diner, Hamburger Heaven, where the locals would go for eight-dollar sandwiches. A few blocks away was Taboo, an upscale restaurant/bar that had affordable pizza as an appetizer and gold diggers looking for husbands. Both have since closed. I also often snuck into The Breakers, and when caught, would fake being someone's lost kid who couldn't remember his room number. Instead, betting there was a Steinberg family as registered guests, I used that name. And I got to use the pool. I have such fond memories of this time, so bringing a celebrity there was not a hard sell to me.

Lara graciously agreed, as did The Jackal, who used the setting to bring glamour and sophistication to a new level. It helped that Lara has such a statuesque figure: tall, lean, and beautiful. The Jackal had no problem getting top designer samples and millions of dollars in jewelry to use for wardrobe. Cliff Lipson was excited to shoot.

Lara came the day before photography, and was witty, sarcastic, and social: the perfect attitude for a day-long shoot. She gave us great behind-the-scenes dish and laughed at our outrageousness. We brought the party wherever we went.

The *ET* rumors were heating up, and several local media orgs pounced on covering our photo shoot so they could dig for dirt. They, too, were unwise to the real story. None of us were *Insiders*.

Our day with Lara went brilliantly. Everyone brought their A-game, and captured each setting beautifully. We shot her in every vantage The Breakers could offer. Our subject was more radiant and interesting than many of the celebrities she covered.

We ended the day with dinner at the hotel's famous Seafood Bar at the back of the main tower and were joined by my mom and stepfather. More than once, I got a raised eyebrow from my mom, who apparently hadn't heard *all* of my more colorful antics.

A few weeks later, Lara emailed me saying she was in New York and invited Super P and me to drinks at The Plaza, which had recently reopened. Celebrities often did this after photo shoots with us because we were rascals. We once did a group dinner in LA with the cast of *The Big Bang Theory*, and drinks with stars like Cote de Pablo, cast members from *The Good Wife*, and a few others. Add to that Lara, who we joined for a night of laughter and stories. I shared details of a particular temperamental actress who we recently shot; she was upset we didn't hire Demarchelier but—sorry, honey—she was not of that caliber. Few were.

"Let a bitch know," was the hilarious response from the makeup artist friend who joined us. That became our mantra.

✧ ✧ ✧

In 2006, AA launched its new Admirals Club first-class cabin with apartment-sized seats that turn into flatbeds. They asked our magazine if we'd like to fly a celebrity to experience this luxury on one of their most popular routes: Shanghai. I enlisted "The Amazing Race" host Phil Keoghan, who loved it but wanted to bring his wife, Louise, and ten-year-old daughter, Elle. That wouldn't be a problem thanks to AA, which comped five first-class tickets to China. I was really starting to love this gig.

Jeremy with *The Amazing Race* host Phil Keoghan in Shanghai. Photo courtesy of Jeremy Murphy.

The flight was longer than twelve hours, and Shanghai in July is terrible: congested, smoggy, and really damn humid. Just getting into the van to the hotel felt like taking a steam shower. Taking a breath of fresh air depends on your purifier's settings. Coffee comes with a side of honking horns and the melody of bells ringing furiously on thousands of bicycles. The skyline is akin to a seizure.

The Shanghai tourism ministry had put together a very packed, weeklong schedule that began at 9:00 a.m. and ended at 9:00 p.m. We had a Sprinter van with three tour guides (two of whom would turn out to be Chinese "minders" hosting American media) that brought us to all the locales: villages, ponds, the Bund, the Pearl Tower, etc. By day four, we were all exhausted and craving non-Chinese food. I swore if I saw a lazy Susan again, I'd add a dead squirrel and spin it back.

Having reached a consensus among our group, I advised our "minders" we needed a day off. They huddled privately in the corner to debate this international crisis and returned to me with a simple answer: no.

That might work in China, but for five starving foreigners who just wanted pizza, it was not optional.

"I understand the situation," diplomat Murphy said, trying to achieve détente. "But we don't work for you. We're tired, hungry, and are taking the day for ourselves."

Another high-stakes negotiation between the three Chinese hosts broke out, and the answer remained the same: no.

The China Missile Crisis had begun.

Again, I kindly advised we would not be in the van the next morning.

Instead, we enjoyed really great food at an otherwise shitty California Pizza Kitchen, which was connected to our hotel.

We were getting ready to do a cover with Mayim Bialik from *The Big Bang Theory* in Paris in 2013. She'd become one of the show's breakout stars, and doing a fashion shoot with an actress not known for fashion was a challenge I wanted. Le Bristol, a five-star hotel across from the Palais de Elysée—France's version of the White House—offered to host the entire crew and provide settings.

Actors are not model sizes. In all my years as editor, I can think of maybe three who fit couture samples easily. Mayim added the extra obstacle of not using anything leather or exposing limbs above the elbow or knee.

Christopher Campbell was one of the few stylists I knew who could figure this one out. He was salty with the challenge—as he was when I assigned him the impossible—but came through brilliantly. For days, he and an assistant collected wardrobe from Paris's most known and most secret vintage shops and couture collectors. They got everything lent to us for a small fee, but with big liabilities if one thread came undone.

Christopher nearly had a heart attack when I pulled a joke on him the day before the shoot. Mayim had just done the fitting, and he was finally starting to relax.

"We have a big problem, buddy," I said. "Mayim can't show her face." His eyes got big.

"I can't...I can't," he said, in frustration.

Mayim's requests for wardrobe were tough, so I knew this sounded somewhat reasonable even if it was a joke.

He can finally laugh about it years later.

Mayim Bialik in Paris at Le Bristol Hotel, styled by Christopher Campbell. Photo by Gilles-Marie Zimmermann.

✧ ✧ ✧

The 2008 financial collapse affected everyone...but us. We existed on barter deals and sponsorships, which eliminated costs and made us look responsible and thrifty, two words that have never been associated with me. I'm their evil twin. The arrangement gave us license to travel and continue our photo shoots.

Crissy Poorman, who I wrote about previously, handled PR for The Ritz-Carlton, Palm Beach and always called with great ideas. Introduced to us by Vivian Deuschl, Crissy gave the hotel a national profile, especially after its near $100-million renovation. The hotel's '80s-era ambiance—oil paintings of dogs, sconces, silk walls, and antique-like furnishings—was replaced by nautical and coastal decor elements, including seashell motifs, coral designs, and beach-themed artwork. It was perfect for a photo shoot, especially after Crissy got the hotel a huge feature in the *New York Times*.

Together, we brainstormed a way to feature the hotel in our magazine, but it was mid-October, which made getting TV stars difficult—they typically don't break until Christmas. Flying to Palm Beach mid-season would affect schedules and filming, which costs money. By this time, I was used to "No," "Are you serious?," "You're delusional," and my favorite, "How's never?" My inbox became a psychiatrist's Super Bowl.

We lucked out hearing Roselyn Sánchez, the smoldering Latina actress on the hit drama *Without a Trace*, was interested and available. Her character was not memorable—none of them were—but she was. Sultry, alluring, and stunning, Roselyn couldn't help but get attention. She was a breakout and perfect for a cover; we were still rookies learning through failure, and she was new to her show. Crissy extended an incredible offer to host our team and give us full access to the resort. It was a no-brainer, but the dichotomy was not just apparent but screaming. Going to a luxury hotel in Palm Beach amid layoffs, foreclosures, wiped savings, and worthless stock gave me pause, mostly for the optics. It just didn't look good. Adding to the uncertainty, Crissy left for a bigger job, leaving the hotel PR-less in the midst of planning.

This is when the good angel on my left shoulder and the evil demon on my right started to quibble. But I'm also an Aries—we are known for being mavericks, risk-takers, and wildly impulsive when following creative vision.

Who am I to argue with the universe?

I summoned our cast of characters—Cliff, The Jackal, and her assistant mostly—and we trekked to Palm Beach, which was due for a tropical storm. I feared this was an omen.

Despite the weather, everyone arrived safely, and we began planning the next day. The Jackal pulled million-dollar pieces of jewelry, designer gowns, and the like from Worth Avenue boutiques. Comically, the makeup and hairstylist we found was based in Miami and did not have a driver's license or credit card; we wound up hiring cars to bring him back and forth.

Shoot day got complicated when the weather turned worse. It was near-hurricane strength, and we were at an ocean-front resort. Without an on-site PR rep for the hotel, we were left on our own. Naturally, we commandeered several locations to use as settings, including its presidential suite, which Crissy had made famous. Mostly for a glass-enclosed collection of shoes inspired by first ladies that lined one of the walls. Designed by Robert Talbert, the repertoire of custom-made heels was a sight to behold, including one pair inspired by Jackie O, replete with a square-toed heel in pink, JFK political button, and heel shaped as a pillbox hat.

Roselyn looks good in any setting. And so does her now-husband, Eric Winter, who flew down to watch us shoot the woman who'd become his wife. Cliff and The Jackal wanted to shoot them together, but Eric didn't come with wardrobe. Not expecting him, we had nothing to dress him in. But capturing them together was too good an opportunity to waste, so I brought Eric into town and purchased a black Hugo Boss suit for his wardrobe. Of course it fit off the rack. He was tall and lean; guys like that don't need a "One day!" closet. It's every day in their world and grist for others' therapists. Making it worse, he was nice and funny. I hate it when the hotties are harmonious; you want to hate them but wind up loving them. He was no exception.

Actor Eric Winter with now-wife Roselyn Sanchez, from *Without a Trace*, in Palm Beach. Photo by Cliff Lipson.

Eric was beyond appreciative of getting a free suit for the photo.

"Stay a bit longer, you might get a car," I joked.

The shoot came together after all, and Roselyn's cover was a big hit. We celebrated its premiere with a media reception at The Capital Grille in Manhattan, which Roselyn and Eric graciously attended. As I scanned the crowd to count the heads, I spied a tall, glamorous woman dressed chic and sleek. She looked familiar.

Where did I know this person?

What little of my brain not soaked by Macallan works like Rain Man. I remember most everything except the current day and what I did five minutes ago. And then it clicked: Christine DiRocco, who I worked with in 1995 when we both lived in Boca Raton and were starting our careers. She looked at me like I was an alien—I get that a lot—but a few reminders triggered her memory. We were buds who were not thrilled with our boring jobs and the people we worked with. Several times we snuck out for lunches that ran very, very long. Christine had become the hotel's new Director of Public Relations and continued giving it a national profile. One idea she had I cannot share in print, but I do when I talked to PR/ marketing classes. Christine brings class and creativity to everything she does, and is still one of Palm Beach's most in-demand PR minds.

And the guilt we felt shooting in Palm Beach during the economic downturn had dissipated; we knew the content we'd just created would offer readers much need glamour, escapism, and beauty.

Jamie and Chris Carbone, left, with Jeremy, center, and Niki Lesson, right.

I made a habit of making my birthday—March 31—an annual get-together for friends and colleagues, who came to know and befriend one another; at one point, I'd become a fifth wheel at my own parties.

It was usually simple: private room at a restaurant with hors d'oeuvres, open bar, music, and laughs. In 2013, I decided to go big and make it a black-tie affair at The Carlyle, New York's toniest hotel.

The only problem? I couldn't afford to because it was expensive... with a capital *E*. To mitigate costs, I made it a fundraiser for the Robin Hood Foundation, a nonprofit started by New York business leaders to give back to the community. I set up a meeting with Pamela Ellison, one of their development directors, and pitched a silent auction concept where my guests would bid on items and the proceeds would go to Robin Hood. Pamela said yes without much hesitation.

Designers including Tom Ford, YSL, Salvatore Ferragamo, Giorgio Armani, Valentino, and Ermenegildo Zegna all donated items for the silent auction to benefit the Robin Hood Foundation.

The Carlyle did too; they actually let me stage the party inside Café Carlyle—where my favorite designer Isaac Mizrahi does a cabaret act—on an off night.

Getting the auction items turned out to be comical for a very legitimate reason: I was high on pain meds after dental surgery and brimming with unusual confidence. Laying on my couch after the procedure, I sent dozens of requests for donations from my Blackberry, each one more ridiculous than the last. To my utter disbelief, every ask was honored. Tom Ford donated an entire beauty collection; Ferragamo, Valentino, and Armani sent purses; YSL Beauty sent a box of fragrances; hotels around the world issued two-night gift certificates; 21 provided a private gourmet dinner; Patrick Demarchelier sent a six-foot original print of supermodel Linda Evangelista; *Vogue* donated a tour of its fashion closet; and *Mentalist* star Simon Baker sent an autographed surfboard.

Even Charlie Siem gifted me with a live performance.

Charlie Siem performing at Jeremy Murphy's birthday.

The night was sentimental. Friends and colleagues came in tuxedos and dresses, Charlie was masterful, the food and drinks were top-notch, and we raised five figures for The Robin Hood Foundation. One bid got competitive: three hotels in Paris—the Plaza Athénée, Mandarin Oriental, and George V—had all donated two-night gift certificates, which would make an amazing trip. My best friend bid on them hard, but a very wealthy couple I *didn't* know—guests of someone who did—continued to top her, and the amount got too high for my friend. I was happy it raised so much but wanted to kneecap the couple for robbing my friend of Parisian luxury.

The Linda Evangelista print must have been eight feet tall in its frame, and, as a one-of-a-kind, it became a big moneymaker. Simon Baker's surfboard also raised a healthy sum.

The next night, as a surprise to a smaller group who had helped me plan the party, I arranged a private dinner in 21's famed secret wine cellar. The restaurant had become a great partner to our magazine and generously hosted (read: it was free!) twelve people for a Michelin star–quality steak dinner. The antics from the night proved highly memorable, including the aforementioned penis puppetry, which shocked and amused to no end. I blocked the door so the servers did not see this unique guest gesture.

The next morning, Charlie was due to depart The Carlyle. I arranged a car to bring him to the airport, and as I guided him toward the idling SUV, he turned to me and said, in the poshest English accent I've ever heard, "Jeremy, you have such interesting friends."

I'd unintentionally set a bar that would be impossible to meet, but I didn't stop trying. The next year, my good friend Iestyn Davies, one of the most famous countertenors in opera, was performing in New York and releasing a new album. He proposed doing a joint celebration and offered as a setting a TriBeCa penthouse owned by very, very wealthy friends.

More than fifty people came to the party that night, and the prime attraction was Iestyn singing to the mesmerized audience. His voice is angelic; it's hard to believe *anyone* can hit those notes. More than a few cried when he sang "Tears in Heaven," and I got misty-eyed when he began "Happy Birthday." Christopher Campbell, the stylist I mentioned earlier, came and brought with him Lazaro Hernandez, who co-founded the fashion label Proenza Schouler (he's the Proenza, his mother's maiden name).

Opera star Iestyn Davies, one of the most celebrated counter tenors of the genre, performed at Jeremy Murphy's 39th birthday.

Stylist Christopher Campbell, left, with Lazaro Hernandez (from Proenza Schouler), and Jeremy at his 39th birthday party. Photo courtesy of Jeremy Murphy.

Throwing events like these is exhilarating but also exhausting. For my fortieth, I invited friends to a local bar/grille called Baker Street Irregulars, a neighborhood joint with great history: it was where the 1988 movie *Cocktail* with Tom Cruise was filmed. I invited about sixty friends to come for beer, wine, and comfort food, and had just as good of a time.

Jeremy at his 40th birthday.

Q&A WITH SOPHIA PAULMIER

Sophia: Can you tell us any good stories Lara Spencer shared?

Jeremy: No, what's said in Palm Beach stays in Palm Beach. But we share a wicked sense of humor. She was a dream to work with.

S: *Have you spoken with her since?*

J: No, I've lost touch with a lot of the talent. I'm no longer in that orbit, but I'd love to see her again. I hope she'd remember me – it was 14 years ago now

S: *Was it surreal staying at The Breakers after sneaking in as a kid?*

J: Yes, totally. I finally realized how expensive it was to be there! For good reason; it's an incredibly impressive, special place to be and provided an amazing backdrop for our photography. They have one of the best PR teams in the business.

S: *Favorite store to shop in Palm Beach?*

J: I could never afford to shop there and I was well-paid! It's luxury on an irrational level. There was a cool surf shop in town, which closed. And a Starbucks. But no, I was not carrying Ferragamo garment bags.

S: *Your go-to Beach in Florida?*

J: I'm a pasty white Irishman; we avoid the sun. Any time spent on the sand turns me into a lobster.

S: *Favorite place in Shanghai?*

J: The departure lounge in the airport. I couldn't wait to leave.

CHAPTER 15

Sunny Weatherly

Michael Weatherly, star of *NCIS* and *Bull*, walking through the Hotel Crillon in Paris. The Jackal, our stylist, convinced French luxury label Faconnable to let us dress him in their tuxedo.

Michael Weatherly was the "First Gentleman" of *Watch* magazine. He got the most photo shoots and most covers of anyone, and here's why: he is the most fun you'll ever have.

The actor was starring on *NCIS*, and later *Bull*, and his impeccable timing, razor-sharp wit, and comedic instincts became the show's secret sauce. Michael had a devil-may-care attitude that spoke to us as a magazine. We loved improvising, going off script, adding the impromptu just as much.

Our first shoot with Michael found me somewhere familiar, on purpose. I'd gotten word he was going to be in Boston over the Memorial Day break in 2006 and rushed to put together a destination-themed shoot for our third issue, sponsored by a place that had become extraordinarily special: The Ritz-Carlton, Boston Common, where I'd spent the week of 9/11. Their kindness necessitated I do something in return, and I called its PR rep Caron LeBrun, who greatly appreciated the opportunity. They hosted us for several days as we photographed Michael throughout Boston, including Fenway Park, Faneuil Hall, Boston Public Garden, Union Oyster House, and at the hotel. Over dinner one night, Caron shared with us the history of The Ritz-Carlton in Boston, including its famous guests. Pianist Peter Duchin, especially. Caron brought his biography to the table, which Michael read.

Aloud.

To the entire restaurant.

It was a you-had-to-be-there moment.

When we got our first opportunity to bring a star to Paris, he was our first ask. Our idea was to photograph him and costar Cote De Pablo glamorously throughout the fashion capital. At the last minute, though, the actress's representative said she wanted to go to Switzerland instead. Which she did not. He just made it up because *he* wanted to go, and when I refused he pulled her from the shoot (we did wind up bringing her yodel land, sadly). It's too bad, because The Jackal had gotten famed Parisian designer Christian Lacroix to lend couture dresses for her to wear throughout Paris' most iconic settings. We were sad to lose Cote but very happy to have Michael.

The actor did not disappoint and flew overnight from Los Angeles hours after wrapping filming of *NCIS* before its Christmas break. The Hôtel de Crillon, in the Place de la Concorde, hosted our shoot, and we pivoted to a James Bond–meets–Cary Grant theme. The Jackal got French luxury brand Façonnable to lend us the wardrobe, which included a tuxedo, suits, and casual wear. Photographer John Filo got what is still today one of my favorite images: Michael walking through the lobby of the hotel looking like he just banged the cheerleading squad. Paris for the first time was sensory overload, and full of sensations I could not process. I could not believe I was finally there. The week we spent includes crazy moments, like eating at Café Angelina, whose tables are so small and crowded, they added a smaller, stool-sized surface. We called it the "Fadapter" because after days of croissants, cheese, wine, and bread, we needed to adapt to our new fat. On our last night, the concierge at the hotel suggested Jules Verne for dinner, not realizing our infinitesimal budget. The famed restaurant is housed inside the Eiffel Tower and includes tasting menus equaling a mortgage payment. We split the bill on four credit cards.

Four years later we got to shoot Michael again in an odd location for a luxury hotel: the Arizona desert. The Ritz-Carlton, Dove Mountain didn't have many doves, but plenty of sand and snakes. Michael was his usual gregarious self, and The Jackal pulled a more rugged wardrobe given the aesthetic. The actor, of course, looked great in everything, including leaning against a motorcycle in the desert. He was a better-looking James Dean. The night of the shoot, the hotel's PR director invited our crew to a group dinner in its signature restaurant, and for some odd reason presented Michael an orange construction hard hat as a parting gift. I never understood why, but after a lot of wine and spirits, everyone wound up wearing it at the table.

As we prepared to leave the next morning, the actor walked into the lobby...wearing the hard hat.

Those were our early salad years, which is all we could afford. In 2013, with the magazine finally making money (thank you, Super P!), we were able to show Michael our appreciation with a setting far more fitting: the South of France. We'd been invited by a small boutique hotel in Vence called Château Saint-Martin & Spa, deep in the Cote d'Azur. The property, which began as an outpost of the Knights Templar in

1550 AD and was later re-imagined by artist Henri Matisse, has only forty-six rooms but also a Michelin-star restaurant, wine cellar dug into a rock, infinity pool, and helipad.

Christopher Campbell pitched me on using photographer Slim Aarons's work as inspiration and aesthetic for the shoot, which was masterful. Aarons's timeless images of beautiful people in beautiful settings was simple, chic, and glamorous, and they transport the eye to a bygone era. Keiron O'Connor was chosen to do the photography, and he brought his own quirky perspective to the theme.

Our final shoot found Michael in London to mark our ten-year anniversary (see chapter 30). The theme was celebration, and we hired three attractive female models to shadow him like an entourage of back-up singers in every setting. One got particularly festive: in a very expensive suite, we used confetti as a prop and threw it in the air as Ian Derry shot Michael dancing and singing in the room with the models. The photos popped, but the hotel PR director and I wound up picking up the refuse on our knees for more than an hour: there was confetti everywhere, including between cushions on the couch. And the room had been booked for the afternoon, which made clean-up more urgent.

Perhaps this was penance for my last celebration in London (at a different hotel, thankfully)?

Once we wrapped, Michael had dinner with our crew, which had grown to include the three models who didn't want to leave. We preferred otherwise, and I politely informed the women the shoot had indeed ended. Hence "that's a wrap."

Michael graced the cover of the issue that celebrated our incredible milestone.

First Gentleman, indeed.

Q&A WITH SOPHIA PAULMIER

Sophia: It sounds like you became friendly with Michael Weatherly. Have you stayed in touch?

Jeremy: We have! I'm literally setting up dinner with him and Super P.

S: The Boston trip sounded like a good time. Have you been back to the Ritz-Carlton since? And has anything changed?

J: Everything has! The Ritz-Carlton sold their historic property across the Public Garden, so the Boston Common hotel became the only Ritz-Carlton in the city. It's still one of the best, but I haven't been back in years.

S: Cote De Pablo's reps pulled her from the Paris shoot because they requested Switzerland instead? Was there more to this story or have anything to do with Weatherly?

J: There's more to the story, lol. It had nothing to do with Michael. Someone on Cote's team played big foot without telling her or anyone why. We found out later it was because this person wanted to go. No one else really cared to see Switzerland, but we wound up going four years later at the same persons behest.

S: Have you worked with Cote De Pablo since and did she confirm this?

J: Yes and yes. We are friends and have a good laugh about it now. It was a great learning lesson in how Hollywood works; often the talent are kept out of the loop in how these things are planned. The requests and demands don't always come from them but their people.

S: Did Jules Verne live up to the hype?

J: It depends who the chef is. Alain Ducasse took over for a while and it got really good. The last time I was there was 2016 so I don't know how it is anymore. I did send a friend who was taking her daughter to Paris for her graduation and got an urgent call: I hadn't prepared her for the prices. It's prohibitively expensive. Eating inside the Eiffel Tower is worth it, once. But the last time I was there I saw tourists in casual wear and sneakers.

S: Did you discover any interesting restaurants or spots while in Arizona?

J: No, we were in the desert! Thankfully there was a really great restaurant in the hotel. I think they might have lost a star solely because of us. We brought the crazy train with us to Arizona!

S: Château Saint-Martin has to be one of the top places to stay. How high would you number it in your top stays of all time?

J: Up there, for sure. It's a boutique hotel I'd never heard of, which are the best kind. I love discovering new places to visit, photograph, and recommend to friends. The property is a few minutes away from a historic restaurant called La Colombe d'Or, which is dotted with artwork from Pablo Picasso, Marc Chagall, and Henri Matisse. The legend is Picasso would visit regularly and pay his bill by sketching something on a napkin.

S: If you could shoot Michael for a new cover today, what would be the location and where would you stay?

J: Wouldn't matter, he's funny anywhere. I think Monte-Carlo would be fun, though. He's got great taste in wine, food, culture.

CHAPTER 16

★

Lights! Camera! Caution!

I wanted this image of Mayim Bialik, by Gilles-Marie Zimmermann for a cover.

Writing this chapter gives me tremors because it's such a hot-button topic/area that inflames passions on both sides. Fortunately, this happened before the most recent turmoil. But it was harrowing nevertheless, and I say that having lost my apartment after it exploded on 9/11.

We'd shot Mayim Bialik from *The Big Bang Theory* two years prior and now had an offer from the Israeli tourism ministry to bring her to Jerusalem and Tel Aviv for a cover shoot. Mayim comes from Jewish ancestry—her grandparents immigrated to the US from Poland, Hungary, and Czechoslovakia—and she identifies herself as Modern Orthodox. She is also related to famed Jewish poet Chaim Nachman Bialik, who is her great-grandfather's first cousin. Given that lineage and the beauty and aesthetics of the land, this would naturally be an easy decision. But it did give me pause.

A celebrity magazine is not a political organ. More than 90 percent of our staff were proud Democrats, but you would not know from our pages. We took pains to strip away any bias from our editorial. If we were to shoot in Israel, it had to be highly *apolitical*.

I agreed to do the shoot but had misgivings.

The first sign was when we got early warnings about our passports. If you had a stamp from a list of countries, which included Syria, Iran, and several other places, you could not enter. I had to cut a few team members who had worked in those areas covering war zones.

Getting the right crew was essential given the sensitivities. Not only did I need staff who could work nimbly and fearlessly, I also could not tolerate drama queens: there was enough already. Gilles-Marie Zimmerman had already shot LL Cool J and Mayim, and his stunning images of the actress surprised people. Mayim is very frank about growing up in Hollywood and never feeling like the ingénue, but Gilles-Marie captured something no one else had ever: transcendence. Together with Christopher Campbell, they showed a Mayim Bialik that no one had seen before but who was always there. Her publicist uses those photos to this day in pitching her for photo shoots. I knew Gilles-Marie was the guy for this.

Christopher had just shot Julianna Margulies in the South of France and had to return to New York, which opened the door to use Fabio Mercurio, the Milan-based stylist who dressed Christine Baranski in Tuscany, Cote de Pablo in Malta, and Matthew Gray Gubler in Park City, Utah. There is no one else like Christopher Campbell, but there's no one like Fabio either. As different as they are, they think similarly: editorially, with fabric, color, texture, aesthetics, and tone as words. How a person wears, looks, and feels in a piece of clothing often tells the story itself. Fabio, too, has deep connections and is able to pull the best pieces from virtually any designer. Dressing Mayim is always a challenge given the restrictions, and Fabio was up for the task.

We needed an awesome crew for the Mayim Bialik shoot in Israel and found one! Photo by Gilles-Marie Zimmermann.

Bruno Weppe, our favorite European hairstylist, joined us, as did Paris-based makeup artist Rafael Pita; both also worked on Mayim's first shoot in Paris.

Our crew met in Jerusalem, and we stayed at The King David, which is the nicest and most heavily guarded hotel in history. Everyone was a bit trepid given our location, but we were in awe of the visuals, especially the Old City.

Shoot day arrived, and we started on a bluff overlooking the Old City. All was going well until our "tour guides," who turned out to be Mossad agents, interrupted the photography and directed everyone into the two Sprinter vans we'd taken.

"Now, now, now!" I remember them shouting with the utmost urgency.

The van I rode in tore out of there like it was in the Daytona 500. I've never seen a vehicle move so fast—it had to be going at least 120 mph. Apparently, word had gotten out Mayim was in Jerusalem and a perfect subject for...well, you get the point.

Our whole crew was spooked, and then it got spookier. Our "tour guides" brought us to a restaurant for dinner, and as we stood at the hostess stand waiting for our table, they again shouted, "Now, now, now!" and snuck us through the kitchen, out the back door, and to another restaurant.

We departed Jerusalem for part two: Tel Aviv, less historic and more Miami Beach. I took a deep breath. That shit gets to you. I was confident we were out of danger until the sirens went off—at 11:00 p.m.

Groups like to launch missiles into Israel randomly—and regularly—but the country knows where they are going to hit. If it's land, they knock it down. If it's the ocean or a barren desert, they let it hit. But the sirens ring loud and let all know there are missiles in the air.

Leaving Israel was a conflicted experience. I won't lie—I was happy to go. Five days fried my nerves; I could not imagine what it's like to live there. But to be there and see and feel the history was something you don't forget.

The photography was as strong as I'd hoped. I made the right calls on everyone we brought. Gilles-Marie's images gave me many options, including a stunning image of Mayim straddling a stone wall and looking beautiful, confident, and fierce. I wanted it for the cover.

But given the "sensitivities," a higher-up threw his considerable weight around and insisted on the smile mandate: cover subjects smiling, as if we were a Sears family portrait studio. I mostly ignored this dictate but on this I was forced to use a less captivating—but still gorgeous—image of the actress looking happy-go-lucky.

Glad someone was.

Q&A WITH SOPHIA PAULMIER

Sophia: Prior to arriving in Israel, did you or your team have any concerns about safety?

Jeremy: it didn't hit me until we arrived. The PR firm that represents the Israeli tourism ministry was very good and laid out the situation/ rules. But being there in Jerusalem is a profound experience. It's a beautiful, stunning city with so much history; unfortunately, conflict is something they have to deal with.

S: Did these "tour guides" know you were there for a photoshoot?

J: Yes, for sure. We had two vans filled with wardrobe, camera equipment, and staff.

S: I'd imagine eating dinner after fearing your safety to be quite difficult, did anyone lose their appetite?

J: No one lost their appetite, but we were all in a bit of shock. The cloak and dagger of it all preys on your nerves.

S: *Is Mayim Bialik anything like her character on* The Big Bang Theory?

J: Yes in the sense that she's modest and likable. But unlike Amy, her character, Mayim is a bit more relaxed and less rigid.

S: *I've heard Jerusalem is beautiful, what was like?*

J: It's breathtaking, but in all honesty, I was scared the entire time. I can't imagine living with that threat every day.

S: *These "tour guides" sound alarming. How terrified were you on a scale of one to ten?*

J: I was glad they were with us! Mossad agents are badass; no one fucks with them. But on the scary scale, I was at a twelve.

S: *Did these "tour guides" eat with you?*

J: Yikes, I can't remember! They were very nice and had almost a paternal quality to them. I felt protected.

S: *Biggest takeaway from this experience?*

J: I'm still processing it nine years later. It was a whirlwind and overwhelming; we didn't have much time to sit around and ponder. I think about it often, but I can't put what I'm feeling into words, which sucks because I'm a writer. I will say that we have it very good here in the US. As Warren Buffett said, if you were born in America, you already won the lottery.

CHAPTER 17

⋯⋯⋯★⋯⋯⋯

Breaking the News (literally)

Don't sing to Ted Koppel. Here's the back story. It was another shitty day in publishing. We had amazing editorial, advertisers were aplenty, but bureaucratic nonsense was making our lives hell; we started calling several divisions "sales prevention." Super P and I went to one of our new favorite "woe-is-me" destinations: the Gilt Bar inside the Palace Hotel, a gargantuan skyscraper across the street from St. Patrick's Cathedral on Madison Avenue in Midtown Manhattan. The hotel was weird because in the front was a courtyard wrapped around an old-school Gilded Age mansion. Behind it, a very tall black glass building that could belong to Chase or Citibank. The Gilt Bar was housed in an ornate, regal room with walls out of the Palace of Versailles: gold, molding, sculptures—you get the idea. It gained notoriety after the first episode of *Gossip Girl* where Blair (Leighton Meester) and Serena (Blake Lively) reunite at the bar. How this hotel let that show—with high schoolers drinking—film on-site astounded me.

I brought "the book"—a binder with all the pages from the next issue—to the bar so Super P and I could slot the ads. We decided which advertisement went next to what page. By now, we had a rhythm— give a little, take a little. We trusted each other implicitly, and still do. Out of the corner of my eye, I saw Ted Koppel, the legendary host of *Nightline*, the daily newscast on ABC that aired at 11:35 p.m. Ted was famous for his journalistic rigor, skepticism, and hair—it was reminiscent of Alfred E. Neuman from *Mad Magazine*. I was three, or many, Scotches in at this point and told Super P I wanted to sing the *Nightline* theme song to Ted. "Please don't," he pleaded. Too late!

An ill-advised, impromptu trip to Paris when Jeremy and his friend befriended members of the Saudi Royal Family, including this hidden member. Photo courtesy of Jeremy Murphy.

Someone royal who was not "vested" in taking my business card.

I went up to "Mr. Koppel," introduced myself, said how much I admired him ("Why, thank you, young man"), and asked if I could sing the song. "No, that's not necessary," he replied diplomatically. I didn't care.

"Doo doo DOOT do," I sang, capturing the urgency of the song, which always signaled major news.

Ted was not thrilled and summoned the manager, who summoned security.

Jeremy ended the party with an unidentified man and a balloon on his head. Photo courtesy of Jeremy Murphy.

Jeremy went to bed in this condition. Photo courtesy of Jeremy Murphy.

Jeremy with legendary Bar Hemingway host/mixologist Colin Field
with Michael Weatherly. Photo courtesy of Jeremy Murphy.

Traveling the world afforded me miles on AA, which I hadn't used until a December in 2009, when I had a drunken idea: go to Paris for New Year's Eve. Because that's what responsible people do a week before the holiday. I booked seats on an overnight flight for me and a friend, and used connections to get a hotel room at the George V. I also cashed in a favor to attend the Ritz Paris's black-tie New Year's Eve party. Mason, my plus-one, and I donned our best and had a quiet dinner in a banquet room, which turned fraternity-house wild after guests indulged in enough bubbly. We crushed the dance floor. As Mason did the tango with an assortment of international strangers, I found myself in Bar Hemingway jumping up and down to the Black-Eyed Peas's "I Gotta Feeling." I was joined by a German father and son amused by the bouncing balloon-shaped American waving his hands in the air like he just don't care. A couple hours in, I found Mason outside smoking... and charming a group of Middle Eastern trust fund babies enraptured with his stories, humor, and opinions. And he was wearing one of their fur coats, commissioning his own photo shoot. I joined the lovefest and talked to the group, who were fascinated by our American sensibilities. As we began to leave, I offered one of the sisters my card, eager to stay in touch.

"Sorry," she said, declining to take it. "I'm not that vested."

I was insulted for a second, then realized it was the best. Line. Ever.

A line of Maybachs was parked outside, one for each, which must have numbered ten. We joined Mubarak, the friendliest of the clan, and the motorcade drove to the Hotel George V, conveniently next to ours. The clan had an entire floor reserved for them, and we continued our late-night—now early-morning—revelry.

"Murphy, you're not in the real world anymore."

Champers the Cat had become our magazine mascot. He had a column—through the voice of writer/comedian Frank DeCaro—as well as a marketing campaign announcing his arrival and even a stuffed animal made in his likeness. All that was missing was an email, which I set up through our IT division. Champers.the.cat@ was his address, and I hoped readers would engage. With a cat.

Meow.

I made myself the administrator—he's my fucking cat!—and added his email to my phone. I'm normally very careful with emails, but I royally fucked up one night when I sent an important email to top executives at our company from—you guessed it—Champers's address.

"Jeremy, don't ever send a message from your fucking cat again," was just one of the uplifting responses I received.

Hssssss!!!!

A big movie star was doing a huge project, and we got a chance to shoot him. It went...OK. Not great, but useable. After the shoot, as I signed invoices, I saw one for a hairstylist: $5,000, which is way beyond what anyone pays in editorial rate. Livid, I picked up the phone and called the actor's manager, who insisted on this stylist.

"Yeah, I got the invoice," I began, laying the groundwork.

"And?" she said, dismissively.

"He's *bald*! He has no hair!"

Expletives flew, but this star was very big, and the powers that be said to just pay.

Gotta love Hollywood.

We got an offer from The Ritz-Carlton, Berlin through Vivian and their terrific on-site rep Marion Schumacher to do a big feature on its "Sleeping Beauty" package. They teamed with a Berlin sleep clinic to show people how to get the best slumber, which of course included Ritz-Carlton bedding, pillows, baths, and nighttime milk and cookies. We hadn't worked with *Criminal Minds* star Matthew Gray Gubler yet and presented this opportunity. To my great surprise and delight, he accepted.

The sleeping concept was brilliant; photographer John Filo got images of him in the clinic, enjoying twilight treats, and even jumping on the bed in Ritz-Carlton pajamas. The hotel was fabulous too.

Berlin, though, was not my thing. The day-time tour of monuments from WW2 was heavy, and the city at night is a strange concoction of eerie and eccentric. The erotic nightlife doesn't just flirt with darkness; it dives headfirst into it, twirling in a dance of macabre fascination with its own tainted soul.

Not my mug of Weihenstephaner.

Naturally, we lightened the mood with our own entertainment. Our crew gathered in the hotel's sultry lounge, and after several rounds for our thirsty team, The Jackal announced, "It's a walk-off!" This dates to the 2001 farce *Zoolander*, when male model Derek Zoolander challenges competitor Hansel ("He's so hot right now") to who can walk down a fashion runway better. We closed the heavy red velvet drapes that surrounded the bar for privacy, and The Jackal lined everyone up to walk through tables—a faux catwalk but appropriate for the occasion. One by one, we sashayed down the runway, including Matthew, and even the wait staff. They were highly entertained by our antics, as were several other patrons who joined the line.

The next morning, the hotel's head of security pulled me aside: our hijinks were caught on tape. He gave me a high five and asked when we'd do it again.

The hotel was my favorite part of the trip and became more so when a last-minute incident almost ruined the trip. One of our crew members' purse—which held her passport—was stolen on an outside plaza. The day we were leaving. Undaunted, The Ritz-Carlton, Berlin security team called the US embassy and raced our crew member to their location to get a temporary passport. This all took two hours.

In Berlin, the magazine staff turned lounge at The Ritz-Carlton, Berlin into a fashion runway. ("It's a walk off!"). See Jeremy, at the end, preparing to strut with a drink in his hand. Accessories, people, accessories. Photo courtesy of Jeremy Murphy.

The Met Gala is the Oscars of the East. An annual soiree for New York's Metropolitan Museum, it attracts A-listers from every industry: actors, politicians, athletes, models, entrepreneurs. Anna Wintour, editor of *Vogue* magazine, rules the roost, deciding who gets invited, who sits where, even when you can arrive. You'd have better luck getting into the White House. I had a crazy idea: What if we brought a big star and did a "night out" feature at the Met Gala?

This would take some effort. We'd have to buy a table first, which was $250,000. That's a lot of money, but I knew we could find a sponsor to underwrite the cost. After all, who doesn't want to go to the Met Gala?

I cold-called *Vogue*, which was a comedy in itself. I've never had more people hang up on me in my entire career. Finally, I got through to one of the planners, who dismissively advised me of the cost.

I didn't flinch. We already had a sponsor willing to pay.

Surprised, she followed with, "...and Anna has to approve your guests."

The table would have ten seats, and each had to go through the *Vogue* screening process, which required bios and visuals.

That didn't faze me except for one thing: I could not risk the sponsor being rejected by Anna Wintour. Telling them *Vogue* said no would not only be heartbreaking but risk future business.

I politely nixed the idea but apparently, no one's ever said no to *Vogue*.

I was fashion roadkill.

Editors rarely go to photo shoots. I was the exception; I loved getting out of the office, meeting new people, finding new hotels. It's an opportunity to bond with your team over beers (and Scotch). But I couldn't go on *every* shoot because someone had to edit the magazine, duh. Doing so on the road is more difficult than it sounds, especially when you often don't bring a laptop (oops, did I forget that...again?). When you miss these experiences, you're envious of the stories your team brings back.

But sometimes you dodge bullets.

A shoot with *Entertainment Tonight* anchor Mary Hart should have been vivacious—those legs were insured for a reason—but I chose the wrong location: a five-star hotel connected to a hospital/wellness center in sleepy Westlake Village, which is in Los Angeles but not really. The vantages to shoot were few, and the photography showed. The images and styling were flawless; the backdrops, less so.

"Ghost Whisperer" star Jennifer Love Hewitt wanted to go to Hawaii. Word was out our magazine was a free vacation, and J. Love had her sights on the Aloha State. I was keen on a free trip to Hawaii myself, but a week before I got notice I was being audited by the IRS. Apparently, my freelance travel writing was seen as a hobby, and costs I'd deducted were not permitted. The optics of me in Hawaii while I was under review would not bode well, so instead I sent The Jackal and Mark Mann, who captured J. Love beautifully. The actress, always a favorite of mine, looked especially gorgeous, which her publicist used as the perfect revenge toward an ex-boyfriend. Paparazzi just happened to capture the star playing tennis in a black bikini. Because that happens every day.

A shoot with an *NCIS: New Orleans* star Zoe McLellan sounded good on paper. She's gorgeous, friendly, talented, and kind. And we hadn't used NOLA as a backdrop for a fashion shoot. But it was end of year and I was busy planning our next shoot—James Wolk, the nicest actor ever—so I sent my team instead. For some unexplained reason, the expertly planned, produced, and choreographed productions we'd become known for turned into a sloppy commercial for New Orleans. I began getting reports from one of the crew of the tumult, which started with a late-night fitting in Zoe's home for the wardrobe, and no car for the stylist to return. Breakfast on day of shoot was non-existent, and lunch turned into an after-thought. My biggest issue was the entire concept/tone. Zoe is stunning, and I wanted a rich, sexy, moody, sumptuous pictorial in New Orleans. Christopher Campbell styled, agreed on, and pulled amazing wardrobe from top designers. But the idea was not shared by several crew members, who preferred her smiling—in graveyards and other dark, haunting settings we chose for mystery. I called Christopher as I began to see the images. Including a tuba band following her for some reason.

In Los Angeles, we photographed the cast of a daytime show, which turned into a political nightmare. Positioning the women in group photos required State Department intervention. They also brought their own makeup and hairstylists and gave Christopher a coronary with their critiques on the wardrobe; some actually brought their own. I was glad to have missed this one.

One shoot I do regret missing was to Malta; Cote de Pablo was filming some stupid movie about doves, or something like that, and it was a big thing. She was the only big thing I was interested in. I hired

British photographer Ian Derry and Milan-based stylist Fabio Mercurio to handle it, and they hit a home run. The photos were brilliant.

For the most part, though, traveling was the best part of the job. I'll stop complaining now.

Psyche!

Q&A WITH SOPHIA PAULMIER

Sophia: Ted Koppel is an icon. And his hairstyle really does reminisce Mad Magazine.

Jeremy: It wouldn't move in a hurricane. They should send him to cover the next one.

S: Did Super P burst out laughing when you started singing?

J: He was amused and horrified at the same time. Super P is as decent, responsible, and professional as they come. I'm the opposite. Maybe that's why we get along so well.

S: Is the Gilt Bar still around?

J: No! And I'm super pissed about it! Around 2011, a South Korean company called Lotte bought the property and did a massive renovation, which was a total bomb. They turned the Gilt Bar into a gourmet restaurant called Villard Michel Richard, which got a zero-star rating in the *New York Times*. Critic Pete Wells called it "awful" and wrote of one of its dishes: "Think of everything that's great about fried chicken. Now take it all away." They put a new bar downstairs called Trouble's Trust, named after its previous owner's dog. When she died, the pooch inherited everything. He shouldn't spend it there. The bar is dark, tacky, there's no reception, or food. The whole hotel is just meh, but I miss The Gilt Bar and their thirty-dollar truffle grilled cheese sandwich.

S: *What were some of the Champers the cat's favorite topics or celebrities to cover?*

J: Frank liked mixing cultural references, fashion, celebrities in what he wrote. Champers had a hot/not list, but with judgements such as "Purrr-fect" and "Cat-astrophe."

S: *Did Champers get his own office?*

J: Yes, my apartment. He treats it like his own.

S: *Bald talent invoiced you 5k for a hairstylist? I assume it was for wigs.*

J: Nope!

S: *Favorite bars and restaurants in Berlin?*

J: I'll be up front: I did not like Berlin. It just has really bad energy, and deservedly so. I preferred to stay at the hotel.

S: *Who won the walk-off?*

J: The Jackal, naturally.

S: *You cold-called* Vogue *to buy a table at the Met Gala?!*

J: Yes! I've never been afraid to do things like that. What's the worst they can say? "No." Like I haven't heard that before.

S: Do you think the sponsors would have gotten the Anna Wintour approval?

J: No. I doubt *I'd* get approved.

S: Aside from The Jackal, who were some of your favorite stylists to work with?

J: Christopher Campbell, for sure. Brendan Cannon. Sarah Nash in London. Maia Liakos in Sydney.

S: What a crazy night in Toronto. Was everyone OK?

J: Everyone got up the next morning! Sometimes you gotta let loose. I hadn't seen my friend who was filming a new TV show in Toronto. He was lonely as well. So we just hit it.

S: Describe Christopher Campbell's personal style.

J: It's funny because on shoot days he wears all black and very basic. But socially, he's brave. He wears clothes I'd never dare to even put on. But he looks good. He likes pops of unexpected color. And his taste always evolves because fashion does. I'm more classic.

S: These 2009 paparazzi pictures of Jennifer Love Hewitt playing tennis in a bikini are well known. Do you think they inspired Kim Kardashian's 2017 tennis paparazzi shots?

J: I have no idea. I try to keep my life—and mind— free of all things Kardashian. I don't understand the phenomenon. They seem nice enough, but they're all billionaires with private planes and I'm still confused what they actually do.

CHAPTER 18

★

Ooo, La-Rue

CSI: Miami star Eva LaRue in Paris during the 2008 Haute Couture fashion shows in Paris.

The writers' strike in 2007–08 ground Hollywood to a halt, much like in 2023. Everything went dark, and actors were bored.

I was too. The magazine was two years old, and it started to feel like *TV Guide*. I needed something cool, exciting, sexy, bold. I also wanted to go back to Paris. I went for the first time in 2006, and it stayed with me. Going back became an obsession.

And more and more improbable given my idea: let's bring an actor to Paris Fashion Week!

The idea was ridiculous. We were a fledgling bimonthly magazine doing dopey features on crime show stars. We had no business even *thinking* about fashion week.

I wouldn't give up. First, we looked around to see what talent was available. *Everyone*. Next, what talent did we *want* to be with for a week? The list got short quickly. My favorite was Eva LaRue from *CSI: Miami*. She is gorgeous, talented, and—according to our intel—nice. We could hang with her. Eva loved it the minute we suggested.

Jeremy with Eva LaRue at the Valentino show. Photo courtesy of Jeremy Murphy.

I hired a freelance producer to arrange tickets to shows and then began scouring for hosts. Every hotel said no except a somewhat pleasant—at least for us—Sheraton, which was eager to get in on fashion week glamour. They offered to comp our entire crew. Airfare from AA, which was sponsoring our shoots, was a given.

Tickets to the shows, however, were not. Getting seats during couture weeks is notoriously difficult, Paris especially. Designers have to accommodate the clients who buy the $100,000 dresses, the stores that sell them, the stars that wear them, and the editors who promote them. A fledgling celebrity magazine was last in line, but luckily the dam broke a few days before we were due to leave. Jean Paul Gaultier was the first to break, but there was a caveat (there always seems to be one or several): we were booked at the wrong hotel. Design houses hand-deliver invitations to where you stay, and there are only a handful of hotels that are acceptable: The Ritz, Le Bristol, Plaza Athénée, Le Meurice, George V, Park Hyatt, and the Crillon. The list has since grown, but the Sheraton was not among the chosen few.

Jeremy commissioned the photographer to take this image
on the Pont Alexandre III bridge in Paris.

This sounded délirant until other designers expressed the same sentiment. Suddenly, I had a hard decision: go to Paris knowing we'd never get into shows or try to get one of the hotels on "the list" to host us. I sweet-talked a wonderful PR woman, Anita Cotter, into hearing our plight. She was the US rep for The Ritz, Paris and brought the on-site PR director Matthieu Goffard into the conversation. After much back and forth, we agreed on the terms, and the Ritz, Paris would be our home for the week. Matthieu has since climbed the ranks in hotel PR.

We arrived on a Saturday morning, and the hotel was as over-the-top as one could imagine. Everything was ostentatious. I warned everyone, including Eva, not to touch *anything* lest we get charged seventy euros for a fingerprint. My room looked like Marie Antoinette's private chamber. Our staff met for lunch in the Bar Vendôme restaurant and the bill—for ten people *without* alcohol—was more than €1,000. They might have discounted our rooms, but this was how they made up for it. I was freaking out.

One by one, we got Eva into shows, and the producer from *Extra*, Yvette Corporon, ran circles around us arranging even better "gets," including a meet and greet with the designer Valentino, who talked to Eva on camera. He was so charmed by the actress, he invited her and Yvette to the Valentino show, which would be the last haute couture collection of his career. The vaunted brand would continue, but he would not. All that sewing and sketching could not rival sunning on his yacht.

His show was set in the Musée Rodin, famous for its sculpted gardens and classical architecture. I was annoyed not to have my own ticket, but happy that at least our star got in; many other A-list stars did not. We drove them to the Rodin in our Sprinter van, which was starting to feel like the Partridge family bus.

As we arrived, I noticed the crowds were overwhelming, requiring a security shield for Eva as she walked through adoring fans and paparazzi. We formed a wall around her and pushed toward the entrance to the show. With utter shock, I realized we had penetrated *their* security; we were in. The seating was also advantageous: grandstands without assigned spaces. We covertly found a row with extra room, and no one was the wiser.

Fashion shows are largely a waste of time; they last twenty minutes, but getting in and out could take an hour. Valentino's was a full production, replete with red roses; models wearing flowing dresses, tailored suits, and evening gowns; starving editors; and blinding lights. At its conclusion, a chorus of women dressed in red, wearing vintage garments from Valentino's near fifty-year career, walked elegantly down the runway. The designer choked up, and so did we. It was an end of an era, and we got to witness it.

Afterward, we made it back to The Ritz and got a bite to eat at Bar Vendôme. A Turkish princess at a nearby table recognized Eva from *CSI: Miami* and invited our group to join hers, which we did gladly: she was picking up the check.

We ended the trip with a drink invitation from a Parisian hotel executive curious how our scrappy little magazine was covering Paris Fashion Week. After hearing our improbable tale, we got him to share stories from his career in hospitality. One was more unbelievable than the next. Working at a resort in the Middle East, he waited on the notoriously quirky Prince Al-Waleed bin Talal, the Saudi billionaire who owns major stakes in Apple, Citigroup, real estate, and hotels around the world. The prince travels on a custom A380, outfitted with a two-car garage, Turkish bath, concert hall, and a prayer room with electronic mats that automatically rotate to face Mecca. He has a staff of more than a hundred and has unusual demands. When the resort didn't have Pepsi, he called the company's leaders and had cases air-lifted the next day. More amusing is what happened after. His Highness had members of his staff stand around the pool, and he issued a challenge. His plane would fly over the hotel, and whoever the pilot heard got $10,000. As the A380 flew past, the staff screamed at the top of their lungs. Of course, the pilot didn't hear anyone, but the prince gave each person $10,000 anyway.

I had trouble believing this was true but later heard more anecdotes from others in the travel industry. In the Polynesian islands,

His Highness works on Saudi time and, more outrageously, includes a harem of little people—they still call them "dwarfs"—in his entourage. They read stories to him at night. I did research on this and found that some Saudis believe little people are good luck because they are closer to the ground.

Now I'm obsessed. I would love to hang out with this dude. On another shoot, staff members of a resort, which the prince also owned, confirmed the little people fetish and revealed his penchant for taking midnight bike rides; the little people ride along with him on tricycles. As does a staff member with a giant flat screen strapped to his back so the prince can watch CNBC.

I'm a screenwriter. I penned a book called *F*ck Off, Chloe*. I've pitched farcical BS for PR clients. And even I couldn't write this kind of shit.

Q&A WITH SOPHIA PAULMIER

> *Sophia: Your honest humility with writing "the magazine was two years old, and it started to feel like TV Guide" is powerful. Have you always known there was untapped potential with this magazine? And if it were still in print and you were still EIC, how would you describe it today?*

> Jeremy: Not at all. I learned on the job. I knew nothing about this business or industry when we started, I just knew I could do it. How well? That's what I worried about.

> *S: Eva LaRue seems like a kind soul and candid sweetheart.*

> J: We had so much fun. I laughed very hard the entire time, and everyone was just excited and felt fortunate to be there, even Eva. I remember returning to New

York and being terribly depressed because I missed the camaraderie and laughter.

S: I've always wanted to go to Paris Fashion Week. Did it live up to the hype?

J: It was a lot better than New York! We got to attend before there were influencers and Instagram, so it was a different experience. It still had that air of exclusivity. Now they're all just marketing stunts.

S: "Designers send invites to your hotel, and there are only a handful that are acceptable." I find this statement fascinating and quite daunting. Do you think it still holds up this way today?

J: I doubt it. I don't think you could get away with it nowadays; someone who can't afford it will sue you for discrimination or having a microaggression. But it was a good lesson in social currency and image: people pay attention to this stuff. What you wear, drive, where you stay gets noticed. People are judgmental, that's just a fact of life.

S: How did the PR team at the Sheraton feel about you switching hotels last minute to The Ritz?

J: They were understanding. I don't remember any drama.

S: "My room looked like Marie Antoinette's private chamber." Did you feel like royalty?

J: It looked like royalty. Mostly, I felt I didn't deserve to be there. I'm a middle-class kid who'd never stayed anywhere fancier than a Marriott until I was seventeen. And here I was, in the world's most famous hotel. I do remember watching *The DaVinci Code* in my room for forty Euros.

S: You got the hottest ticket of the week by scoring Valentino's last haute couture show. What was it like watching the final collection walk down the runway? And had you died and gone to heaven?

J: It was surreal. We were watching living history. This was the last couture he, as a designer, would create. The brand has continued, but he did not. Valentino's signature color is red, and at the end, a stream of women in red gowns came walking down the runway. People were crying; I think he was too.

CHAPTER 19

······★······

"That's Not What the Macarons Are For"

Good Wife's Matt Czuchry, author Jeremy Murphy, photographer Ellen von Unwerth, and co-star Archie Panjabi at Le Meurice during the photo shoot.

*T*he *Good Wife* kept on winning awards and acclaim. Viewers loved it, as did our readers. I'd heard two of its stars—Archie Panjabi and Matt Czuchry—had become good friends, which sparked an idea: platonic pals in Paris, featuring all the indulgences the French are known for, except one: sex. I wanted to show men and women can be friends and bond over life events.

Archie and Matt liked the idea, but Archie wanted more of a backstory. At my thirty-sixth birthday party, which both graciously attended, she asked for a playlist so she could capture the essence of the character she'd play. This was new. I'd never considered that before, but for a classically trained actress, it was not a surprising request.

Around the same time, a very crafty agent from an otherwise respectable agency brought Ellen von Unwerth to my office for a meet and greet. She is the provocative, super edgy German photographer famous for the highly saturated Guess jeans ads with Claudia Schiffer. She was kooky, but I like my characters. They make life interesting.

Ellen is also a name, which advertisers demand, at least the fashion ones. I hired her for the shoot once Archie and Matt were 100 percent in.

The Dorchester Collection, which owned The Plaza Athénée in Paris, offered to host us at Le Meurice, a five-star property off the Rue de Rivoli and across from the famous Tuileries Garden. The hotel is designed in a Louis XVI style, unabashedly French, and almost too precious to touch.

The Rue de Rivoli is an interesting location to build a five-star hotel because it's a tacky avenue filled with shops that cater to tourists. Fanny packs galore crowd its sidewalks, as well as a McDonald's, which adds luster to the setting. Still, the hotel is famous, and it was new scenery, rich in details and history. Salvador Dalí was a regular guest and known to pedal down its steps on a bicycle. He also once brought with him a herd of goats. Other notables like Queen Victoria, Tchaikovsky, Franklin Roosevelt, Elizabeth Taylor, Picasso, Charles Dickens, Kate Moss, Justin Bieber, and Leonardo DiCaprio have enjoyed its potent French-iness.

Archie arrived first and made a scene. Well, her dog did. It basically exploded on the marble floors, emitting everything you can imagine.

We're here!

The Jackal and her assistant did the wardrobe styling, which included classic French labels like Yves Saint Laurent, Dior, Givenchy, and other noted fashion houses. The hotel's on-site PR director, who wore torn T-shirts and leather pants, gave us full use of its Belle Etoile suite, which featured a 360-degree view of Paris, 7,000 square feet of space, and a private terrace.

Ellen was delightfully avant-garde, and came with only two assistants and no equipment. That was concerning, but she's Ellen, and her work is unmistakable. As we began the shoot, I was highly entertained by her style. When she moved, the assistants on each side moved with her, holding the flashes. It was like belly dancers slithering and grooving in unison. She shouted, "Yah, yah," in her German accent, signaling her pleasure with each image.

An early setup was intended to be a childlike image of Matt and Archie in pajamas, sitting cross-legged in their bedroom surrounded by macarons. Our staff had worked the previous day convincing the famous Angelina Café to provide the desserts, which numbered more than a hundred. The crew placed the macrons stylishly around the suite when Ellen asked everyone to leave. She wanted to shoot Matt and Archie in private. The space was small anyway, at least after we filled it with desserts. Super P and I went to the lobby bar—as an editor naturally does mid-shoot.

After an hour, we returned to find Matt and Archie in bed, feeding each other the macarons. Ellen had turned besties into lovers. The "yah, yah, yahs!" became more frequent and enthusiastic with each click of the camera.

My stomach nearly dropped. Our magazine had pushed the line several times, but this was drawing a new one that would be hard to sell when your publication is on newsstands at Walmart. Still, Ellen's work would give us an edge we hadn't had, and who was I to argue with a photographer of her esteem? I kept my reservations to myself, but worried it might be too hot. Ellen continued with the unexpected theme, including Archie shaving Matt provocatively in the mirror, Archie licking a spoon in the bar, them feeding each other seductively in its restaurant, both walking through the Tuileries in post-coital bliss, and other family-friendly scenarios. The images were impossible to see because she didn't let you; her assistant downloaded the memory card into a laptop and covered his head with a giant hood, shielding us from peeking.

The rest of our group found their way to the bar for post-shoot elixirs, which lightened the mood. So much so, we snuck back into the suite and had a dance party atop the roof as well as many orders of room service.

The next day we had off I spent in Le Marais (or "SoMa" as the French call it), a district in Paris's 4th arrondissement that included boutiques, galleries, and gay bars. I was too fat to wear any of the high-priced garments sold in these ironic-for-no-reason stores but found an absurd painting in a dilapidated art gallery: Papa Smurf dressed as Karl Lagerfeld. This I *had* to bring home.

The hotel packaged it up and sent it back to New York, which triggered a call from the US Customs Office. Sending undeclared pieces of art is illegal; I'd have to pay considerable taxes before they'd release it from custody.

"It's a painting of a Smurf, for heaven's sake," I said incredulously.

The agent surveyed the painting and laughed.

"Never mind," was the response.

Back in New York, I worried the photography would be *too* tantalizing, but Ellen quickly relieved me of that sentiment. Her work was evocative and brimming with sexual energy. It almost felt primal. What she saw was something different, sure, but it worked. We wanted a different style and tone to our images anyway, and Ellen had found a storyline that told a new narrative, but one that gave a double take. It was just what we needed.

What I took away from this experience was a good lesson: Trust the photographer. You hired them for a reason.

Q&A WITH SOPHIA PAULMIER

Sophia: I loved *Matt in* Gilmore Girls, *but I'm not too familiar with Archie. Can you tell me more about her?*

Jeremy: She tends to do more high-brow work. *The Good Wife* was her first network TV show. She's petite and almost seems delicate, but she's strong inside and out. She's got impeccable taste and chooses her projects carefully. Ridley Scott is a big fan.

S: "I wanted to show men and women can be friends and bond over life events." I assume you've heard of the When Harry Met Sally *theory.*

J: I thought of that, but they hook up at the end, which destroys the whole theory.

S: "She asked for a playlist so she could capture the essence of the character she'd play." I love the depth of this idea. Do you remember any songs you suggested?

J: No, she wanted me to create one. The concept for the shoot was mine, and she wanted to understand the character.

S: Ellen von Unwerth is known for brilliant black and whites. Were you nervous to see her do color for your magazine?

J: No! We actually ran a few in black and white too.

S: Ellen is a true artist. Had you been able to hire her again?

J: I would have, but she had a very wily representative who tried to trick us on costs. I wouldn't work with *him* again.

S: *This can't be the same Rivoli with one of the biggest museums in the world! Next to some of the most famous shopping streets that it houses all the main fashion labels.*

J: Yes! The Louvre is down the street from the hotel. But the sidewalk is filled with tacky tourists.

S: *Salvador Dali's McDonald's order?*

J: He was known for exploring "subconscious imagery," so I'm guessing some kind of wrap where he could guess what's in it.

S: *The "Belle Etoile suite, which featured a 360-degree view of Paris, 7,000 square feet of space, and a private terrace" sounds breathtaking. How would you rate this on your top hotel stays of all time?*

J: We didn't stay in the suite! I got a very small room that was cozy. Their mascot is a white dog, and they left a plush stuffed animal on my bed, which was very sweet. I took it home. The hotel was wonderful, but I don't like the neighborhood.

S: *Ellen sounds like a true cheerleader. Did Matt and Archie enjoy her as much as she enjoyed shooting them?*

J: I think they were in shock. Like, what just happened? Ellen was like a whirlwind, full of energy—more than we had experienced. No one said a cross thing about her though. I think they enjoyed it once the "what the fuck?" sensation dissipated.

S: *You borrowed one hundred macarons? And nobody ate one?*

J: I'm sure people did. I didn't, I know that.

S: *So, you walk back to set and catch the two stars playing with whipped cream. Did you fear the worst?*

J: It was certainly unexpected. Our magazine went into peoples' mailboxes so I couldn't afford anything too risqué.

S: *How did you handle that? When you heard the "yah, yah, yahs," did you scream, "No, no no!"?*

J: I did not. I was too insecure, and she is Ellen von Unwerth. This was only our fifth year of publishing, and she's had a brilliant career. I hadn't yet built up the confidence to speak my mind to someone of her caliber.

S: *Did you feel Archie and Matt were still comfortable in this shoot or had Ellen crossed the line with them at this point?*

J: I think if it got inappropriate, one or both would have said something. Actors like danger, the unexpected, improvisation. I think there was a "this is interesting, let's see where it goes" feeling.

S: *"We snuck back into the suite and had a dance party atop the roof as well as many orders of room service" I would pay to see Logan Huntzberger do the Dougie. What type of music did you guys dance to?*

J: We had some "go-tos" in our crew. Soulja Boy's "Turn My Swag On" always got played. I insisted on "Kids" by MGMT. Something by Britney for sure. We also had a cheesy habit of singing "We are the World," and each of us doing a part. I always went for Stevie Wonder because he gets really sassy at the end.

S: *"Ellen had found a storyline that told a new story, but one that gave a double take. It was just what we needed."* *These photos came out incredible, did you take more risks with photographers after this shoot?*

J: A bit, sure. But celebrities are not models who you can do whatever you want with. Actors, especially on well-known TV shows, have their own image and brand, as well as publicists. That prevents you from experimenting too boldly. They don't want to tarnish their reputation or do anything too risky.

S: *Last time you crossed paths with Archie or Matt?*

J: It's been years! But we're all still in touch. I email Matt frequently, and Archie recently commented on a photo I posted on Instagram.

CHAPTER 20

★

J'adore De Pablo

NCIS star Cote de Pablo modeled Christian Dior's 2012/2013 Fall Collection outside the Hotel Plaza Athénée Paris, which made the cover of WWD. Photo courtesy of WWD.

Christian Dior revolutionized fashion with his "New Look," a post wartime aesthetic that emerged in 1947 as a counter to utilitarian design. The couturier recognized women wanted to look elegant and feminine again, and began experimenting with luxurious fabrics, clinched waists, exaggerated shoulders, and A-line silhouettes. The result was groundbreaking; a new optimism that marked a return to high fashion and opulence after years of austerity.

Cote posed in the "Dior Institute" spa inside the Hotel Plaza Athénée again wearing its 2012 Fall/Winter Collection. Photo by Gilles-Marie Zimmermann.

We had convinced the top PR people at Dior to let us photograph their fall/winter 2012-2013 collection, but had to do it in Paris, where the design house in based. Its original atelier still exists on Avenue Montaigne, which happens to be a block away from our favorite setting: the Hôtel Plaza Athénée, where Dior often presented his collections. They were natural partners.

We needed to find our own. Here is the dirty secret about celebrities: few are "sample size," which are the measurements fashion labels use when showcasing their designs. For women, it's especially unforgiving, rarely exceeding size four. Models fit this effortlessly because that's their job. Celebrities, not so much.

We needed to find an actress who could not only sell copies on the newsstand but fit the clothing while looking elegant.

There aren't many. At least before Ozempic.

NCIS star Cote de Pablo had stayed in our sights after two previous photo shoots in Laguna Beach and, weirdly, Switzerland (don't ask) Though she played an Israeli on the show, Cote is a native Chilean, and has a magnetism you cannot ignore. She's stunning in your eyes, and more so the camera. Photographers love shooting the actress, whose luscious black hair, olive skin, dark eyes, and exquisite features jump off the screen.

She's also really cool. I'd gotten to know the actress, once even hosting a dinner in my apartment for her and my best friend Branko Karlezi, who is also from Chile. He is more of a bitch than I am and vouched for her personally.

We extended the offer to shoot her for the cover, but with trepidation. We didn't know *how* restrictive the Dior samples would be.

Still, it was Dior, which became our entire theme. The design house epitomizes Parisian glamour, which we would showcase in its home. Our team storyboarded setups for the shoot, which included the hotel, Avenue Montaigne, and the Eiffel Tower. A late suggestion made the production more complicated but fit with the storyline: Cote carrying shopping bags outside Dior, surrounded by three chiseled men as her entourage.

The Idea was great; the application, unfeasible. It was now Sunday, the day before the shoot, and finding three male models in that short of time was nearly impossible, made more difficult by it being election day when France's president Nicolas Sarkozy would lose his job to dullard François Hollande, the most boring man in politics; he doesn't get to bang Carla Bruni.

Gilles-Marie Zimmermann, our favorite French photographer, really wanted the shot, and I was determined to make it happen. With no modeling agencies open, I got inventive and commandeered the hotel bellman to walk with me down the Champs-Élysées, where a new Abercrombie & Fitch had opened. The brand is known for employing ripped, chiseled pretty boys who love being photographed, which was exactly what we needed. Surely, there would be a few shirtless douchebags available.

Just not to us. We looked super creepy; me, wearing a hoodie and sneakers, and the bellman in full uniform, including a top hat. And offering cash to be photographed.

Out of options, I called Gilles-Marie's agent, Angela de Bona, to break the bad news. Somehow, she found three models that evening who fit the part.

Cote arrived the same day and looked effervescent—youthful glow, dewy skin, lean frame, and a timeless essence that perfectly captured the Dior aesthetic. This was before hair and makeup, mind you. To everyone's relief, she fit the samples seamlessly.

The next day, Gilles-Marie photographed her from nearly every vantage—on the Avenue, at Dior, inside the Plaza Athénée, in front of the Eiffel Tower. We even "rented" French poodles for Cote to walk past the hotel, wearing a chic Dior suit and millinery. Every setting lit up the camera, but one proved complicated. In the Royal Suite, we positioned the actress on a chaise longue surrounded by the three male models. On-screen, perfection. In layout? Gang bang. That's when Photoshop proves its worth.

With the clothing, photographer, stylist, and crew based locally, our production was nimble, which allowed me to invite two friends—actor Matt Lanter, from the 90210 reboot and action series *Timeless*, and his then-girlfriend, Angela—to join us (they were in Europe anyway) in the City of Lights. I knew Matt was going to pop the question and what more romantic place? The original plan—to propose on a boat cruising down the Seine—was ruined by a rainstorm, so Matt improvised later on a discreet, cobblestone street at night. The next day, when we shot Cote, I arranged for Gilles-Marie to take Matt and Angela's official engagement portrait overlooking the Eiffel Tower, her wearing the Dior.

While in Paris shooting Cote, author Jeremy Murphy invited friends Matt Lanter (*90210*, *Timeless*) and his now wife Angela to join them at the Hotel Plaza Athénée. Matt planned to propose to Angela while in Paris, and to celebrate, photographer Gilles-Marie Zimmermann took this engagement photo on the hotel terrace with a special monument behind them.

All the effort we'd put into this paid off. The New Look looked timeless and modern, embracing the Dior aesthetic and radiating Parisian glamour. The brand, as well as their parent company, LVMH, were stunned we pulled this off.

Not so much the termites, who disparaged the photography on a conference call, not realizing I was secretly listening. They critiqued all the images, pointing out flaws that didn't exist. I was furious, and let it be known later I had heard their commentary. In truth, they were angry not to have been invited on the shoot, a tradition I continued.

Gilles-Marie's photography helped Super P and me land our first Dior advertisement. The Hôtel Plaza Athénée licensed several photos for a coffee table book published by Assouline. And *WWD* put the portrait of Cote walking poodles down Avenue Montaigne on its cover.

Chew on that, termites.

Q&A WITH SOPHIA PAULMIER

Sophia: What's Cote De Pablo like in real life?

Jeremy: Normal, funny, kind. Twenty million people watched her every week on NCIS, and you wouldn't know it. We've become friends and text regularly.

S: Did she enjoy being the first to wear Dior for the magazine?

J: We'd always use Dior garments from Saks or Bergdorf, but this was the first time the designer let us pull from their showroom—and from a collection that hadn't been shown in stores. Everyone realized it was an incredibly special milestone for our magazine. She was especially gracious expressed gratitude, which she does to this day. I framed the WWD cover for her as a memento.

S: Europeans not working on Sundays is a bad thing because...?

J: I was joking! But it's actually illegal in France for bosses to contact employees after 5 p.m. on weekdays. What was the line from *Emily in Paris*? "The French work to live; Americans live to work."

S: Did Dior have any restrictions with the use of their collection in your cover shoot?

J: Return as you received. Also, we couldn't alter them in any way.

S: Did Abercrombie & Fitch ban you from their store for trying to recruit their staff to model in your shoot?

J: I didn't stay long enough to ask! Looking back, it's so creepy but really fucking funny.

S: You tried to help Matt Lanter for a special his proposal to his girlfriend; did he invite you to their wedding?

J: Yes, it was beautiful. Matt had a crew of Storm Troopers bring him into the reception.

S: Aside from Matt, have you helped plan any other celebrity proposals?

J: No. Too much pressure!

CHAPTER 21

···········★···········

Big, Bang, Bust!

Something always unexpected happened during our photo shoots, but the talent usually left with a fun experience. Until *Big Bang Theory* star Kaley Cuoco, who likely still has a dart board with my photo in the center. For good reason. I fucked up royally.

Here's the lesson: never do a cover shoot with a big star on a commercial jet flying overseas. I learned this one painfully.

As editor, I befriended a lot of important people, including Mike Flanagan, who was a top PR executive representing American Airlines. I met him on a trip to Miami, and we struck up a friendship, which later led to a years-long sponsorship for all our photo shoots.

Mike and I both were dreamers and discussed many ways to work together. Out of these conversations came a crazy idea: the first magazine cover shoot on a flying plane—with passengers. Mike did not seem fazed, but the obstacles were endless. This was 2009. Travel was still weak after the 2008 financial collapse, and airlines needed all the publicity they could get. Mike was confident he could get this through.

The first hurdle was AA: He had to sell it through the chain, right up to the CEO Gerard Arpey. Then we'd need all the "constituents" to sign off—pilots, pilots' union, flight attendants, their union, onboard services workers, and their union (even *they* get one?), FAA, TSA, the airport (JFK), and several others.

Ha! Good luck with that one.

2009 turned to 2010, and we'd discuss the idea sporadically, but nothing was moving—until it did. Somehow, Mike got everyone onboard. We'd get the entire first-class cabin of an AA jet flying to London, where we could do our shoot.

I was shocked, and now worried. The ball was in my court.

The first question was who to bring. We'd just done an incredible shoot with Kaley, so she was a natural. Everyone loved her, and she's gorgeous. We also had our sights on Matt Czuchry, who we had yet to work with in 2011.

Both agreed enthusiastically.

The Jackal would style—that was non-negotiable; I wouldn't use anyone else—and I hired photographer Jeff Lipsky, who we'd just used for Michael Weatherly and Archie Panjabi. Jeff was awesome, and his assistant was one of my favorite people ever: Nate Bressler, who is now a photographer on his own. He's the coolest cat you will ever know.

Here was the issue: The plane would be flying, and we could not use electricity. Everything had to be battery-powered, which limits options with photography. On any shoot, there are many pieces of equipment requiring juice. Jeff and Nate would need to use handheld, fully charged flashes.

A week before the departure date, and after two years of planning (now 2011), I got a call from Matt's publicist, who told me he couldn't do the shoot on the dates we booked because *The Good Wife* cast was needed at the SAG Awards in Los Angeles. She insisted we change the dates.

That was impossible. We were locked into the schedule. Matt pulled out.

We shot Kaley solo the previous year, and I thought it would be redundant with just her again, so I raced to find another male counterpart. I really wanted Matt Lanter, the incredibly handsome young actor from the *90210* reboot, but he was not available.

I gave up after a few days of robo-calling, but in all honesty, we already had the gold. Kaley was—and is—a big star. *The Big Bang Theory* was the hottest show on TV, and she was a lead.

Of course, nothing is easy. Two days before we were scheduled to leave, a wonder woman named Sundae May, who books all the media seats for AA, called with a heads-up: someone had reserved a seat in our first-class cabin, which I assumed we had blocked. I began to think of the complications and panicked: Kaley would be changing outfits; the stylists would be running through aisles; the videographer would be filming. Having a stranger watching was impractical, and frankly, weird, as well as distracting.

Sundae, who I'm convinced fights crime at night while making every journalist happy (a rare feat), somehow solved the issue and we got the cabin to ourselves, again.

On the day of the shoot, we all met at the Palace Hotel, where Kaley was staying. We had three vans to accommodate our huge crew: Kaley, her plus-one, publicist, me, producer, second producer, model, hair, makeup, videographer, stylist, assistant stylist, photographer, assistant photographer, writer, photo editor, and a journalist from *Tribune*, who was writing about this crazy endeavor.

AA and JFK had reserved a big space for us to prepare Kaley for the first shots, which we would do in front of the plane's door connected to the Jetway. Kaley did makeup and hair and reviewed the wardrobe. On tables were soggy sandwiches, sad pasta, warm cans of soda, and hard-as-a-rock cookies. No one savored.

Across the room, I did my usual song and dance, talking with the crew, sharing war stories, cracking jokes. Basically, trying to set the tone.

I made a huge mistake: not properly attending to the talent. Kaley sat on the other side, *unattended*. There were others there, but I was not. Kaley was doing this shoot as a favor to us, and I was not showing the appreciation and gratitude I should have.

After several hours of preparation, we boarded, took our seats, and waited for the plane to reach cruising altitude before we could begin. Meanwhile, Kaley's publicist approached me to share she hadn't eaten and was hungry. My heart broke, but the options were limited. Thomas Keller was not fileting salmon in the galley. They barely had salad.

Kaley was a trouper and rallied, and we began the shoot. Jeff did his best under extremely trying conditions—the lighting was atrocious—and the photos were good given the limitations. Without known male counterpart (we used model Matt Merrell, who is gorgeous in any setting) there was little drama, tension, sex. It was just a beautiful woman on an airplane, with little context.

Fortunately, we had a part two: a fashion spread outside London in Ascot, which is a very posh suburb deep in horse country. A new resort, Coworth Park, had just opened, and they invited us to use the property as a backdrop for our cover. Once we landed, I played traffic cop and began loading people into four Sprinter vans we'd reserved, each headed to Ascot. Once there, everyone breathed a sigh of relief.

It didn't last.

Coworth Park became high school: a makeup artist we hired stirred the pot, creating unnecessary drama and gossip, and assembled a clique that did not include most of our crew. Nor me. I understood why.

Instead, the uninvited met in the lounge of the hotel and let loose, which included dancing, singing, laughs, and levity. I genuinely loved the crew we brought with us and licked whatever wounds I had with a night of liveliness.

"The other side" did not have as much fun, and someone in the group let me know as much.

Again, I took my eye off the ball.

Shoot day began without a hitch. It was seamless, except the tension was raw. It had bad mojo. Kaley crushed every shot; the styling was impeccable; the setting proved luscious. Yet no one was having fun.

Turns out the evil makeup artist was talking smack about everyone the entire time, and into Kaley's ear.

We ended the English countryside shoot with muted cheers. Yay. No one was high-fiving. The irony was the images were exceptional.

That night came word of a huge snowstorm headed to the northeast, affecting everyone's departure. Our crew spent hours working with Sundae May at American Airlines to rebook thirteen flights ahead of a blizzard.

Unfortunately, this distracted me from making peace with Kaley, who was now visibly disappointed...and rightfully so.

The next morning, no one greeted her in the lobby to say goodbye. It was incredibly rude and insensitive. I was exhausted from the whole experience and used the next day off to sleep in. You'd think someone in our ridiculously sized crew would have suggested the gesture, but it fell on me. As it should have.

Everyone returned home safely, and life went back to normal. Until I got a heartbreaking email. Kaley sent me a message from her personal address and expressed her thoughts.

I could not argue with any. She was right about everything.

So, to Kaley Cuoco, I apologize profusely.

Q&A WITH SOPHIA PAULMIER

Sophia: Previous to this shoot, what was your favorite memory of Kaley?

Jeremy: Doing the "Justify my Love" homage in 2010 with Patrick Demarchelier. It was the first time we'd worked with him, and he shot her tinged with sexual energy but tastefully. Kaley was the perfect subject.

S: Had Kaley been a handsome male talent, say Matt Czuchry, do you feel you have handled this situation differently?

J: I honestly don't know; it was a new circumstance. I hope not, and that my screwups are gender blind.

S: "Without a male counterpart, there was no drama, tension, sex. It was just a beautiful woman on an airplane." Does one need a male counterpart to create drama on a flight? Or do you think that maybe the story of her on the flight wasn't quite thought through?

J: We shot her solo for a cover the previous year, so to do so again felt repetitive. And doing a shoot with just one person limits your options creatively.

S: *How did Kaley acclimate to the experience, without someone looking after her?*

J: She brought a publicist and her friend, but I got completely overwhelmed with the details, I forgot the most important part: making the talent feel comfortable, valued, and safe. This was all my doing and I readily admit to the fuck up.

S: *It sounds like the lighting was another problem on set. Did your crew bring a generator to power lights on the flight or were they just planning on using flash?*

J: We had several fully charged batteries and anything else we could use that would not drain from the plane's hydraulic fluid. The dynamics of this shoot were especially complex. We had very restrictions from American Airlines, the FAA, TSA, and every other entity you could imagine. The airline was very supportive about our shoot, but also had a full plane of passengers who they had to service and protect.

S: *"I was insensitive, distracted, overwhelmed, and did not do my job." It must be hard to look back on this shoot in this day and age. Do you have anything else to add or to say to Kaley?*

J: I've thought a lot about this since. It was incredibly hard, and I was overwhelmed with the circumstances. Dealing with so many agencies, the airline, unions, a full crew, hotel, and the talent was not something I was accustomed to. And I didn't delegate – I took all this on my own shoulders. The result was a shitty experience for everyone. And that's on me. I sent a heartfelt apology when Kaley expressed her disappointment, but it could have been less defensive. Today, I'd just say I'm genuinely sorry. It's one of my biggest regrets in my career and I learned and grew from the experience. She was justified in everything she said. We're all human; hopefully time heals wounds.

S: *Looking back, what was it that would have changed the mood of the set?*

J: I don't know. We were exhausted having pulled this off and concentrated on the wrong things. I should have enlisted more support for the logistics so I could focus on the most important part of the shoot: Kaley, who took time out of her personal life to do this for us.

S: *Looking back, did anything from this experience affect or change you?*

J: Immensely. It was a great learning experience and becoming a grown up. I also realized talent relations is not my thing. It's really fucking hard and I'm too A.D.D. to manage what goes into that.

S: *Lastly, should you bump into Kaley again, what's the first thing you'd say?*

J: A genuine apology. I haven't seen her in over a decade so I'm not sure how she would receive it, and I'd understand why. But I've followed her career since. "The Flight Attendant" was terrific. And I read she's a new mother, which I think is terrific. She has a natural warmth and love of life that is infectious. Her kid won the lottery.

CHAPTER 22

· · · · · · · · · · · · ★ · · · · · · · · · · · · ·

Murdering the Lens

Author Jeremy Murphy with Neil Patrick Harris.

NPH. Everyone knows who I mean. Even my cat, and he plays with his poop.

Neil Patrick Harris has been a star since his childhood when *Doogie Howser, M.D.* premiered on network television and became a surprise hit. This is when TV networks *had* hits because there wasn't a lot else to watch. Neil played Doogie, a sixteen-year-old doctor who balanced life-or-death scenarios in the hospital and high school.

The show—a single-camera comedy without a laugh track—was created by Steven Bochco and David Kelly, mostly known for gritty or glossy dramas like *LA Law* and *Hill Street Blues* where people died, cried, went to jail, or practiced law in Los Angeles. A thirty-minute show about a child wunderkind is the last thing people expected. They were shocked when it became a hit; the series was consistently a ratings winner. In its 1991–92 season, it outrated *Seinfeld*.

After ninety-seven episodes, the series ended and his career waned, as happens with teen idols. It took a cameo in the movie *Harold & Kumar Go to White Castle*, in which he spoofed himself, for NPH to turn the tide. In the stoner pic, Neil was a stripper-loving drug fiend—the anti-Doogie. Audiences howled, and the creators of *How I Met Your Mother* noticed. Craig Thomas and Carter Bays had the perfect character in mind for the actor: Barney Stinson, a suit-wearing playboy who never grew out of the frat house. Neil got the best dialogue ("A bro is always entitled to do something stupid, as long as the rest of his bros are all doing it"), most farcical storylines, and the most laughs.

He was the perfect choice for a cover, but every other magazine thought so too. *Entertainment Weekly* was still a reader favorite. *TV Guide* was always tough to compete with. And we had little in comparison. As always, we were last in line. To get his attention, I needed something that others couldn't offer: the famous Orient Express train, legendary for its posh trappings, scenic routes through Europe, and being the center of Agatha Christie's mystery novel, *Murder on the Orient Express*.

Our good PR contact Geoffrey Weill represented the company that owned the train, and he came to us *at the same time* with a tantalizing offer: do a photo shoot onboard as it made its way from Venice to Paris.

Ummm, who wouldn't jump at this?

Neil is a fan of mystery novels, including Agatha Christie, who was the John Grisham of her day. He and his now-husband, David, eagerly accepted the invitation.

Wow, this was too easy. It's like when soldiers hear silence. What's next?

Arduous work, that's what. I'd need seats for him and David, me, stylist, writer, photographer, and videographer. Which also meant flights, hotels, meals, and so on. This was only my third year as editor, and I got confused with my own online bookings (military time always fucks me up.)

I assembled a great crew—Cliff Lipson to shoot, Jim Colucci to write, The Jackal to style, and Kevin Egan to film—and began planning the logistics with my team.

The Orient Express is a one-night trip that starts in Venice, goes through the Swiss Alps, and ends in Paris. Each guest gets their own cabin to rest and sleep, and then a gourmet dinner is served in the restaurant car; guests wear tuxedos and gowns as they savor the cuisine. There is no direct flight from the US to Venice; everyone would need to land in Rome, where we planned to photograph Neil at all the landmarks.

Geoffrey's team found a hotel—the Cavalieri—to host, and they arranged a two-day itinerary. I met Neil and David when the crew arrived, and remember being caught off guard by how casual and friendly both were. This was our first time meeting, and I'm always prepared for celebrities to be assholes. Not so with them. Neil stuck out his hand and said, "Hi, I'm Neil."

Rome provided great scenery, but the real story was the Orient Express, whose ride begins in Venice. After three days, we took a train there, and I was awestruck by a setting that almost themed inauthentic, as if "imagineers" at Disney World designed the floating city. It was too perfect, with every vantage providing a postcard moment. Of course, Venice has a rich history of art, culture, and architecture, which is apparent at every turn. The Orient Express company (now called

Belmond) also owns hotels, and its property in Venice—the Cipriani—
is among the city's (and world's) most glamorous hotels. Situated on
the island of Giudecca, the property features ninety-six guest rooms, an
Olympic-sized pool, gastronomic restaurants, and beautiful people to
make you feel inferior. Our crew needed two boats to get to the hotel.

With an hour to shoot Neil in front of the Orient Express train, the
crew prepares hurriedly. Photo courtesy of Jeremy Murphy.

That afternoon, evening, and the following day were reserved
for atmospheric shots of Neil and David at various locales throughout Venice, which included the Grand Canal, St. Mark's Square, Rialto
Bridge, a gondola, and the Cipriani.

We scheduled a group dinner that night, but Neil and David wanted
some alone time, not surprising for a couple in a romantic setting like
Venice. I was just tired and bailed on the group dinner as well. While
exhaling over a cocktail in the hotel bar, I found The Jackal felt the
same. We ate by ourselves, sharing stories, jokes, and ideas while savor-

ing fifty-euro martinis. Neil and David had done their own date night and, upon returning to the hotel, joined The Jackal and I for night caps. Now relaxed and "off camera," Neil revealed a more philosophical, self-deprecating persona, laced with his impeccable timing and wit. David was charming in his own right—expressive, funny, and smart. Night caps became early morning caps as we shared stories, thoughts, and opinions. I was relieved Neil and David shared our concern the shoot could easily become a cheesy, celebrity travel feature if we didn't do it right.

The cover for this package was scheduled to shoot in front of the Orient Express, and we had an hour to do five wardrobe changes before boarding ourselves.

I've never seen a crew work faster. The Jackal dressed Neil in the bathroom, ushering him back and forth to change looks ("Quick like a bunny! Quick like a bunny!"). Cliff had a local digital tech—the guy who downloads images from your camera and lets you know if they're good—named Luca, who might as well have been on strike himself. After every setup, he'd download the memory card, light a cigarette, take a long, leisurely drag, *then* check out the images. We'd wait with anticipation after each setting as he finished his smoke. Finally, "It's OK(a), it's OK(a)" he said in a heavy Italian accent.

We barely made it on the train and retreated to our individual cabins before meeting for drinks in the bar car, where Cliff shot more portraits.

Dinner would be black tie in the dining car, which presented a small problem: our crew had stuffed their faces, and one or two tuxedos suddenly got too snug. The Jackal spent the afternoon as a seamstress, doing whatever she could to make the clothing more comfortable. In her styling kit was thread, needles, even buttons, which came to good use: mine flung off and might have blinded the porter. The dinner was five-course gastronomy, but what I remember most was our crew reenacting *Murder on the Orient Express*. Neil played victim and laid on the ground pretending to be dead. Cliff photographed him, then took mug-shots of the suspects: everyone else. We made a movie poster out of the images, and it hangs on my wall today.

After staging our own "whodunnit" about the Orient Express,
a poster of our production had to be made!

After night caps in the bar car, we retreated to our cabins to find the couches had been turned into beds. I had one of the best sleeps of my life as the train rocked back and forth, plowing through snow covered towns, villages, and mountains.

We arrived in Paris the next morning and went to our next hotel: Fouquet's, which sits atop its namesake restaurant off the Champs-Élysées. The consensus of our crew, after our other accommodations, was a collective "meh." My room was odd: the toilet was in a different room than the shower. This makes overnight nature callings complicated.

The last night of our trip, Neil called again: he and David asked The Jackal and me if we'd join them at Robert et Louise, an old-school French restaurant that only grilled meat—ribs, T-bone steak, lamb—over an open wood fire.

We ended the trip the next morning, the Muppets going separate ways.

Back in New York, I started going through the images, which were phenomenal; Cliff captured the rarity of the experience. They were timeless, nostalgic, and with a relaxed, "bella figura" sensibility. But the cover setup, in front of the Orient Express, sparked a kerfuffle with someone who was angry because they were not invited. This person found any reason to criticize the images.

"The train is floating" was the complaint.

It wasn't. Neil was smoldering and confident, intense in the Ermenegildo Zegna suit that The Jackal had gotten the designer to lend. He looked like the rich, handsome playboy who bangs you in the cabin and never calls again, and you don't regret a minute.

We were at a standstill, but I wasn't going to be held hostage. I found a freelancer to help prepare it for the cover.

The issue came out, and the cover looked very *GQ*. Neil was booked for *Late Night with David Letterman* the next week, and the host showed the cover on-screen, and spent an entire segment of his appearance talking about the trip.

Geoffrey Weill and his PR team were ecstatic. They won a huge award for all the press the trip had generated.

Sophia: Neil Patrick Harris comes off so down to earth and kind.

Jeremy: I spent enough time with him to confirm that is true.

S: Did anyone end up murdered on The Orient Express?

J: I didn't see Poirot interrogating any of the passengers! Our reenactment was the closest it got.

S: How limited was the space for a photoshoot on a moving train? Did you have room to style and setup? What was the lighting like?

J: Shooting in tight spaces is already hard. But on a moving train? Cliff got really great photos despite the circumstances.

S: Was it more or less difficult than shooting on an airborne plane with Kaley?

J: Nothing was as difficult as the plane photo shoot.

S: How was the train ride? Did you see some great views of the Swiss Alps?

J: It was dream-like. At night, the train would pass small villages in the mountains, and they looked like Christmas settings.

S: What's the food like on the Orient Express?

J: Delicious! Meals on planes and trains are notoriously bad, but this was gourmet cuisine. We got to see the kitchen, and damn, we thought we had a small space to work.

S: *Did you sleep well or was it hard to fall asleep on a moving train?*

J: I slept like a baby.

S: *Favorite shot by Cliff Lipson?*

J: The cover! Neil is Brad Pitt.

S: *Giudecca in Venice looks breathtaking. How many nights did you guys stay there?*

J: Two nights, I think.

S: *Favorite Italian restaurants?*

J: OMG, yes! On our day off we found a hole-in-the-wall restaurant on a side street called Vino-Vino. I had the best plate of spaghetti of my life.

S: *Pasta or Pizza?*

J: Both.

S: *Rome, Venice, and Paris. Which city did everyone enjoy most this trip?*

J: Venice, hands down. Rome was "meh." I had more fun hanging out with our crew than seeing monuments.

S: *Did the Orient Express ever ask you back?*

J: That was a one-time thing. Our entire trip was comped. I couldn't afford to ride today.

S: *Has Neil reached out to you since?*

J: We email occasionally. I was trying to get the train to host Neil and David for a ten-year anniversary from our trip in 2019 but the dates never worked. Neil also did a video for my company's five-year anniversary sizzle reel.

CHAPTER 23

....

Snow, Surliness, Stars, and Safari

Commentator/author Fran Lebowitz was a guest we hosted at our annual "salon" at The Surrey hotel, where famous/noted talents gathered for "fireside" chats. It was a big hit with advertisers and the media, but not a big higher up, which is why author Jeremy Murphy continued to do more. Here he is with Fran in the image he calls "I'm Not Going to Pay a Lot for This Muffler" photo. Photo courtesy of Jeremy Murphy.

Thomas Gibson, who starred on *Criminal Minds* (and was Greg in *Dharma and Greg*) could not have been nicer on a trip to Lake Tahoe, where we asked him to do a skiing feature. My good friend Steven Holt hosted us at the newly opened Ritz-Carlton, where *I* caused the drama. On the first night, the fire alarms went off at 1:00 a.m.; all guests had to leave the premises. I was very annoyed to be awoken and went back to bed. Five minutes later, photographer Mark Mann knocked, and still sleepy-eyed, I opened the door when Mark shouted that we needed to leave. Oblivious to the gravity of the situation, I responded, "They'll call back if it's important," then closed the door and returned to bed. It turned out to be a false alarm anyway.... The next morning, we hit the slopes, which I did literally; I plowed down a family as soon as I started the course. I was then required to take beginner ski lessons with a group of eight-year-olds and got super offended when the instructor kept yelling "Pizza!" and "French fries" in my direction. Jesus Christ, lady; I'm not that fat. Turns out they meant the position of your skis; pizza means to turn your feet in, and French fries is to keep them parallel. Finally, I was due to meet our crew at the top of the mountain for lunch. The natural place to put a restaurant. No problem, they had a ski lift. That doesn't stop when it gets to the top. It just flings you off, and it flung me down the other side of the mountain. I have not skied since.

✧ ✧ ✧

We did a salon once with Fran Lebowitz, the curmudgeonly commentator on society, politics, art, entertainment, public policy, and New York. She specifically hates tourists, Times Square, and not being able to smoke in restaurants. I've loved her for years and lobbied to book her as guest speaker. After a few back-and-forths with her agent, I got her to agree and began booking the appearance. And was delighted to learn her only "ask" was a turkey club sandwich she could bring home. Fran was a home run. Everyone loved her ruminating on any topic you could ask, which got a witty, smart reply. She also stayed to mingle and take photos.

Matt Lanter was starring on The CW network's *90210* reboot; he also is the voice of Anakin Skywalker in the *Stars Wars* animated series *The Clone Wars*. My publisher, Super P, told me his son was a huge fan, so I had Matt call his home and talk to his boy as Anakin. Childhood moment, indeed! And shows you what a good guy Matt is.

More than Halloween, I hate nature. I'm a city boy. I like creature comforts: AC, electricity, television, streets, and buildings. If land, grass, cows, trees, squirrels, or whatever floats your boat, fine. We can meet later at the bar. So when I got an offer to bring an actor on a luxury safari to Africa, I yawned...and deleted the email.

Next!

This was the advantage to editing a magazine that at this point had no money and no readers: no one gave a shit. But the PR firm the safari company hired was really, really good and kept at it. I couldn't deny that getting lions, zebras, giraffes, and other wildlife on our pages would spice things up, so we began figuring out *how* to do it; bringing a crew to South Africa is not for the faint of heart. It's a very long trip, and we didn't have an airline partner to fly us direct. Or much money.

Eric Close, who starred on the hit TV drama *Without a Trace*, had just done a shoot for us in Chile, and our team bonded with him and his wife, Keri. We had too much fun and all became friends, and I knew Eric had the travel bug. He also liked nature, which I tried not to hold against him. Of all the talent we had worked with at this point, Eric was the easiest. Asking him to go was never a question, and it wasn't for him either.

I put together the leanest crew I could get because this would cost us a bit and we didn't have a bit. Erica Berger, an incredible photographer I'd met through friends, joined our crew, as did videographer Kevin Egan. I also brought a plus-one to do very important work that was to be determined: my buddy Mason, with whom I went to Paris for New Year's and wound up partying with Middle Eastern royals.

Eric Close from *Without a Trace* on an excursion in Ngala, South Africa.

Everyone flew from New York to London to Johannesburg separately. Mason and I went first, and the flight from Heathrow to "Joburg" still gives me nightmares. British Airways stuffed us in the last row on the plane, middle aisle, middle seats, with no overhead compartment. I had to put my carry-on under my feet and sit like that for sixteen years...in coach, which on BA might as well be in steerage; they practically throw the food at you as if you're peasants. Two hours in, I summoned the flight attendant and ordered whatever liquor was left. After six "nips" of less-than-premium booze, aided by a couple of Xanax, I passed out for the remainder of the flight. "I think you flatlined," Mason said upon landing. "You died there for a few minutes."

I wish I had.

Johannesburg is filthy. Sorry! I know that's very un-PC to say, and I'll probably get tased by some HR person, but it's true. Fortunately, we were going to Kruger National Park, which is north of Joburg in Ngala; I write this as if I know where the fuck any of that is. We flew on a propeller plane for three hours over lands I was not interested in landing on, and finally got to our home for the next week: CC Africa (now part of &Beyond), a luxury safari experience deep in the African bushland. The resort was expansive, with many "cottages" spread throughout, including some for guests. Mine was very large and was stylishly decorated like a set from *Out of Africa*, which I was hoping my eventuality. At night, monkeys and other assorted vermin climbed on the thatched roofs. Also, you're advised not to leave your hut in the dark because you might get eaten by a roaming lion.

Our crew in Africa on an excursion.

Everyone loved it except me. I was miserable. My first morning, I awoke to find elephants walking feet from my window, which is not my normal experience. Nor preferred. Also, the food was too spicy, and the nightly entertainment with tribal dances grew tiresome. Being guided to your room at night by a guard with rifle did not add to the charm. We also had a white tracker with a fancy South African accent, which usually means they have controversial opinions on apartheid. I really didn't care because I had my own opinions about *him* and his fascination with birds (read: flying rats). For the first few hours of our inaugural ride through the bushland, this dude talked incessantly about the horrid species and pointed them out in places they were hiding...which meant we didn't see them. He also passed around a book about birds for our group's reading (dis)pleasure. Fed up, I attempted to throw it off our truck, which Mason blocked, and I instead shouted, "Can we see some fucking lions?" Our guide got the message, and we soon saw many, and more creatures I never thought I'd be near.

Giraffes are cool—they're like the supermodels of the jungle: tall, thin, long eyelashes, only eat leaves, and judgmental. They are fabulous, and they know it. Zebras are very high on themselves; they think they're very special, but the lions do, too: on their lips. Hippopotamuses are gross. Elephants are basket cases; highly emotional, they never forget sadness or buried water, and their ears wave like flags in a windstorm when they're annoyed or angry. Like someone you're dating who's upset you didn't text seconds after the date.

The entire experience was like an acid trip, which might have happened because the drug doctors give you to prevent malaria is known to trigger such sensations. Tripping out when monkeys are dancing on your roof is an experience no one should experience. Or maybe they should.

We spent four days in the "luxury" resort and then two nights in the real wilderness where our hosts set up tents with furniture. The days were somewhat interesting, but the nights more so, thanks to the medications: I was so whacked out on the Malariad meds I dreamt a lion dragged me by his teeth to Studio 54, where I danced on a thatched-roof floor with Halston and Liza.

That's an awesome hallucination, come to think of it. Never mind!

On the morning we were scheduled to leave, I awoke to loud squawking outside my tent. "Fucking birds," I cursed, not happy to be awoken by their terrible species. It got louder and louder to the point I ran out to find Eric and our videographer, Kevin, mimicking bird sounds.

"I don't care if it's a Monet. It clashes with the wallpaper." Having a
serious discussion on a nighttime excursion in Africa.

As we left, the manager of the resort raced up to me with very
important news: we had a bar bill still open and owed one million
RAM, or some absurd amount like that.

Shit, I thought to myself. *That sounds like a lot, even for us.*

Converted, it was twenty dollars. I gave them one hundred.

Nancy Grace is most known as the shrill, permanently disgusted former
prosecutor who hosted a talk show on some variation of CNN, which is
likely now a Spanish language soccer channel. She rode the wave of the
Scott Peterson and Casey Anthony trials, and her ratings skyrocketed.
Viewers loved her opinions, sneers, and when she interrupted guests.
Her fierce advocacy for victims—which sometimes went overboard—
was easy to understand: her fiancé was murdered at an ATM, which
inspired her to become a district attorney, victims' advocate, and inven-
tor of labels like "Tot Mom."

Nancy became a source of public fascination, celebrated and ridi-
culed. You know you've penetrated the zeitgeist when Amy Poehler is
imitating you on *Saturday Night Live.*

In addition to CNN Whatever, she began to host a syndicated series called *Swift Justice*, and in the run up to its launch, we got an opportunity to interview and photograph the Media Snarler in her Atlanta home.

I was expecting the worst. Frankly, she scared me.

Not the one who answered the door. *That* Nancy was unrecognizable: no makeup, helmet hair, or sneer. She was welcoming, warm, and gracious we'd made the trip. I asked my crew if we went to the wrong home.

The host even took breakfast orders from McDonald's and drove herself, returning with bags of Egg McMuffins and other artery cloggers.

Where's Nancy, and what have you done with her?

As we prepared for the photography, Nancy smiled.

"I have to put on my bitch face," she joked.

Thirty minutes later, the Nancy people love and loathe emerged. It was a startling transformation.

After the photos, we left charmed. She was self-deprecating, kind, accommodating, and fun.

The camera does lie.

Q&A WITH SOPHIA PAULMIER

> *Sophia: While you were in Lake Tahoe shooting Thomas Gibson, the hotel had a fire alarm go off in the middle of the night, and after Mark Mann woke you up and told you it was an emergency you went right back to sleep?*
>
> Jeremy: Yup. It was the middle of the night, and I was in pajamas. I'm not standing outside in the snow. I figured if the hotel was really on fire, they'd call.
>
> *S: You are a character straight off a sitcom. What's your show titled?*
>
> J: "Fuck Off."

S: *Did you enjoy skiing once you took some lessons?*

J: No, I hated every part of it. My body hurt in places I did not know you can hurt.

S: *Favorite spots in Lake Tahoe?*

J: I didn't stay that long.

S: *Was sledding Utah more fun than skiing in Tahoe?*

J: Getting a hang nail was more fun than skiing in Tahoe.

S: *Summarize Fran Leibowitz in a few words.*

J: Acerbic with wit that came easy and a natural command of the room. She has a reputation for being surly, but we must have gotten her on a good day. She stayed after her Q&A and even posed for pictures. I have an image of the two of us together, and neither of us are smiling. I call it the "I'm not going to pay a lot for this muffler" photo. You have to be older than forty to get that reference.

S: *Matt Lanter is a real-life Jedi for calling Super P's kid as his favorite character, Anakin. Did Super P ever thank him?*

J: Profusely. What a great experience for his son.

S: *What's Nancy Grace's McDonald's order?*

J: We all ate Egg McMuffins!

S: *Did she spill any tea with you?*

J: No, we didn't have time for that. It was friendly but professional.

CHAPTER 24

⋯⋯⋆⋯⋯

Going Aeropostal

This chapter is a little tricky because it involves something serious that I'll try to make funny. But in interests of protecting the guilty, I am changing identifying characteristics.

We'd set up two photo shoots in Paris—again—with Archie and Matt from *The Good Wife* and Oliver Hudson from *Rules of Engagement*. I naturally flew in earlier, but *much* earlier this time. I used the opportunity to bring my mom, and it was more enjoyable than I'd expected.

The morning she left, my crew was scheduled to arrive. I was, frankly, relieved. Pretending I wasn't a reckless heathen for a week with my mother was exhausting, although I'm guessing she knows the truth.

As I said goodbye, the phone in my room rang. It was a colleague advising me that a member of our crew had been arrested...on the plane. We'd caused a lot of trouble around the world, but this was new. Surprisingly so. I'm frankly surprised it hadn't happened before.

Tom was a relative newbie and stood out for being responsible and not drunk. He'd given up drinking for a while and impressed me with his discipline and can-do attitude. I hired him as a manager, and he quickly proved he could do anything.

Except Ambien.

Tom joined others on the overnight flight, took the normally safe sleeping aid, and knocked out. And then knocked in. As in, sleepwalking. This is a very rare side effect with this drug, but it happens. Tom began to troll the aisles speaking incoherently, asking other passengers if they were "with him," and even tried to bum a cigarette from someone coming out of the bathroom. He didn't even smoke.

He also began shaking the head of the seat in front of him, enraging the passenger who stood up and slapped him in the face *Knots Landing* style. It didn't help that he was wearing a hoodie and sunglasses, looking like the Unabomber.

After enough disruption, the crew and other passengers quartered him to his seat for the rest of the flight. Upon landing, the pilot announced there had been an "incident" and asked everyone to remain seated. The gendarmes—French police—entered the plane and put our guy in handcuffs.

The colleague who advised me of this situation arrived at the hotel—we had others who would handle the situation at the airport—and we met in the lobby lounge, where I got the lowdown.

Here's what normally occurs when something like this happens: you assess the situation and advise your superiors, especially when someone is in legal trouble. I've never experienced said trouble, but I'm also not a rat. I really liked Tom and wanted to protect him. Something like this could ruin his career; it would have definitely got him fired. In the Google age, he might have not worked again.

I didn't want to get fired either and risked a lot not reporting this, but I really didn't give a shit. Going down for one of my teammates would have been an honor.

I decided on radio silence. I wouldn't say anything unless someone else did, and in that case, I would have pleaded his case. I *was* worried it would get out—American arrested on plane!—but thankfully, this was before Instagram stories. Ten years later, it would most definitely have been filmed and posted.

Except in France. For them, this was apparently a "meh" incident. They threw him in the drunk tank until he woke up and let him go. The airline was also not interested in delaying the return flight with paperwork. They had to turn the plane around and didn't want burdensome reports to delay departure.

Tom emerged unscathed, as did I.

There's a lot in my life I'm not proud of, but covering this up is something I am damned sure am.

Sophia: This is on the same trip as Archie Panjabi and Matt Czuchry?

Jeremy: Yes!

S: When you first got that call from your colleague, what were you thinking?

J: At first, I assumed he was joking. This hadn't happened before, and it never happened after. It seemed too farcical. How do you get arrested on a plane? What was he, the Unabomber? Did he accidentally bring peanuts or say a girl was pretty?

S: Was he maybe paranoid?

J: No, he was sleepwalking! This can happen on sleep meds. I think it's listed in one of the ten thousand side effects they mention really fast at the end of commercials.

S: What did you say to Tom when you saw him?

J: I didn't have to say anything. He was mortified, and frankly it wasn't his fault. He really thought he'd lose his job. That wasn't going to happen if I could help it, and it didn't. We were able to protect him and keep it silent. Although we teased him about it quite a bit. We still do. The first night, I took the staff to dinner, which was becoming customary, but Tom opted to stay behind at the hotel. He felt incredible shame, which was unfortunate. I wish he'd have joined us.

S: No Michelin-star restaurant for you!

J: "Go to your hotel room at the Hôtel Plaza Athénée! You're punished!"

S: *I'm just thinking of like your crew panicking on how you would take the news.*

J: I was easy to talk to because I'd usually done worse, and I always enjoyed hearing about the trouble we'd caused. Maybe not the arrest, but this would be an awesome story if we could keep it covered. Tom was very lucky it happened in France. They tend to take a laissez-faire attitude to these types of situations. I'm surprised the gendarmes didn't offer him a cigarette and glass of wine. Had this been in the US, he'd have been a news crawl on CNN.

S: *So your crew members weren't afraid to ever tell you things?*

J: I think so, unless there are things they didn't. I don't freak out in these instances; I tend to go into battle mode and just get shit done. I'm good in crisis, especially mine, which are many.

S: *It's what you want from a PR person too. Somebody that does not freak out.*

J: "Don't panic, adjust." The fifth grade teacher I mentioned before, Mrs. Porter, instilled this mantra in me in 1985, and I've embraced it since. I lost touch with her for thirty years and recently got a message through my company website asking if it was me. "Are you Jeremy Murphy from Forrest Glenn Elementary?" We made contact and talked for hours by phone and now text regularly.

S: *What did she think of you?*

J: She thought I was incredibly quirky. On one assignment, I wrote how much I enjoyed ham and cheese sandwiches while watching *Santa Barbara*. I was ten.

CHAPTER 25

★

Long Live the King (Cole)

Jeremy in front of the restored mural of Old King Cole in the famous
King Cole Bar. Photo courtesy of Jeremy Murphy.

Don't sing to Mary J. Blige. Especially at a bar.
This is one life lesson I would impart to my children if I wanted
or had any. Honestly, I don't know why my tribe fought for this right.
It used to be the best part of being gay.

We'd just done a photo shoot at the Peninsula Hotel on Fifth
Avenue and 55th Street in Midtown Manhattan and were ecstatic
with the results. Patrick Demarchelier exceeded our expectations with

his images, which were sultry, sexy, and timeless. It was our first time shooting with Patrick, and it could not have gone better. We were in the mood to celebrate.

Our crew went across the street to the St. Regis Hotel, which houses the historic King Cole Bar, otherwise known as our watering hole. There had to be ten of us, and the servers—Michael, Francis, and George—always gave us the best tables. We got an entire corner: prime seating that gives you vantage of the entire bar.

As the drinks poured, my confidence grew. So much so, upon seeing "Her Blige-ness," I felt the urge to sing.

"Mary J. Blige! No more pain, no more drama!" I crooned, hitting each note perfectly.

She was ready to hit *me*. Instead, she raised her index finger signaling me to stop. It was a full Whitney.

"I'm sorry, Mary J. Blige," I responded sheepishly.

I rarely tell this story, but this one has been confirmed by several people with me, including The Jackal.

The King Cole Bar has a unique history in New York. Opened in 1932, it has hosted celebrities, artists, royalty, business titans, and legends, including Salvador Dalí, John Lennon, and Marilyn Monroe. Dalí, who lived on-site, brought his ocelot (a wildcat) to the bar regularly. Legendary *Vogue* editor Diana Vreeland was discovered dancing on one of its tables by *Harper's Bazaar* lioness Carmel Snow.

Its mood is dark, clubby, and exclusive, and it's well known for the giant mural draping its wall: Old King Cole sitting on a throne with servants and guards on each side. Except the artist, Maxfield Parrish, got cheeky and painted in two jokes. First, the king has an agitated look on his face, and the folks standing beside him scowl as if they smell something foul. Because they do: the king just farted. Second, Parrish so hated the hotel's owner, John Jacob Astor IV, that he put his face on the king.

More recently, the bar was featured in films like *Hannah and Her Sisters* and *The Devil Wears Prada*, where Anne Hathaway goes to get the *Harry Potter* manuscript from Simon Baker.

It was this movie that inspired me to check it out, and on a very stressful day in 2006, I summoned two colleagues, including The Jackal, to join me in my exploration. We wound up closing out the bar.

Building a publication from scratch is tough. I was not only editor in chief, but I was the general manager and responsible for every operation—editorial, marketing, circulation—except advertising. That was Super P's domain, and his prowess helped us become what we became. We built it together, including moving boxes from the shipping docks to our offices, handing out copies in the rain, stuffing envelopes, what have you. It was arduous work and required liquid sustenance. Which came with quasi-scandals.

On one boisterous night, I got plastered with a colleague, then awoke the next morning fully dressed on the top of my bed, not knowing how I'd even gotten home. I searched my pockets for evidence from the night before and found a sales order for a $5,000 Sub-Zero refrigerator. I'd somehow bought a major kitchen appliance in a bar, with no memory of doing so.

"Did I buy a refrigerator last night?" I asked my colleague.

"Yup!" he responded, laughing hysterically.

The sales order had a woman's name and phone number. I know I didn't sleep with her, but stranger things have happened. The rate I was going, I very well could have. I called the number and got "Lizzy," who squealed with delight when I contacted her, then asked for a credit card.

Click. I hung up instantly, having dodged another bullet.

Halloween 2011 was farcical. I was meeting a friend for drinks before he went off to some all-night rave. I hated that idea, and I abhor Halloween. Honestly, it's children at your door begging for food. If you're that hungry, you shouldn't have spent so much on your costume.

My friend spent none. He came dressed as Jesus, complete with white caftan, thorn crown, and blood on his hands. In a bar at a five-star hotel. To my relief, other patrons found it as hysterical as I did. One even asked him to bless his lotto ticket.

On another night, a coworker and I had a typically crappy day in magazine world and sulked over pricey Macallans. By round three,

we decided to document our displeasure with a website called www.
YouKnowWhoElseIFuckingHate.com? We bought the URL from the
bar and began making lists of everyone who pissed us off, and it got
very long. As did the night. We never did create the website and lost the
URL rights a year later. I still think it's a great idea.

The most scandalous incident at The King Cole involved a couple
from the Midwest, impeccably dressed prostitutes, and my crew. Five-
star hotels in New York are notorious for high-end escorts trolling for
new clients; most of the hotels hold their nose and look the other way.
The amenity may not be on their menu, but it's available for guests who
feel frisky. The King Cole Bar inside the St. Regis is not an exception
to this phenomenon.

As the night continued, the couple began to make noise. In particular, the woman seemed angry. Her husband tried to console her to no
avail. Finally, he stood up and approached the three prostitutes, spout-
ing not-very-nice words, including "whore." His wife seemed to think
the women were pointing and laughing at her for some reason.

I assure you, no one was pointing at her or him. For whatever reason, she thought otherwise, and he felt chivalrous. As the confrontation
got more heated, people in our group stood up and entered the conversation, trying to make peace. The man was drunk, and it looked as if
violence was coming next.

It did—toward us. Super Hubby did not appreciate our intervention and directed his anger at us, pushing me against the wall. We were
ready to fight, but a colleague pushed him back and warned him she'd
break his arm if he tried that again. Instead, insults were hurled, accusations spouted, and threats came aplenty.

The couple finally left; she in tears and he embarrassed a woman
had prevented him from coldcocking me.

We sat back down and recapped what happened with the three
prostitutes, who were delightful. "Misty," "Cindy," and "Claudine" (I
think) were very grateful we defended them and bought several rounds
of our drinks. I was surprised to find them well-educated, worldly, and

sophisticated. They also looked fabulous, as one should at their caliber of...service.

The corn-husking couple hadn't finished though. They went to security to complain, and we were asked to leave.

We were also banned for six months.

Q&A WITH SOPHIA PAULMIER

Sophia: Favorite Mary J. Blige song?

Jeremy: "No More Pain!"—the song I sang to her!

S: Go-to order off The King Cole menu?

J: Macallan 12.

S: Favorite cocktail to recommend?

J: Macallan 12.

S: I've read that there's only one table you can reserve at The King Cole, and it costs $2,500 to reserve a secret six-course tasting menu with a rare selection of wines and whiskeys. Have you ever had the pressure of dining this sought out experience?

J: No! That's new information! I'm fortunate to have been a regular, so we never had to reserve a table. We just got right in.

S: I can't believe you hate Halloween. Is this why you missed my Halloween party?

J: Yes. I avoid all Halloween-related activity. It's a stupid holiday.

S: What's your favorite holiday?

J: Not to be Debbie Downer, but it used to be Thanksgiving. My father would take my brother and I to Washington, DC, every year and we'd stay at the Willard InterContinental for three nights, see all the sites, and eat at my favorite restaurants—Clyde's, The Old Ebbitt Grill, Capital Grille, 1789. He died in 2005, and I tried to keep up the tradition with my mom and stepfather, but it wasn't the same and not fair to them. I started a new thing by bringing friends somewhere cool everything Thanksgiving—Paris, London, Dublin, Cancún—but that ended for whatever reason. It was such an amazing time in my life, and we had such fun and laughs. Aside from crashing a wedding by accident, there was no scandal.

S: *You protected three women from being physically harmed, which is a courageous act. Have you considered changing careers to superhero?*

J: My territory would be 1st Avenue between 63rd and 64th.

S: *What surprised you more, the educated sex worker or getting banned from the King Cole Bar for six months?*

J: Neither surprised me, they were bound to happen.

S: *Where do you think today's artists meet?*

J: Somewhere I couldn't get into. I'm not that cool. I'm frankly surprised I've been able to do what I've done. I collected Smurfs and watched *Santa Barbara* as a kid!

S: *If the King Cole Bar named a drink after you what would it taste like?*

J: A tall glass of Macallan!

S: *If you opened your own bar, what would you name it?*

J: I've thought of this! It would be "JeMur."

S: *Most overrated bar in New York?*

J: Anything at the Gansevoort Hotel in the Meatpacking District.

CHAPTER 26

······⋆······

Shake, Rattle, and Roll

Author Jeremy Murphy in the Rock & Roll Hall of Fame.

While developing the magazine idea, I helped a fledgling TV network write its annual advertiser presentation, which basically includes cliches like "Game-changer!," "We're firing on all cylinders!," "We're swinging for the fences," and "It's a rebuilding year, and we have a bold new strategy." They say this all the time so you can see how great the strategy is. On this particular year, the network hired Usher to perform, hoping his lilliputian dance moves would convince advertisers to whip out their checkbooks. Because that's what one does after seeing Usher.

"Damn he has moves. Let's stay in the moment and buy $12 million of commercials," said no one ever.

I confess to not knowing who Usher was. For a second, I thought the ticket taker might be dancing on stage. This was before AI/ChatGPT, YouTube, and Wikipedia did your research for you. I scoured online to find how to fill three minutes, which is a lifetime on stage. Finally, in the spirit of the occasion, I just thought of as many cliches I could customize to the circumstances: a star singing and dancing for suit- and dress-wearing media buyers.

"Yo, 10:00 a.m. at MSG. This is when the party's usually ending, not starting," I wrote for him.

Usher read it whole, and well.

Cleveland was not a "must" with our crew or talent. I'd never been, but the images of an industrial giant rusting its way into oblivion was my perception. But it's the home of The Rock and Roll Hall of Fame, and *that* piques my interest. The museum, designed by famed architect I. M. Pei, was opened in 1995 after Cleveland won over many cities with—what else?—money to help build it. But it has ties to the genre—WJW radio DJ Alan Freed was an early proponent of the music style, and he coined the term DJ. I'm sure the Rolling Stones also stopped in a local McDonald's to use the bathroom.

This was 2007. The rock hall offered to host a shoot, but I had to get there and bring talent. No one wanted to go (we barely did), but an assistant on the floor of our building had gotten me interested in *The Young and the Restless*, and I began to think there was our answer.

Y&R is, or was, the number one soap opera on daytime, famous for when its theme song was used as Olympic gymnast Nadia Comăneci's performance music in the 1976 Summer Games. The sudser was famous for its snail-like storytelling, tight camera close-ups of actress Melody Thomas Scott crying, and unintelligible dialogue from Eric Braeden as Victor Newman. For this, we chose two of its newer, younger stars—Bryton McClure and Christel Khalil—to do a fashion shoot throughout the museum. The Jackal would style, and Cliff Lipson, naturally, would shoot.

With barely a budget, but not eager to stay in a Holiday Inn—I had enough of that through my youth—I desperately hoped there was a hotel appropriate to bring talent. To my great surprise, Cleveland had a five-star property whose marketing director was interested.

I quickly got the hotel to agree to put us up in exchange for taking photos of the actors enjoying the property. That shouldn't have been a problem. But, as I waited at the gate for my flight, its corporate office called.

Here's the thing with luxury brands: they're fanatical about who uses, buys, and experiences their products. Soap and reality stars are a particular no-no for travel. They feel it sullies their brand. I, frankly, think that's ridiculous. More people watch *Y&R* than most primetime shows. The hotel, thankfully, made me a deal: they'd honor the trade, but we could only feature the hotel in a *separate* story *without* the actors. As long as I wasn't paying, that was fine with me.

Christel and Bryton joined our crew for dinner the night before, where I made my first *d'oh!* I had begun to watch *Y&R* and commented how great I thought both actors were. Bryton called my bluff and asked me what storyline his character was going through.

OK, I didn't say *which* storylines I watch. The truth is, every summer *Y&R* thinks teens will suddenly shut off their phones and say, "Let's watch a soap opera that never ends!" The show puts its older, more established stars on the back burner for the season and focuses on young, ripped, and busty young actors with storylines that require little clothing and dialogue. So I fast-forward to Nikki, Victor, Jack Abbott, Cricket, and other legacy characters.

The next morning, we photographed the actors in eight different settings throughout the museum, which was incredibly accommodating, collaborative, and provided backgrounds with scenery steeped in history and color. While preparing the wardrobe, which we did on-site, The Jackal fretted she didn't have Christian Louboutin high heels for one of the settings. "Where should we get them?" she asked.

"Honey, honey, honey," responded her assistant Daryl. "We're in *Cleveland.*"

We used what we had, but every time I see Daryl, we say that line on cue.

"Honey, honey, honey! We're in Cleveland."

The shoot turned out stress-free, and the images were fun—the actors were having a great time, the clothes reflected the setting, and the museum was depicted just as intended. Afterwards, we brought our crew to the hotel lounge where things got wily. Daryl and Paula, The Jackal's other assistant, got especially frisky and raided the wardrobe to dress like Russian rock stars, complete with fur hats, sunglasses, and other whimsical accessories. They created a back story—Boris and Natalia from Belarus—and talked in accents for the rest of the night, including to other patrons.

Author Jeremy Murphy, center, between "Natalia" and "Boris" at The Ritz-Carlton, Cleveland. Photo courtesy of Jeremy Murphy.

As we built our fashion cred, I began to get invited to black-tie events with people who can afford to attend; I was still eating Lucky Charms for dinner and relied on plus-one invites. At one dinner, I sat next to people from Ralph Lauren and made the mistake of saying it wrong. I used two syllables: La-Ren. A very haughty woman from the brand corrected me sternly. "It's *Lauren*," she hissed. One syllable. She was obnoxious, which required me to respond in-kind: "I'm sorry for mispronouncing your *fake last name*," I hissed back. Ralph changed it from Lifshitz. I would have too.

✧ ✧ ✧

The Greenbrier is a stately resort in West Virginia steeped in history, tradition, luxury, blah blah blah. The truth is it's a giant turd. Here's why: I arranged to do a photo shoot with TV sports reporter Tracy Wolfson, who covers the NFL, at the "resort" at the behest of its New York PR agency. They'd been kind to us, and I felt obligated to return the favor. I shouldn't have.

Located in the Allegheny Mountains near White Sulphur Springs—as if I know where any of that is—The Greenbrier occupies 11,000 acres with 710 guest rooms, 20 restaurants, 35 retail shops, and a casino. As you arrive, you see a giant white mansion that looks like a funeral home/rehab facility. The interiors are worse. Designed by the hugely overrated Dorothy Draper, it's complete sensory over*board*, as if a Jolly Rancher and a Starburst hooked up and birthed this monstrosity in a Texaco bathroom. Green, purple, red—all the worst color combinations—assault your eyes as you enter.

The property is so big it could rival the Mall of America, which would have been a better setting. My room resembled a set from *The Golden Girls*, and the hallways were so vast, I got lost several times.

The Greenbrier loves itself more than anyone else. So much so, its owner plastered pictures of him and his family throughout the hotel. There was even a large cardboard cutout of him in the gift shop.

I brought Christopher Campbell to style, and he was as visually offended as me. Combined, we could not identify any settings to shoot Tracy. Neither of us expected *Deliverance* as the backdrop.

The next morning, as Christopher and his assistant prepared the clothing, we got an SOS message: it was likely, but not definite, Tracy would not be able to come. It had to do with weather, riots, Armageddon, whatevs.

FUCCCKKKKKKKK!!!!!

There we were, in nowheresville for no reason.

Christopher and I strategized, and we decided to hire a model to at least shoot the wardrobe, which was top-notch. Try finding a model in West Virginia with teeth.

We settled on a good-looking blonde woman from the DC area and sent a car to bring her to The Greenbrier, but she got stuck in torrential rain, and the drive took sixteen hours. The model arrived half asleep, but there was no time to spare! Poor girl, we put her through the ringer. The irony was that Tracy managed to get there the following day, so we shot her too.

Jeremy with Mary Ann Winkowski, the inspiration for "Ghost Whisperer." Photo courtesy of Jeremy Murphy.

A key selling point to The Greenbrier is the worst selling point you can imagine: buried below the hotel is a nuclear fallout shelter for Congress. There's literally a mini city underground, complete with housing, cafeteria, medical facility, and other necessary functions. The hotel gives tours of the facility, which is super creepy and not the amenity I'd be selling. And, quite honestly, who the fuck is going to West Virginia when the big bomb goes off? Radiation sounds more appealing.

Our magazine was beginning to make a name for itself with splashy photo shoots in Paris and the like, which were often chronicled in *WWD* and other media. People in the industry began to notice, including a high-powered studio head looking to bring her family to Paris over the holidays. Her assistant called me and asked if I would help plan the itinerary, which I was happy to oblige. I was flattered to even be asked.

Which didn't last long.

"Suggestions" soon became "Can you do it yourself?," which rendered me a part-time concierge. As I edited the magazine, I also juggled making breakfast, lunch, and dinner reservations in the City of Light, which I hoped would turn dark. I got some relief when I was asked to book the hotel, which was easy: the George V. It's not only one of Paris's top properties but also has the best concierge team in hospitality...who soon became my allies. Together, we booked, cancelled, rebooked, cancelled, and rebooked reservations for a week, which was beginning to feel like a year.

The demands became more comical by the day. When I was asked to book cars for the airport pick-up—three SUVs for her and husband, nanny and baby, and luggage—I made the mistake of requesting the flight number and time of arrival.

"She doesn't fly commercial," her assistant sniffed, then gave me the private plane's tail number and hangar.

Working with my new family at the George V, we put together an itinerary that would make the Royal Family gasp: reservations at Michelin-star restaurants throughout Paris, at optimal times. I was ready for a victory lap, but it soon turned into a marathon. The executive requested I go with her, but separately...and invisibly. I was to be "insurance" in case anything went array.

Problem? This was over Christmas, which I actually celebrate. And my stepfather had recently died, and I didn't want my mother to celebrate the holiday alone. I politely passed on the opportunity.

That fell on deaf ears. A higher-up at our parent company knew of the situation and "strongly" recommended I change my mind. Budget was no object, which is music to my ears.

Thus began the most ludicrous holiday one could imagine. My mother and I flew first class to Paris, stayed in suites at The Shangri-La hotel, and had all our expenses covered. Upon arrival, I checked in and savored a full night's sleep, given the executive's arrival the next day. The only obstacle was annoying lights flashing through the drapes of my room.

"Can you please do something about that?" I implored the front desk.

"Monsieur, that is the Eiffel Tower," he responded, incredulous.

I pulled back the curtains, and there it was: the world's most iconic monument, twinkling.

I'm the first hotel guest in history to complain.

The executive and her family arrived the next day, and the real work began. An hour before each booking, I went to the restaurant, inspected the table placement, and showed her headshot so they'd recognize and fawn over her. I bribed each maître d' with hundred-euro bills.

The George V concierge staff had become my heroes, and I became their Santa Claus. Before I left, I purchased each one a gift: scarves for the ladies and ties for the men.

Her trip was flawless, and I've never been so happy to hear a plane had taken off.

Returning to New York, I expected to find a thank-you note, bottle of wine, some gesture from the executive. Nada.

What did I get? A thank-you note and photo of the twelve concierges holding champagne flutes, saluting me for the gifts.

Turned out, it was the best thank you I could have received.

✧ ✧ ✧

Ghost Whisperer had become a quasi-hit. It was based on the real-life story of Mary Ann Winkowski, a Cleveland housewife born with a unique gift: seeing ghosts. I had gotten to know her doing freelance work, and she's legit. Relatable and smart, she's like a big hug. I had a kooky idea: let's go ghostbusting with Mary Ann! Again, I'm bipolar and was likely drunk when I came up with it.

Mary Ann loved it and agreed to go wherever we chose. A PR friend knew of a resort in upstate New York called Saranac Waterfront Lodge, which was said to be haunted. It was remote, buried deep in the mountains, and was made of logs, or whatever they use to make log cabins.

We brought Mary Ann for a two-night stay, and she went to work immediately. At dinner, she asked the server if the bathroom in the basement was still locking people in. "How did you know that?" the server asked.

Mary Ann explained a ghost was having fun ("tomfoolery!"). She also knew the dishwasher in one of the kitchens was constantly breaking plates.

The next morning, we did the real sleuthing and began trolling the hotel for spooky thrills. One of the log cabins piqued her interest, so we brought her in.

"Right there," she said, pointing in the air at nothing. "He's standing right next to you."

Our photographer began to take images but was using a super expensive Nikon camera with built-in computer, satellite uplink, and tickets to Taylor Swift.

"Digital cameras filter out what they don't understand," she said, then advised we buy a wind-up camera at a drugstore. We did, then took photos wherever she pointed.

The store processed the film, and wouldn't you know it: there were weird orbs floating everywhere she pointed.

That night, a fire alarm went off at 2:00 a.m., waking everyone up dramatically.

Ghosts' night out, I assume.

After Mission Impossible: Paris, word had gotten out I was a good concierge. Another industry executive inquired if I could help him and his entourage get into an exclusive club/lounge in Amsterdam, and not of the hedonistic kind. Somewhere cool *befitting* his stature. Having never visited, I was at a loss but confident Google could help. It did, in an unexpected way.

My initial searches proved futile until I found use for a set of Louis Vuitton city guides resting on my desk, which I thought were décor. In them, I found an obscure reference to a hot club called Door 74, the most exclusive venue in Amsterdam. So much so, it didn't have an address or contact information.

This is when Google *could* help. After scrolling though sixty pages, I found a vague reference to someone named Timo and a phone number associated with the location. Desperate, I sent a text with no expectation of a response but got one almost instantly. Timo was the doorman, and was impressed I had his digits. He did his homework to make sure I wasn't sending the Kardashians and extended a rare invitation. And the best-kept secret in Amsterdam: its location.

This is when victory turned comedy. I didn't get an address but directions. Go to random street, make a left; make a right when you see a red tricycle; continue however many feet and turn at the corner with dead tulips; when you see a red door, knock three times. The password is whatever. In all honesty, I am writing this from memory so the details are sketchy (red bicycle is for real).

I sent the instructions to his assistant, who quickly called me back.

"Are you out of your fucking mind?" she snapped. "I can't put this on his itinerary."

You asked!

Fortunately, this executive was known to have a good sense of humor and laughed. I was hoping the revelry would last.

"If this blows up, it's on you," the assistant warned.

No stress there!

To my great relief, he and his guests had a blast. Of course, I got no thank-you. The only gesture of gratitude came from me...to my new friend Timo. He got a bottle of Macallan.

Q&A WITH SOPHIA PAULMIER

Sophia: If you like Dorothy Draper, you'd love the foyer in my apartment.

Jeremy: The Carlyle is the only work of hers I've ever liked. That green/pink/purple watermelon aesthetic she used everywhere else is hideous.

S: You spent Christmas in Paris organizing the trip for a "higher up." Did they ever thank you for their trip?

J: I never got thanked. You don't get thanked for anything in Hollywood, including organ transplants, providing alibis for talent, and doing your job.

S: Was the trip a success?

J: I wasn't yelled at or fired, so I consider it so.

S: Did your mom have a nice Christmas in Paris during this trip?

J: No, we were both miserable. I felt so bad. It was so stressful, I was glued to my Blackberry and coming and going the entire time.

S: Would you have planned another holiday trip for this "higher up" again if you were asked?

J: I'd rather stick a fork in my eye.

S: *You were "not to be seen" during this Christmas trip to Paris. Have you seen season two of* The White Lotus?

J: I have not. By the time this comes out, I will have.

S: *You went ghost hunting with the legendary Mary Ann Winkowski?!*

J: Yes, it was an insane idea. I was fortunate that she has a sense of humor because, in retrospect, it's a rather insulting question.

S: *Was any part of you nervous to piss off a bad spirit?*

J: No, but there was a woman on our trip who had really bad energy, which Marianne picked up on. And, according to her, the ghosts. We'd known this for years.

S: *What was the most important thing you learned on your ghost trip with Marianne Winkowski?*

J: Ghosts are not evil. They are "earth-bound spirits" who leave the body but don't cross over. They usually stay because they're scared or they need to settle some unresolved conflict.

S: *Had there been any cities or hotels that you wish could have hosted your magazine for a photoshoot?*

J: I really wanted to do something in the Seychelles. But organizing that would have been a beast.

CHAPTER 27

·············★·············

Spring Love

Beth Behrs is showered in a rain fall of rose petals at The
George V Paris. Photo by Patrick Demarchelier.

When I envisioned the magazine in 2006, it was with words. Interviews, profiles, Q&As, essays. I'd spent my career up to that point telling stories. Now, as editor, I had to *show* them.

Part of the learning curve was developing an eye. Not just for photographs, but design, text, color. I'm lucky to have had great teachers in Beth Tomkiw, Ed Mann, Kate Betts, Patrick Demarchelier, The Jackal, Christopher Campbell, and many other talents who taught me the emotional reaction is just as important as the rationale. I might not be able to express *why* an image or design affects me, but I gained confidence in recognizing it had, and I sought to understand the reason.

Sensations stay with all of us. For me, it's the feel of my cat's fur when I pet him at night. The smell of my father's Cigarillos. The taste of cashew-encrusted grouper I remember eating at the Beach Bistro when I was a starving reporter. The sound of Charlie Siem playing Paganini.

And the sight of Jeff Leatham's flowers at the George V, which affected me viscerally.

Beth Behrs with Jeff Leatham, center, and Jeremy.

I first witnessed his work in 2006 when I brought my brother to Paris for a bonding trip after our father had passed. The hotel was as stately and regal as I had read, but the explosion of color that greets you in the lobby is awe-inspiring. Jeff, a modest, self-deprecating native of Utah, explodes your mind with a kaleidoscope of the unexpected: oversized florals, color blocking, three-dimensional arrangements, mirror and glass installations, and neon accents. They are stunning in their audacity.

I arranged a quick meeting with Jeff in the lobby, and he disarmed me with his humility and graciousness. A former male model, he learned he had this talent when he began designing the lobby at the Four Seasons hotel in Beverly Hills. His adventurous, assertive, and imaginative displays captured people's attention, and acclaim. When the Four Seasons announced it was renovating the legendary George V hotel in Paris, Jeff was recruited to create the aesthetic and ambiance of its public settings. And did he ever! He is one of the few Americans to be awarded the Chevalier de l'Ordre des Arts et des Lettres, which is bestowed by the French Ministry of Culture for contributions to arts and culture.

Whether staying at the George V or not, I always went to see what Jeff had envisioned next. We got to know each other casually, and when our magazine launched Muse, he was one of the first profiles I commissioned. I remember being there when we photographed him on the hotel rooftop playing air guitar with a bouquet of roses.

Just as I was developing an eye for visuals, I was also learning to trust my instincts. What Jeff was doing wasn't just design; it was art. And the inspiration for a 2014 cover story.

The idea was deceptively simple: renewal. This was for our spring edition, and the same month we were debuting the marketing campaign with Charlie. I wanted to evoke hope, optimism, and elation, and Jeff's creativity provided the perfect aesthetic.

Jeff was game, but getting the George V to let us shoot on property took time and persuasion. The Four Seasons had become a fantastic partner, but this was their crown jewel, on par with the Hôtel

Plaza Athénée a few blocks away. I developed a relationship with its PR director Caroline Mennetrier, who appreciated the editorial we had given the hotel over the years. Once we ran the profile of Jeff, she became more receptive to something bigger. I pitched my spring concept and threw in dessert: Patrick Demarchelier.

As with any cover, we needed a worthy star. By this time, we were turning them down. With only six issues a year, our covers had become prime publicity real estate, as well as free vacations for the actors. This issue was especially important, and its theme limited our options. Television was deluged with crime scene procedurals, crass sitcoms, and tacky reality shows. Pickings were few, but one talent had already charmed us with her positivity and kindness: Beth Behrs from *2 Broke Girls*. Beth is tall, lean, blonde, and sunny, and her show had become a big hit. The George V agreed without hesitation, as did Patrick. She was the perfect complement to Jeff's whimsy.

Choosing the right stylist proved difficult. The Jackal had expanded her work beyond dressing stars, becoming a much-in-demand creative consultant, manager, and advisor. Christopher Campbell was booked for four of our other covers. And we hadn't yet met Fabio. I needed someone I trusted, and who could work confidently with Patrick and Jeff without becoming a wilting flower. Whoever we hired needed to bring their own perspective and *add* to the conversation.

Cannon was an interesting option; he already styled Josh Charles and *Entertainment Tonight* host Rob Marciano, but his earlier working dressing three actresses from *Criminal Minds* demonstrated a plucky fearlessness I hadn't seen. Still, I hadn't worked with him on a scale like this and was unsure if he was the right choice. We met several times, and I became more confident as we discussed the concept, setting, and challenge of not competing with Patrick and Jeff's visuals, rather, accentuating with *his* voice.

We also agreed it had to be Parisian but newly wondrous. Coco Chanel was not known for her embrace of color. Raised in a convent by nuns, she turned the color of their habits—black and white—into symbols of empowerment (hence, "The Little Black Dress.") The designer, and those that came after her, emphasized modernity with neutral palates, impudent sizing, and inventive uses of fabrics like tweed. Even the playfully mischievous Karl Lagerfeld respected the house DNA.

My challenge to Cannon was to prove this wrong and find vintage Chanel designs that embraced color, but not obvious or commercialized. I wanted to see if there were jackets, dresses, blouses that defied the code with color and expression.

Cannon accepted the challenge and spent weeks prowling through private collections, archives, vintage stores, even online. What he was able to pull was stupefying. He found garments in varying palates, including red, white, yellow, green, gold, and silver.

The wardrobe was mesmerizing. Patrick shot Beth with a heightened exuberance, adding a playful twist to reawakening. In one portrait, he photographed her standing in a pool of floating roses while showering her with petals. He also captured her perched on the concierge desk, legs crossed elegantly; exquisitely framed between long-stemmed lilies in the lobby; sprawled gracefully across a divan in the hotel's signature restaurant; emerging from a pool in a Chanel bikini; and standing atop the George V roof wearing a shimmery silver jacket and Chanel suspenders covering her nipples. Jeff's exquisite sense of shape and color gave each photo renascence.

The creative force behind the Beth Behrs in Paris shoot. (Left to right) author Jeremy Murphy, Beth Behrs, Patrick Demarchelier, and stylist Cannon. Photo courtesy of Jeremy Murphy.

The shoot exceeded already high expectations and put us on the radar with Chanel, which had resisted buying ad pages because we were not in their "brand neighborhood." Super P and I tried everything. Our efforts had landed Dior, Valentino, Ferragamo, Givenchy, Oscar de la Renta, and Fendi, but Chanel proved elusive.

Finally, though, we captured their attention. Super P's relentless pursuit and our stunning homage by Demarchelier had convinced their marketing team to meet with us...on their turf. We hopped on a red-eye flight to Paris and spent the next day preparing. Chanel is the Holy Grail in luxury, and this was our chance; we needed to overawe, and what better way than Chanel itself? We'd be meeting with one of their top male executives, who was known to be smart, savvy, and discerning. As a gesture of appreciation, we purchased a rare Chanel men's tie in its Rue Cambon flagship boutique and presented it as a gift. It was a cheeky choice, admittedly, but did the trick. He loved it and gave us an hour of his time, which Super P used to sell the merits of our magazine with his signature "sophistiqué."

A few weeks later we got word we'd likely be on their next media plan for fragrance, but timing worked against us. Print was in freefall and budgets were being slashed. Including us.

Still, it was an incredible experience to be in Paris, pitching a top marketing executive at the most revered brand in fashion.

Q&A WITH SOPHIA PAULMIER

> *Sophia: Who discovered Jeff Leatham first, you or the Kardashians?*
>
> Jeremy: I'm claiming credit. I'm sure my 10 Facebook followers at the time can attest.
>
> *S: Aside from the shoot with Demarchelier, have you ever worked with Jeff for an event or shoot for another client?*

J: Not with the magazine but Jeff and I continue to work together. He is so warm, funny, talented, and off-the-charts creative. My mom loves flowers and gardening, and in 2017 Jeff was appearing at a show in Palm Beach. She'd just had eye surgery but it didn't stop her from wanting to see and meet him. The photo of the three of us together is priceless: she is squinting. That's when it dawned on me; I'd taken my mother to a flower show and wasn't sure she could see the flowers. Son of the year!

S: Chanel was (and still is) very difficult to land licensing rights of use in any photographs. It contributes to the brand being so highly thought of. How do you feel with the overshare of photographs and videos on social media have affected the status of their brand today?

J: I don't think anything affects Chanel at this point. They're impenetrable. Social media has helped brands – at least those who do it right – reach audiences they never have and introduce to them a new world that inspires aspiration.

S: Had you landed the ad with Chanel how big do you feel the impact of the magazine would have changed and would it still be around today?

J: It would have given us a new luster but nothing could stop the migration of print readers to other mediums.

CHAPTER 28

★

Ghosts, Glam, and Glitz

LL Cool J and Jeremy posing in front of the Maserati, which legend
has it the star purchased. Photo courtesy of Jeremy Murphy.

NCIS: Los Angeles was about to premiere. It was the hottest show of
the season—spin-off of a huge TV hit, with LL Cool J and
Christopher O'Donnell as leads. Both were huge stars in their own
right. It was a coup for a crime show procedural to get them.

NCIS, the mother ship, was generating huge ratings. The storytelling was abysmal, but the cast was top notch—Mark Harmon, Michael

Weatherly, Cote de Pablo, Pauley Perrette, Brian Dietzen, and other great actors. Every week, they probed crimes in the military, which turned out to be the most dangerous place in America; it was the new Cabot Cove, the sleepy New England village decimated by murders that Angela Lansbury uncovered every Sunday (and so obviously committed herself).

With that many viewers, *NCIS* was natural for a spin-off. Although it doesn't have any nearby military bases, producers chose Los Angeles as a setting for the new incarnation. Everyone was buzzing about the show, which made it a shoo-in for a cover. Given its setting, we decided to shoot both stars in LA at The Peninsula, one of the most exclusive hotels. The usual cast of characters joined us—Cliff, The Jackal, me—and the concept was simple: LL and Christopher in LA. It did not take an engineering degree to figure this one out.

At the last minute, of course, Chris's publicist gave us a heads-up on an issue. He was filming on the day we were scheduled to shoot. Could he do the following? That's typically not a problem, but LL was filming that day. We could not get them together.

Rather than lose the shoot, we decided to get them separately and then Photoshop them into the same pictures. But it doubled our costs. We now had *two* shoots to pay for.

Both stars were easy; LL more friendly but Chris warms up once he feels comfortable.

For one setting, Super P had gotten Maserati to lend a very rare model of a sports car, which we damaged. LL, wearing a metal belt, leaned against the vehicle and accidentally scratched the door, which no one but Super P noticed. He worked his magic and made sure it didn't become an issue, or expense.

A few months later, Super P saw LL and reminded him of the shoot and the Maserati.

"Remember it? I bought it!" he said.

I hope it wasn't still scratched.

Soap opera actors are among my favorites to work with. They're hot, easygoing, up for anything, collaborative, and not monsters yet. When we started the magazine and had little to show for it, they were the only talent willing to work with us. As we got bigger and more successful, I still championed using the actors because I'm loyal and like to work with people who supported us.

In 2008, *As the World Turns* was still on the air and doing decently in the ratings. Daytime was dying as cable, streaming, and the internet gave people other options to watch in the afternoon. The days of Luke and Laura on *General Hospital* attracting fifteen million viewers were long gone. Soaps were lucky to get a fifth of that crowd.

Stars Ewa Da Cruz and Dylan Bruce posted as Jackie and JFK.

It was an election year, and everyone knew Obama was going to win. We were planning our Jan/Feb 2009 issue and wanted something election/inauguration-themed but couldn't be so bold as to predict the winner, even though we all knew who it would be. Instead, I searched Google to find archival images of inaugurations past—JFK and Jackie, Ronnie and Nancy, Bill and Hillary, and even George and Martha. We'd recreate the photos with a modern-day twist, using actors styled to match the photos.

As the World Turns was not known for its hotties, but there were four who'd fit the bill: Austin Peck, Terri Colombino, Ewa Da Cruz, and especially Dylan Bruce, the show's main eye-candy who turned out to be an incredible actor. He's since gone on to starring roles in Orphan Black, Heroes, Arrow, and Midnight, Texas. We became good friends for many years but lost touch during the pandemic. I still cheer for him anytime I see him in a new movie.

The Willard InterContinental in DC agreed to host our shoot, and we brought all four actors down by train to play the role of presidents and first ladies past on swearing-in day. I gave The Jackal the images to use in recreating the wardrobe, and that she did. The four actors photographed exquisitely; you don't get on soap operas if you don't. Especially the younger ones. Chiseled faces and toned bodies were requirements, acting optional.

We shot them throughout the Willard, including George and Martha Washington (Austin and Terry) in a very seductive scene in bed. Also, JFK and Jackie (Dylan and Eva) walking out of the front entrance.

The concept was novel—enough for the Washington Post to spend a day with us doing a behind-the-scenes feature on our shoot. A giant photo of Dylan and Eva made the cover of the Style section. Both leapt off the pages, especially our JFK. Had Jack looked similar, he would have banged more than Marilyn.

The actors were fun and joined us for dinners and drinks. The night after the shoot, one actor joined our crew in a Jameson drinking contest in the hotel's historic Round Robin Bar, whose space is so tight you have to suck in your stomach to get around the counter. At least we did. The actors had no issues.

Stars from *As the World Turns* recreated famous inauguration photos of presidents and first ladies past. (Left to right): Austin Peck, Terri Colombino, Jeremy, Ewa Da Cruz, and Dylan Bruce.

The bar became our hangout spot (surprise!). The day before the shoot, our staff gathered for a late lunch, but it was too late for lunch and too early for dinner. Instead, we got a surly waitress not happy to be working. We were not asking for the moon but did inquire about crackers and cheese.

She rolled her eyes, walked away, and went to the bar to discuss with her colleague. We could hear enough to decipher the best line ever.

"Bitches want cheese."

It became a catchphrase the rest of the shoot. So much so, we made a rap song out of it.

The feature turned out great. In addition to the *Washington Post*, *Capitol File* did a huge photo spread, and a local network affiliate aired behind-the-scenes video.

As the World Turns was cancelled two years later, but the memory of that shoot lives on.

On our first shoot in Paris, with *NCIS* star Michael Weatherly, we had a minimal crew and no producer. Or permits. We went commando in how we used the monuments as backdrops, including one of the fountains in the Place de la Concorde, a historic square in the middle of Paris most known for the site of Marie Antoinette's beheading. There are worse places to be decapitated.

Actor Michael Weatherly in front of the Fountain Concorde, which The Jackal, our stylist, quartered off: even from Parisians.

Crafted out of marble and bronze sculptures, the fountains are breathtaking in their majesty, attracting a lot of tourists, as well as local Parisians walking through the square.

The Jackal, photographer John Filo, and I whisked Michael across the street for the image, but there was a sizeable crowd blocking our vantage. We had a specific angle we needed Michael to be in that didn't include spectators.

The Jackal blocked it off, much to the chagrin of the French observers.

"Vous ne pouvez faire ça! La fontaine n'est pas à vous!" ("You cannot do this! The fountain is not yours!") a man shouted angrily.

The Jackal, who spoke French, was nonplussed.

"C'est aujourd'hui!" she yelled back.

"It is today."

Ian Somerhalder starred on the CW drama *The Vampire Diaries*, and his twinkle-in-the-eye mischief as bad boy bloodsucker Damon Salvatore brought humor and levity into the teenage sci-horror soap opera. He stole every scene, and so did his cheek bones. A former male model, Ian is head-turning hot. You cannot look away. We did several shoots with him, including in Atlanta, where the series filmed. I'd met the actor several times and I knew him to be relaxed and easygoing. For someone so good-looking, you'd expect a degree of arrogance, but he emitted none. Ian is just a cool dude. I knew just who to use for the shoot: London photographer Ian Derry, who brings British swagger to every shoot. I knew they'd click (pardon the pun), and they did.

Modesty aside, the best photo to come out of the shoot includes me sitting next to the actor in a Tesla.

Ian Somerhalder with Jeremy in Atlanta. Photo by Ian Derry.

***

In a previous chapter, I wrote about "ghostbusting" with the real-life ghost whisperer Marianne Winkowski, whose life and abilities formed the basis for the popular drama series. I left out my own busting experience at home.

In 2005, after my father passed, life returned to a new version of normalcy by September. Until it didn't. I began experiencing weird sensations and events in my apartment: sudden drops in temperature, shadows racing across reflections in pictures hanging on my walls, furniture moved randomly. The last straw came when something grabbed my leg in the middle of the night.

Oh, hell no. I never believed in ghosts. I don't buy into the hippie-dippie spiritual bullshit. Instead, I wear my cynical, sarcastic gay badge with honor. But shit was getting weird in my apartment, and I needed answers. I convinced the publicist who handled *The Ghost Whisperer* to put me in touch with Marianne, who could not have been nicer (this was before our ghostbusting adventure). After telling her what I'd been experiencing, she instructed me to call her landline that evening—from a landline phone in my home—and leave a two-minute message on her answering machine.

This sounded ridiculous, but so did the whole thing. I did as I was told, then returned to work the next morning doubtful anything would be resolved.

My phone rang, and it was Marianne.

"You have a ghost," she confirmed. "You were in your kitchen when you called, and he was standing behind you. Then he raced upstairs and hid behind a leather club chair in the left corner of your bedroom."

What. The. Fuck. I did not tell her anything about my apartment, including having two levels.

My options were limited. I could fly Marianne to New York, but that would have been prohibitively expensive—even ghost whisperers don't want to fly coach. Nor do, I imagine, the ghosts.

I was left to several options, the first being to have my home blessed by a priest.

The last time I went to church, my skin began to melt. As a lapsed Catholic, I'm the last person who should call a member of the clergy. When I was a kid, my mom dragged us to Saint Andrew's for Sunday mass, and I spent the service causing my usual mischief, including tying people's shoelaces together as I crawled under the pews. Years later, in after-school Jesus lessons, I got nabbed hiding *People* magazine inside my "Jesus Loves You" workbook. In my defense, it was the "50 Most Beautiful People" issue and Cher was on the cover.

I called around to churches around the Upper East Side, who were outraged I'd even ask for something so outrageous.

"Hi, I know I haven't attended mass in fifteen years, and I might in fact be the demon seed, but could a priest come and bless my apartment so the ghost will leave?"

It's sad when even someone at church hangs up on you.

I finally got a church in a less wealthy zip code to come in exchange for a cash donation. The priest came on a dark, rainy Saturday morning that began to feel like a scene from *The Omen*. The lightning and thunder were violent, as was the wind. Perfect atmosphere for an exorcism, or however they rid homes of evil.

"Would you like the blessing in English or Latin?" he asked.

A question I get regularly.

The sound of the lightning grew more and more intense, as did I.

"Latin," I said.

Why the fuck not? I'd come this far.

He put on a sash and lit sage or something to that effect and began walking through my apartment, chanting prayers in Latin that sounded creepier each second. I expected Linda Blair to pop up any moment.

The smoke from the sage filled the apartment, and he began flinging holy water in various directions.

"Over there! Over there!" I instructed him. "Don't miss that corner."

I was stage directing a priest in where to splash the blessed water throughout my home.

You cannot make this shit up.

The ghost left but returned a few days later. This time, Marianne suggested I try myself. She sent her own sage sticks, which I lit and filled my apartment with its smoke.

It worked. The ghost left.

The next time I saw her, I asked if she ever knew who it was.

She smiled.

"It came with your father," she replied.

The ghost had been following him, and when he moved in with me, it stayed.

I found this creepy but amusing, and it inspired an idea for a sit-com: Katzper, the Jewish ghost who doesn't want to leave the Upper East Side.

Q&A WITH SOPHIA PAULMIER

Sophia: Favorite actor on NCIS?

Jeremy: I think Michael Weatherly and Cote de Pablo. Their characters were so unique, and there was genuine chemistry between them.

S: I love Scent of a Woman. What's your favorite Chris O'Donnell film?

J: I'd agree about *Scent of a Woman*. It's a brilliant film, and that scene where Pacino and Gabrielle Anwar do the tango is a classic film moment.

S: If you could travel the world with a personal trainer, a stylist, or a chief, which would you choose?

J: Stylist for sure. The trainer would be stuck hanging with the chef making low-calorie kale while the stylist and I went shopping.

S: LL's metal belt scratched the Maserati during the shoot. Was this the belt he's photographed wearing next to the car in the magazine?

J: Yes, it was a new model delivered to us for the shoot.

S: Which president was your favorite to recreate for the photo?

J: JFK and Jackie. The actors—Dylan and Ewa—captured the "Camelot" sensation in the portrait. Plus, Dylan is unnaturally handsome, and Ewa is a classic beauty.

S: *Which shoot do you think was The Jackal's personal favorite, and who did they favor to style?*

J: I think Pauley Perrette in the impressionist paintings was a favorite for everyone. It was our first time doing a big glamour shoot in Paris and shooting at the Hôtel Plaza Athénée. Pauley was incredible and collaborative, and people brought their A-game. It was a love fest, and we all felt we were creating something really special.

S: *This ghost you felt in your apartment...did it ever haunt you again?*

J: Maybe. I had a really stressful week in January of 2010 and felt a weird energy again, but I was not in the mood and screamed "Go the fuck away."

S: *Did it make you more creeped out or more aware of the spiritual world?*

J: More aware, for sure.

S: *Have you come in contact with any other ghosts since then?*

J: Not that I know of, but I swear some people I worked with came from Satan.

S: *Favorite ghost film?*

J: *The Sixth Sense.*

CHAPTER 29

★

Swan Song

NCIS star Pauley Perrette in the St. Regis King Cole Bar.
Photo by Patrick Demarchelier.

I stumbled upon a niche: making iconic images and paintings modern with TV stars. After Pauley Perette (*NCIS*) recreating impressionist French paintings in Paris and *Big Bang Theory*'s Kaley Cuoco as Madonna in "Justify My Love," I was hungry for another challenge. I'd be reading a lot about socialite Babe Paley, who was one of the glamorous "swans" author Truman Capote swanned about. Mind you, this was 2011—thirteen years before Ryan Murphy expertly captured their relationship in the FX drama *Feud: Truman vs. The Swans*. For the first time in my life, I was ahead of the curve; normally, I'm on the side of the curve disparaging it with clever bon mots and a cocktail.

Pauley proved the perfect muse, and I was eager to work with her again. The actress epitomizes cool, and her lithe figure and porcelain skin are a photographer's dream. She had become a friend, as had her best friends Darren Greenblatt and Sam Hunt, who joined us on the first photo shoot in Paris.

For an unexplainable reason, I could not get Pauley out of my head as I imagined Babe Paley. They could not be more different. Babe was a socialite married to a media baron—privileged, pampered, perfumed. Pauley, conversely, drove a used car stocked with food for homeless people. She wore vintage clothing on red carpets, drank Bud Select out of bottles, and recoiled at luxury. When I suggested buying her a Louis Vuitton purse for doing our first shoot, Darren suggested a donation to the Los Angeles Food Harvest charity instead. I sent $1,000.

The dichotomy intrigued me. I loved twisting the narrative. Pauley took a minute to decide but saw in it, too, something outlandish and whimsical.

Were we celebrating or mocking this rarefied moment in society? I loved the contradiction.

After putting Pauley in tutus in Paris, I knew The Jackal was the perfect person to bring this insane idea to life. And Patrick Demarchelier, who was photographing *Vogue* covers, could capture the "ladies who lunched" in societal context. Babe, with her husband, William, kept a suite at The St. Regis in midtown, which I thought the perfect setting. The hotel is revered with people who can afford to revere, and they had a very astute PR rep named Meg Connolly, who smartly surmised these photos could go viral.

I selfishly scheduled the shoot the weekend of my birthday so Pauley, Darren, and Sam could come, as well as actor friends Dylan Bruce, who starred on *Orphan Black*, and Jay Jablonski, the lead on the hit independent film *Everybody Wants to be Italian*. The night before the shoot, everyone gathered in the apartment of Matt Merrell, a tastemaker/designer/model, who prepared an incredible gourmet dinner with his friend Lexi Tavel that we ate communal-style on a long, indoor picnic-like table. It was so joyous a gathering and the perfect precursor to an incredible experience.

Pauley, center, with colleagues Super P, left, and Jeremy, right.
Photo courtesy of Jeremy Murphy.

Shoot day started flawlessly. The Jackal had not only pulled a rabbit out of her hat, but a unicorn, leprechaun, and lotto ticket. When Demarchelier saw the wardrobe she had pulled, he smiled profusely and whispered "voila" under his breath.

Pauley *became* Babe Paley. Not just aesthetically but capturing a subdued suffering she hid under a superficial veneer. The actress unearthed her quiet distress in a way that was intimate, revealing, but respectful. Patrick's eye caught it brilliantly. The portrait of Pauley dressed in a green suit and yellow scarf in the King Cole Bar transcends time, as do the other photographs. The one image that didn't make it was intended to be our cover: Pauley posing in front of glass-blown bulbs adorning the wall of the hotel's restaurant. Patrick's coiffeur created a very bold, chic, unexpected hairstyle, which photographed beautifully, but it was maybe too extreme for the actress, who nixed the image. I did everything I could to save the photo, including nearly sixty rounds of retouches and cover samples that nearly put one of our top editors, Sam Mittelsteadt, in a strait jacket. Pauley never asked for anything so this was an ask I was going to honor, however painful.

All the images told the story, but adding context was writer Michael Musto, who scribed an incredible profile of Babe Paley and the rarefied world she lived.

This was my third shoot with Patrick, and I knew we'd finish early. Our crew celebrated the end at the King Cole, and, as usual, a few of us raised the bar. We were keeping our equipment in one of the hotel suites, and naturally used it for a drunken game of fake laser tag, which extended to the hallway and included sound effects ("pew-pew"), somersaults, and other gymnastics.

The next morning, I anxiously watched a network morning news broadcast that covered our shoot; Pauley did an on-camera interview during her lunch break, and we were excited to drum up excitement for what we'd soon be publishing. To my horror, the story included everything *but* our magazine. There was no mention of *why* Pauley was posing as Babe Paley. I called the control room and called BS, then sent very curt emails to the producers; they ran a second, abbreviated story the next day.

I was mightily disappointed but did not let it spoil the riches we'd been given. Patrick's imagery was peerless. So much so, Super P and I knew we had to seize this opportunity to make it our own moment. We slotted it as our 2011 September issue—the most important of the year—and launched a marketing campaign that included a cover wrap in *WWD*. The day the issue hit newsstands, we hosted a party at The Monkey Bar, a nostalgic restaurant in New York City that *Vanity Fair* editor Graydon Carter and his partners had turned into a rare hotspot in midtown. Super P catered to dozens of ad/marketing reps from all the top luxury brands, while I minded all the great minds we'd recruited: writers, editors, designers, photographers. Pauley also graciously appeared at the party and posed for photos for more than an hour.

The party made a few headlines, but the issue made more. The St. Regis PR rep was prescient: a story by Tribune Media Services writer Jay Bobbin about our photo shoot hit the wires and appeared in hundreds of newspapers and sites across the globe.

Q&A WITH SOPHIA PALMIER

> *Sophia: Sending money to her favorite charity instead of gifting Pauley a Louis Vuitton bag was such a kind act. Did you find that a rare thing as a celebrity ask?*

> Jeremy: Only time it's ever happened.

> *S: Having a birthday dinner attended by many actors -- did anyone improv scenes of famous lines?*

> J: I don't think so but I was probably blacked out within an hour!

> *S: Pauley truly channeled Babe Paley in these photos at the King Cole Bar. Did she enjoy this shoot as much as you did?*

> J: Yes, very much so. It was a rarefied experience. There was a timeless feeling about the whole day, like we were winding back the clock but through a modern lens.

S: Has Pauley reached out to you about this shoot since the announcement of Ryan Murphy's new show, and did she use these photos to be considered for the role of Babe Paley?

J: I haven't talked to Pauley in a while. I have no idea if she was considered for the role, but it would have been brilliant casting!

S: What's your impression of Feud: Capote Vs. the Swans?

J: I'm five episodes in. It has a heaviness I didn't expect. None of the characters are particularly likeable.

S: What was the asking price to rent out the King Cole Bar for a photo shoot?

J: We did it before it opened! Patrick shoots very fast so we were never pressed for time.

S: Laser tag in the hallways of a five-star hotel sounds fun. Who thought of this idea, you or Pauley Perrette?

J: She wasn't involved. It was just our crew after a very long shoot and a lot of drinks. We generally tried to keep talent away from trouble.

S: Along with the press coverage on the morning news, this shoot sounded like a defining moment for you and the magazine. Would you say this is when you discovered the magazine's niche?

J: We'd done a few recreations but this brought it to a new level. We bought a huge cover wrap in WWD to celebrate the milestone, then threw a huge party at The Monkey Bar. The entire experience was wistful.

CHAPTER 30

★

From Doubt to Decade

Buster Poindexter brought the house down at the *Watch* magazine's 10th anniversary party.

Ten Fucking Years.

We'd made it. Against all odds, our magazine survived. We'd done photo shoots around the world; hired the best photographers, stylists, makeup and hair artists, and talent; and had the most glamourous hotels as our settings. Not to mention the advertisers we'd signed: Dior, Ferragamo, Tom Ford, Oscar de la Renta, Givenchy, Valentino, Armani, Ritz-Carlton, Mercedes, and more.

I wanted to celebrate the milestone because who knew if we'd see twenty? No magazine was thriving at that point. Print was dying.

We needed to change the narrative with something big, the kind of event people talk about long after it happens. New York Fashion Week was scheduled for February 2016, and that seemed the perfect opportunity given the inroads we'd made with advertisers. Of course, getting something like that approved would be impossible. Belts were being tightened, expenses questioned, budgets not approved. A party seemed frivolous to many. To me, it was important to show how far we'd come. I just needed the budget—*someone else's*.

We had a working relationship with a fashion week magazine called *The Daily Front Row*, which covered all the shows, designers, models, parties, and media. The editorial is fun—colorful, sassy, engaging, and witty. It doesn't take itself too seriously, which is why everyone in fashion reads it. *The Daily*, as it's known, is owned and operated by a shrewd, no-nonsense but kind woman named Brandusa Niro, who is also creative and entrepreneurial. She likes a big idea as much as me, and I knew she'd be receptive.

My pitch was a bit unconventional. I proposed *The Daily* doing a big package in their print edition celebrating our anniversary, and we'd sell the ads. With those proceeds, *The Daily* would also throw us a party. Brandusa was intrigued but not sure we could pull it off. We'd need to raise almost $100K in ad revenue to pay for everything. I wanted this badly, so I went to work with Super P; together, we got vendors, divisions of our parent company, and sponsors to buy pages congratulating us on the anniversary.

Money in hand, *The Daily* went about planning the special issue and party. We nixed a couple of locations, but the Gramercy Park Hotel caught our interest. For a long stretch, it was the hottest spot in NYC. Designed by Ian Schrager and Julian Schnabel, the property featured dark interiors, high-backed chairs, a giant metal chandelier, and red velvet banquettes. The aroma from the lobby fireplace completed the cozy ambiance. Owner Aby Rosen filled its walls with priceless pieces from his art collection, including a room filled with Andy Warhol paintings on the rooftop.

I knew we were in good hands with Brandusa and went about dreaming other stunts to herald our ten-year survival.

The first was obvious: a special edition of *our* magazine, which included a cover story with *NCIS* star Michael Weatherly in London, and then an oral history about the publication from its inception to anniversary. Hud Morgan talked to everyone to get their memories, and he put together a fantastic story that captured the experience. What was interesting was reading between the lines of some of the quotes. We'd still been plagued with naysayers who did not want us to succeed, and their contributions to the story must have been made through gritted teeth.

My next idea was also celebratory. We had made a name for ourselves with our covers, usually shot by top editorial photographers, and this presented another opportunity to showcase the quality of our editorial. My idea was to create eight-foot-tall installations of our four favorite covers and position them throughout the lobby of our building. It sounded insane, but most of my ideas were. I scoured online to find a company that could produce this kind of installation and found a firm called Ralph Appelbaum & Associates, which created exhibits for museums and other venues. They loved the idea and agreed to work with us, and for two months we went through our archives to find the four best covers. We settled on three by Patrick Demarchelier (Bridget Moynahan, Beth Behrs, and Julianna Margulies) and one by Art Streiber (the cast of *The Talk*). In addition to a giant, blown-up image of the cover, we added text to give the backstory: who, what, when, where, yadda yadda yadda, as well as quotes from our staff about the experience. Of course, this got political; a couple people on our team were pissed that their quotes weren't used. I couldn't give two fucks at this point. What Ralph Appelbaum & Associates created was breathtaking, and a big hit with the company, visitors, and media. We even did a time lapse video of the exhibits being built.

With party, special issue of our magazine, *The Daily*, and the cover exhibit in place, I wanted to cap off the week-long celebration with something refined and exclusive. We had begun doing salons for advertisers and VIPs to come and hear/talk to artists, musicians, and authors in a private setting at The Surrey hotel. They provided the penthouse, and we worked with the Cornelia spa and beauty brand to make sure it was filled with A-list speakers and guests. In two years, we'd hosted opera singer Iestyn Davies, commentator/speaker Fran Lebowitz, and author Kate Betts. Advertisers loved attending our salons because they were intimate and gave them face time with our honored guests. I especially loved doing salons because someone at the company hated the whole concept. He constantly tried to sabotage our events, which had the adverse effect: people started paying attention. The Surrey and Cornelia loved the idea of doing another salon, and we lined up my friend Charlie Siem to perform, doing a Q&A with fashion star Derek Blasberg, and answering questions from the audience.

The week kicked off on February 4, 2016, with the special issue of *The Daily* celebrating us. Included in the twenty-plus pages were the ads we sold, an oral history of the magazine, and features on our stars, including Super P and Christopher Campbell. Mark Mann also took a staff photo of us on an elaborate newsroom set Marla Weinhoff created.

The party came Tuesday night, and what a whirlwind that was. Charlie Siem was our main attraction, and he and a twelve-person orchestra played the song he'd written and performed for the magazine. We also debuted our new brand video featuring his music, B-roll from photo shoots, and narration by Julianna Margulies. At the entrance, guests walked down a red carpet, and the celebrities who came posed in front of paparazzi standing behind a banner with our logo. There were hors d'oeuvres, open bars, great music, and a crowd that grew to over two hundred people. The big surprise came at the end: I secretly arranged for Buster Poindexter to close out the party with his band. "Buster" was the persona of David Johansen, lead singer of the '70s band the New York Dolls. David morphed into the martini-swilling, cigar-chomping lounge singer with a pompadour that reached the sky. He starred in the '80s Christmas movie *Scrooged* and had a hit single "Hot Hot Hot" later in the decade. At the time, Buster was performing at Café Carlyle, and I took a colleague to see his act, which was equal parts cabaret, jazz, and commentary. At the end, he started a conga line to "Hot Hot Hot" that went around the room. Naturally, I was first in line.

This is how I wanted to close out the party. I reached out to his wife, who was his manager, and hired him to perform. The rate was less than I imagined, which made it better.

As the night ended, Buster hit the stage and got everyone dancing and singing, and then he ended his set with a conga line around the Gramercy Park rooftop. To this day, people remind me what a magical moment it was. *Who the fuck gets to walk a conga line with Buster Poindexter?* More special was doing it with my mom, who had flown in for the party.

Buster closed out the night with a conga line to "Hot Hot Hot" around the
rooftop of the Gramercy Hotel. Photo courtesy of Jeremy Murphy.

I've always had a problem living in the moment. It's not until later that I realize how much I enjoyed an experience, and then I get sad it's over. I've been this way my entire life; my mind always wants to know what's next, next, next. On this night, I was *in it* and laughed uproariously. I can say it was one of the most fun nights of my life. It was a strange sensation standing there, seeing a room filled with love, supporters, history. All the struggles, setbacks, disappointments, petty grievances, and trouble I caused vanished for those few hours. I finally felt joy. The hard work we'd all put in was worth it.

Later in the week, we held the salon with Cornelia and The Surrey, and Charlie was mesmerizing and gave a terrific interview with Derek. Our guests were also "in the moment."

Our "event-ized" anniversary ended that Thursday, and Friday was a breather for our staff. I took most of them out to Serafina, an Italian restaurant on Madison Avenue, and we toasted the week over wine and pizza. I also gifted my publisher with race car cufflinks.

The week was finally over, but so was an era. At least for me. I knew my time was ending—see chapter thirty-two—and this was the perfect way to bookend an incredible ride.

Jeremy in front of one of the photo exhibits for the magazine's 10th anniversary. Photo courtesy of Jeremy Murphy.

Q&A WITH SOPHIA PAULMIER

Sophia: Prior to this big fucking party, had you been a guest to any other magazine parties in the past, and did they have an influence on you for yours?

Jeremy: Yeah, several. When budgets were big and you could drink and be wild without the fear of HR tasing you for telling someone they're attractive. Those days are sadly over.

S: Did you have any gift bags or giveaways for the anniversary party?

J: Yes! We put in our anniversary issue, copies of *The Daily Front Row* that featured our milestone, moisturizer from Kiehl's, and gift cards to various entertainment subscriptions.

S: When was the first time you met with Brandusa Nero and The Daily Front Row?

J: In 2011, we bought a cover wrap in *WWD*, which put us on her radar. She called, we met, and she sold me on a spread in one of the issues distributed during that year's fashion week.

S: Did Kate Betts give you any critique, compliments, or advice on your magazine?

J: Once she began doing her "Best Betts" column, we established a very positive and friendly working relationship. So much so, I asked her to critique every issue before publication. I'd bring the layouts to a chosen restaurant for lunch, and she'd offer suggestions on how to improve every page. For some reason, I remember doing this at Locanda Verde, Robert De Niro's restaurant in TriBeCa. Kate's insight was invaluable. She was constructive in her feedback, but also kind and funny. I miss working with her.

S: *Same question but about Derek Blasberg.*

J: He was unique. I wanted someone with fashion cred, and Derek had made a name for himself by then. I reached out blindly, and we offered him a nice paycheck. I also wrote the questions for him, which he read verbatim. Nice work if you can get it.

S: *Iestyn Davies has such a beautiful voice, did you have the honor of having him perform at one of your exclusive gatherings?*

J: Yes! He did one of our earlier salons, where he sang, answered questions, and schmoozed.

S: *As the lights dimmed, giant flat screens debuted the video to much applause. What was that moment like for you?*

J: It was a "pinch me" moment. A decade of memories in a two-minute video that encapsulated the experience in its entirety. We made great effort to plan its presentation, from the equipment to the positioning, sound, and timing.

S: *Buster Poindexter closed out the party with a conga line. Could anything ever live up to this moment?*

J: Nope. It was a moment in time. I feel incredibly fortunate to have experienced it.

S: *In that moment, did you feel like every up and down, every roadblock, every setback, every rude greeting, and every overspending anxiety was worth it?*

J: I always felt that way because we produced something tangible you can hold in your hands. Every struggle was made better once the latest issue came out. The party was on a grander scale, and it felt like a bookend to a crazy ride. It wound up exactly that.

S: *Would you do it all again tomorrow? And if so, would you change anything?*

J: I don't have that kind of energy, sadly. I was young, wide-eyed, not yet cynical, and bursting with ideas and dreams. Also in the right place at the right time. You can't replicate that kind of experience. Now I'm old, surly, lazy, and looking forward to retirement.

CHAPTER 31

★

Crowns, Cameras, and Charges

90210 stars Matt Lanter and Jessica Lowndes as Queen
Elizabeth and Prince Philip. Photo by Ian Derry.

I always knew if a photo shoot would work by the energy on set, and
the first setup by the photographer. You just feel it. A creative concept, a photographer who understands it, and the right setting brings
an idea to life before your eyes. One such instance was when we recreated iconic photos of a young Queen Elizabeth and Prince Phillip. We'd
developed a niche doing these types of features—Babe Paley, presidential inaugurations, etc.—and anything royal always excites Americans

(except Meghan and Harry; enough already). I found very rare images of the couple through stock agencies, and then enlisted London's most legendary hotel, The Dorchester, to host.

Choosing which talent to use was also easy. Matt Lanter from the CW's *90210* remake had become a favorite of our magazine, and his costar, Jessica Lowndes, was interested and available to play Lizzie. Our sponsorship with American Airlines was coming to a close, but I got this last one in. Barely. There weren't enough tickets to bring a whole crew, so we hired locally. Ian Derry, who photographed Rachelle Lefevre for us later, liked the concept but knew the challenges. Recreating photos from the late '30s through the early '50s was going to be tough. Where the fuck do you get tiaras, swords, sashes, and other regalia? Ian said he'd do it but asked that we use London stylist Sarah Nash, who also worked for us many times later. Sarah recreated every photo with wardrobe spectacularly, as did Ian, who captured the sense of time and history with each setup. The Dorchester was the consummate setting and host. We had no problem matching backgrounds to the photos. And Matt and Jessica embraced their roles with perfection.

The images were mind-blowing; how similar they look—even today—is eerie.

Going back to NY, I was excited to package this whole feature. Normally it would include profiles of the actors, but the story was the story: Queen and Prince. I hired Kate Betts to write an essay on the sovereign's influence on style; to my great surprise, Kate was effusive, which in hindsight is deserved.

"But her unswerving style is part of her message of consistency. And there is certainly a degree of comfort in her lack of spontaneity," she wrote with flawless and elegant perspective. "When she visited New York in the summer of 2010, even 103-degree heat could not melt the rigorous style favored by this mother of all style icons. In her floral print suit, matching hat and sturdy black pumps, she addressed the United Nations, laid a wreath at Ground Zero and walked through the British Garden in Hanover Square to pay her respects to the families of the 9/11 victims—all without breaking a sweat. When the heat index hit

106, she didn't change outfits—as some public officials might have—for another appearance. With her regal poise and stately sophistication, she remains the ultimate style icon."

The feature ran in our big summer travel issue, accompanying the *2 Broke Girls* shoot in Milan, and created more buzz for the novel concepts we'd been producing.

Being shameless, I sent copies of the issue to Buckingham Palace; a friend had gotten me the contact info for someone in their press office, and I dutifully sent it Federal Express to London. A month later, I got an official letter from the Queen's Lord Chamberlain thanking us for the feature. I heard offline her Majesty saw it herself, and smiled.

It was time for a press check, which is an inspection of where our magazine was printed. Somewhere in Virginia. Truth was, I didn't give a shit. What was I checking? The ink? Paper? Drug tests for the operators? It always seemed like a useless exercise, which is why I avoided it up to that point. But in 2009, I found out that a five-star hotel and restaurant I'd longed to visit, The Inn at Little Washington, was nearby. What a perfect excuse to start caring! A colleague and I visited the big printing facility, buried deep in the Virginia countryside, and it was as bland and boring as could be. Very cute, though, how important they thought we were when they also printed *Time*, *People*, and *US Weekly*—magazines with far more readers. After a couple of hours feigning interest, we drove to The Inn, and it was as fabulous as I imagined. It's housed in an old gas station/garage restored into a charming, cozy retreat with a Michelin-star restaurant and eighteen rooms designed by London set designer Joyce Evans, who's filled it with hand-painted murals, whimsical sculptures, artwork, decorative frescoes, flowers, and plush furnishings. We stayed overnight and had dinner in its award-winning restaurant, helmed by celebrated chef Patrick O'Connell. After ordering off a well-curated menu, a server approached our table with two bags of popcorn. "We always believed dinner is theater," he said. "Enjoy the show." That we did.

Anyone who's traveled with talent will tell you to always remember their hotel room number. For emergencies, naturally—like covering up your bar bill. They don't even read the room bill because they aren't paying, and talent expenses rarely get questioned. And if it does, let them take one for the team, like one actor did in 2009. He had gone with us overseas and never cared to join our crew for drinks and laughs. Who cares, he'd have ruined the mood anyway (read: zzzzzz). It didn't stop us from signing the bar bill to his room every night. The amount got so high, the bill was questioned by a bean counter back home, who was owed the truth: the actor had a very serious drinking problem, but that was his journey and we needed to respect his time and privacy.

✧ ✧ ✧

Nancy O'Dell is as close to a Barbie doll as you can get: tall, lean, gorgeous blonde mane, golden tan, flawless skin, and a bubbly personality. She was a natural to replace Mary Hart as a cohost on *Entertainment Tonight*. I'd heard really good things about Nancy, which made her a natural to do a fashion shoot. I commissioned a crew—photographer Pavel Havlicek, writer Ali Prato—but was told Nancy wanted to use the wardrobe stylist from *ET*. She looks good in anything, so I wasn't overly concerned, but I was a bit miffed I couldn't bring The Jackal.

ET tapes in Los Angeles, which sucked. Especially where we ended up.

The Ritz-Carlton inside The Staples Center, a giant sports/stadium/restaurant/bar/hotel complex that had recently opened as a way to revitalize downtown LA, home to the country's largest skid row. What a great place to lure people with Laker games and award shows! Like New York's Hudson Yards, I find the whole concept offensive, a celebration of crass commercialism and greed. The buildings have no artistic value.

The "entertainment complex" is as heinous as it sounds. It's like a giant petri dish for dumb people eager for an afternoon or night of mediocrity and carjacking. Cheesy casual dining restaurants, tacky mall shops, and theme-park accoutrements fill its concourse. I was more interested in leaving the premises to go to the movie theater across the street, where I saw "Horrible Bosses," which turned out to be the best part of that trip. And a fucking funny movie.

The pièce de résistance is a giant glass tower housing three hotels in one: the Marriott, JW Marriott, and The Ritz-Carlton, none of whom deserved such a prison. It was the last place I wanted to do a photo shoot, but our options were slim, and the hotel was offering to host our whole crew and give us the run of the building.

Beggars can't be choosers.

I hated it from the moment we arrived. There were so many doors that required swiping your room key, it began to resemble a hospital ward. My room was spacious but nondescript; no sense of place except views of I-10. That's not in the brochure.

The room also had a bathroom covered in mirrors. I know people from LA like to look at themselves, but I don't. Not like that.

The "signature restaurant" was an Asian fusion venue, whatever that means. I'm not a fan and was pissed that its only restaurant didn't have continental fare: would it kill them to cut a steak? To eat a real-person meal, a foreign concept in Los Angeles, admittedly, you had to go down to the concourse where guests of all three hotels could sample micro-waved fare at an assortment of grills, taverns, ale houses, and whatever else they choose to call themselves.

This shoot should have been easy: Nancy in a hotel wearing designer dresses and outfits, but it was further complicated by the *ET* stylist who wanted us to shoot *her*. For what purpose, I don't know, but she brought a closet full of clothes, shoes, handbags, jewelry—more than Nancy. She overwhelmed us with her needs instead of the talent's.

Making it more complicated, the executive producer of *ET* wanted us to photograph her with her niece and write about how she'd mentored the young woman. In an entertainment magazine. I knew there was some kind of ulterior motive, but I was too distracted to care.

After shooting the *ET* stylist for what seemed like eons, Nancy came ready to shoot. But she's a perfectionist. Makeup and hair monopolized much of our time. The irony is she didn't need it: the woman is a knockout.

Finding places to shoot in this Habitrail of a hotel proved challenging; there were few. And we were hours behind schedule.

There was also a weird thing with "body butter." A makeup stylist covered Nancy in this orange cream that made her tanner. Again, unneeded. For anyone.

The cream wound up leaving an imprint on multiple pieces of furniture, which we'd have to pay for.

An all-day shoot with ten setups turned to five. Even the rooftop pool shot proved difficult; we missed the sun. Pavel had to shoot her in the dark.

We finished, but no one was in a mood to celebrate. We were tired and stressed.

Back in New York, I saw the artwork and was impressed with what little Pavel was able to get.

I never heard feedback from anyone and didn't know if it was even read.

Q&A WITH SOPHIA PAULMIER

Sophia: What's the Dorchester like?

Jeremy: Very English! But with a gloss that bridges tradition with modernity. It's a walk-through time.

S: Did you get afternoon tea while at the Dorchester?

J: Yes! I felt very posh!

S: How did it feel hearing the Queen smiled at your reenactment photos of her and Phillip?

J: That was secondhand information but I'll take it! I remember getting the letter from Buckingham Palace at my desk and couldn't believe what they'd sent. It's not something you get every day!

S: Go-to bar in Los Angeles?

J: The older I get, more I want cozy, comfort, and class. I don't need Nicki Minaj blaring or $50 roof top Cosmopolitans. The lounge at The Hotel Bel-Air is my favorite.

S: Describe Nancy O'Dell with a few words.

J: I didn't get a lot of time to really get to know her. She was friendly but focused. It was very much a "let's do this" feeling, even though hair and make-up took forever. I thought that was interesting because she didn't need a thing. I saw her on arrival and she was flawless.

CHAPTER 32

⋯⋯⋯★⋯⋯⋯

Out with a Bang!

(Left to right) Allison Janney, Jeremy Murphy, and Anna Faris. The last photo shoot Jeremy oversaw during his tenure. Photo courtesy of Jeremy Murphy.

By 2016, the winds upending magazines had reached hurricane-like strength. In just the previous few years, Condé Nast folded *Details*, decapitated the top leadership of *Allure* (including its founding editor, Linda Wells), and closed *Lucky*, its once red-hot shopping magazine. Bauer ended the run of laddie chronicle *FHM*. And Hearst, the best-managed company, wasn't immune to the trend.

The days with six-figure photo shoots were coming to an end. High-priced photographers were not en vogue, or in *Vogue*. I'd spent ten years making the magazine happen, and now it was fleeting. I did not want to go backwards; it's not in my DNA.

Better to go out like a lion, and I wanted a roar.

At the same time, I'd taken a pitch by an incredible studio publicist from the new-ish TV comedy called *Mom*. The series starred Anna Faris and Allison Janney in a three-generation family living under the same roof, two of whom were recovering alcoholics. Created by Chuck Lorre (*Two and a Half Men*, *The Big Bang Theory*, etc.), the writing was razor-sharp, clever, and featured perfectly executed dialogue by Anna and Allison.

I'd grown up watching *The West Wing* and loved C. J. Cregg, the sarcastic, occasionally clumsy White House press secretary played brilliantly by Allison, who went on to win numerous Emmys, and deservedly so. And Anna captured my heart in comedies like *The House Bunny*, *Take Me Home Tonight*, and the *Scary Movie* series, which spoofed the horror genre (specifically *Scream*). Anna could play dumb and kooky but with a wink and smile. You couldn't help but root for her.

They were naturals for a big glossy photo shoot, and what better destination than Paris? By this time, we'd done ten covers in the City of Lights and knew the destination well. We also had a great relationship with Hôtel Plaza Athénée, which hosted most of them. Their PR rep Isabelle Maurin, still my "Flawless Friend," invited us eagerly.

This would be the last time we could spend properly, and we used it to assemble an all-star crew including Demarchelier, Christopher Campbell, Bruno Weppe for hair, Rafael Pita for makeup, Hud Morgan to write the story, and two male models to play catnip for the actresses. Choosing Bobby Konjic for this was a given. Picking the other was an assignment I savored. My first pick was Bertil Espegren, a Norwegian who moonlighted as an artistic director, specifically furniture. I'd bought several pieces from him, including a leather club chair he found at a vintage market in Paris, and grew to admire his sagacity. Unfortunately, our dates conflicted. Bobby suggested his friend Johannes Huebl, another in-demand face who's become a tastemaker and budding designer. Johannes took a bit of convincing but was worth the effort.

Jeremy, middle, with Johannes Huebl, left, and Robert Konjic, right. Photo courtesy of Jeremy Murphy.

Our concept for the shoot was simple: Allison and Anna would play besties enjoying a weekend getaway, and the models would be their dessert. I didn't want anything overly complicated or, frankly, hard. It was a free trip to Paris in a super chic hotel.

It should have been a breeze, but when the weather is too nice, it's sometimes the calm before the storm. This sure was.

The first indication came when the cars for the New York team didn't arrive at the airport to bring them to the hotel. I was taking thirteen people to Paris for the shoot, and that morning, I started getting messages from very annoyed passengers who'd just flown overnight. Then, on the walk-through of the hotel, the schedule was nowhere to found except on someone's iPad. As if we could all telepathically read the screen. I could tell Patrick was nonplussed. Isabelle, thankfully, had the front desk make copies.

That same morning, the actresses came at different times, which complicated the room assignments. Anna and Allison were supposed to each get a grand suite, but Allison arrived earlier than expected, and her room wasn't ready yet. Instead, a crew member told the front desk to give her a smaller one.

That is a no-no when you're traveling with more than one star of equal ranking. Everything has to be equal, from room size to airline cabin, quality of wardrobe, and overall experience. Otherwise, the one who gets less also gets cranky. In such situations, you offer them a drink, lunch, and spa treatment until their intended room is ready.

Luckily, Allison was cool, but a rep on her team in Los Angeles was not. They went online, compared the grand suites' square footage, and let loose a tirade that could have blown over the Eiffel Tower. On me. Allison never heard any of this and would have been mortified to know.

There was a weird intensity among our crew. Everyone was super tense. To break the ice, I arranged a dinner with the team—a ritual dating back to our first shoot in Paris with *NCIS* star Michael Weatherly—but even over Châteauneuf-du-Pape, people were stiff. The conversation around the table was short and uninteresting. No one was enjoying the experience.

It would get less enjoyable.

The next day, our first setup was set in the lobby of the Plaza Athénée, signaling the girls' arrival to Paris. Our time—9:00–10:00 a.m.—was set in stone because international guests tend to arrive in the 10:00 a.m. hour after overnight flights, and the hotel did not want our shoot to affect their check-in.

Patrick was not as enthusiastic and playful as he had been.

"Who iz ze star?" he asked, growing impatient, and rightfully so.

His team had set up the lights and equipment, and Christopher brought the women down from the wardrobe suite; each looked ooh-la-la in French couture. Everything seemed on point except one small thing: the Louis Vuitton trunks we rented as props had not yet arrived, delaying the start.

I'd worked with Patrick on five previous shoots, and he'd never said a cross word to me—until now. Arguably one of the most famous photographers in fashion lit into me.

Finally, everyone/thing appeared, and we got the shots at the eleventh hour, but it wasn't a great way to begin the day.

Also, I'd brought a social media person as an experiment to see what kind of on-the-fly content we could generate. It was a noble effort, but the crew found it invasive. Hilariously, the male models were the first to express concern. Given both had worked on huge campaigns, I listened intently. And fixed the problem.

For a shoot that was supposed to be easy, this was getting harder. I deputized a colleague to be shadow producer, and he finished the job expertly. But there were several shots outside the hotel, and Paris in March is cold. No one thought to bring bathrobes or coats for the actresses and models standing in the frigid air. Anna, especially, had a sleeveless dress and was shivering. Our producer, thankfully, raced to get what we needed.

The rest of the shoot had similar hiccups. The girls were rock stars, though, and brought their best. As with any Demarchelier shoot, we finished early despite the delays.

That night we met at Le Bar, the hotel's lobby lounge, and everyone just exhaled. All I wanted was a drink, to stretch, and to look at the images. The assigned "producer" had the drive in his room and was supposed to be choosing selects for us to see, and that I could send back to New York. The images never came that night.

The shoot was ending just as it had begun—on a bad note. The casual eye would not have noticed. There were no raised voices, arguments, walk-outs, slammed doors. But it was sloppy, ill-prepared, and lazy.

The person to reinforce this is the last one I expected: model Johannes, who met me for breakfast the next morning and listed point by point what an unprofessional production this was. My first instinct was to defend my team, which I did, but Johannes's feedback was honest, reasonable, and correct. He wasn't mean, petty, or out of place. Just hyper-observant, as we should have been.

This was a lot to swallow. And not something I could hide from. I'd need to make changes. I also wanted to save this trip from being hostility hotel. For once, I had the right solution.

LVMH, the company that owns Louis Vuitton, Dior, Tiffany, Moët-Hennessy, and most other luxury fashion brands, had heard we were doing a big shoot in Paris and made a tempting invitation. The company had a very private apartment in Paris's 8th district and suggested hosting a dinner for our crew, complete with gourmet cuisine, premium wine, cocktails, and cordials, and a stunning view of the city. Of course we said yes. Who wouldn't? Besides, we were still trying to get Louis Vuitton as an advertiser, and face time with its executives would be a great time to sell our magazine.

The mood amongst our crew—Anna and Allison as well—finally turned festive and continued all night. The food was exquisite, the wine pairings perfect, and the conversation hysterical. At one point, we went around the table requiring everyone to sing their favorite song, or at least one they could recite. By this time, we'd had plenty of alcohol, so my memory is hazy, but I do remember singing "Shoop" by Salt-N-Pepa. Another crooned "Killing Me Softly" by Lauryn Hill, and Hud sang "Tu Vuò Fà L'Americano" by Nicola Salerno and Renato Carosone; those are the ones I remember.

After dinner, we went to a posh study for extremely rare Hennessy cognac Richard France from 1765. When we returned to our rooms, we each found a gifted bottle of equally rare Paradis France cognac.

The gesture had softened the intensity from the shoot, and everyone left Paris somewhat pleased, even though we still did not see images.

Returning to New York was somber. The winds affecting the magazine business not only changed, but they also uprooted trees.

April 25, 2016, was my last day as editor in chief. It was an ideal time: ten years, kick-ass anniversary party, and a photo shoot in Paris as departing memories.

Q&A WITH SOPHIA PAULMIER

Sophia: Allison Janney has had quite the film career. She's like a Philip Seymour Hoffman who had a great career playing supporting actors until he hit it big. What is your favorite performance and movie of hers?

Jeremy: *I, Tonya*, in which she played Tonya Harding's foul-mouthed mother. She stole the whole movie.

S: What's she like in person?

J: Very delicate, like a wounded bird. I was shocked. *She* was thanking *me*.

S: Did you ever ask Anna Faris which Scary Movie *was her favorite?*

J: I don't remember. If I did it, would have been at the LVMH dinner, but we got so smashed I don't remember much.

S: Anna Faris is known mostly for doing comedies, but my favorite role for her was when she embodied Cameron Diaz as an actress in Lost in Translation. *What was your favorite performance by her?*

J: *The House Bunny*, when she does the creepy voice.

S: Mom *brought to light many real-life issues, addressing dark themes such as drug addiction, alcoholism, and domestic violence that most family sitcoms don't dare go near. Did you feel it was ahead of it's time for that?*

J: I really don't like when sitcoms do that. Situation comedy. It's in the name of the genre. There's nothing to laugh about with those topics.

S: *Would this be your last stay with the Plaza Athénée?*

J: I'm a fan for life. I've been back three times.

S: *It sounds like there was a lack of preparation going into this shoot. Was there someone new hired or had your team not planned everything out on this one?*

J: We didn't plan. I'd set the wrong tone and was too laid back. I take full responsibility.

S: *Did you feel the first dinner was stiff from the room and car mix-up or was there more tension to it?*

J: There was more to it. We were normally boisterous. I used to joke that if security wasn't called, it wasn't us. This dinner felt like a library.

S: *Did you ever find out why the rented trunks were not there?*

J: We didn't do our job.

S: *How did you take Patrick's frustration?*

J: I was devastated. This was the most important relationship I had with a photographer.

S: The weather played a part in this shoot as well. Did you feel your A-game was slipping away from you when you noticed the talent shivering?

J: The weather is like that all the time. We just didn't consider it.

S: So you sang Salt-N-Pepa's "Shoop" at private dinner hosted by LVMH?

J: Yes! I know it by heart and can sing it on cue.

S: What did Hennessy from 1765 taste like?

J: I could swim in it.

S: I picture the meme of Frank Sinatra sipping bourbon from a helicopter. Was it something like that?

J: More *Thomas Crown*. I love the 1999 remake with Pierce Brosnan.

S: If you could go back to that last shoot and change anything or say anything knowing it'd be your last, what would it have been or said and why?

J: Good question. I think I would have been more relaxed. The hiccups wouldn't have gotten to me as much as they did.

S: Your last shoot with Patrick was a sour one. Did you two ever reconnect and smooth things over?

J: He had a memory like a goldfish. Got over it that morning. I worked with him and his agent after to try to bring his Paris photo exhibit to New York.

S: Did you ever see Anna and Allison again?

J: I texted with Allison for a few months, but that's it.

S: *Had any talent reached out to you in the six years the magazine continued without you and admitted they missed working with you?*

J: Many. Except for one celebrity, I always made it fun for the actors.

S: *Final word to describe this end of an era?*

J: Over.

Acknowledgments

········★········

To Sophia Paulmier, thank you for joining me on this crazy adventure! You are so talented, and I am lucky to have you in my life.

To Marni, thank you for you.

To Bonnie Rubin-Schultz, thank you for copyediting *Too Good to Fact Check* (at least what I could send by deadline!) and being honest with your feedback. You made it a better book.

To Robert Konjic: Thank you for talking me off the ledge and being the best wingman and friend.

To Champers: Meow, meow, meow, meow.

To Suzanne Herbert: Thank you for being a great friend, Sunday night drink date, and a great sounding board.

To Paul Krasinski, my second guardian angel: Thank you for your friendship and being a source of support during shitty 2023.

To Faith Zuckerman, Scott Hart, James Brolin, and Andrew Cooper: Thank you for believing in *House of Medici*!

To Barbara Bahny: I hope Heaven is as good as The Willard. You deserve the best, and we miss you dearly.

To Patrick Demarchelier: (unintelligible) (unintelligible) (unintelligible) (unintelligible) voilà! Très jolie! Magnifique, (unintelligible). We miss your exquisite eye.

To Beth Feldman, Dan and Susan Fox, Kenny Kim, Stephanie Garland, Claudia Lake, Bobby Konjic, Garrett Neff, Dana Brown, Kim and Kelly Kahl, Steven Holt, Kim Myers Robertson, Stuart Eliot, Luis Miranda, Kenny Kim, Niki Lesson, Angelique O'Neil, Nanci Grasso, Sahib Faber, Christopher Carbone, David Morton, Mark Grgurich, Josephine Hemsing, Sarah Cairns, Kendra and Jake Rogers, Darren Greenblatt, Sam Hunt, Luis Miranda, Eric Rutherford, Lyss Stern, Matt Pisanelli, Ben Widdicombe, Diego Serrano, Jay Jablonski, Anna Carbonell, Cathie Black, Luis Toledo, Tom Harvey, Steven Holt, Isabelle Maurin, Jamie Roberts, Pat Canole, Maurie Perl, Colleen Evans, Jay

Braff, Simone Rathle, Angela Jackson, Vivian Deuschl, Cote de Pablo, Stephen Payor, Michelle Payer, Tammy Petersen, Cassin Duncan, Sarah Stanndard, Leslie Lefkowitz, Jennifer Cooke, and Branko Karlezi: You're all awesome, and I'm honored to have your friendship.

To Neil Patrick Harris, Cote de Pablo, Michael Weatherly, Pauley Perrette, Brian Dietzen, Emily Wickersham, Julianna Margulies, Christine Baranski, Matt Czuchry, Archie Panjabi, Alan Cumming, Cobie Smulders, Beth Behrs, Bridget Moynahan, Rachelle Lefevre, Emily Proctor, Lara Spencer, Mayim Bialik, Johnny Galecki, Matt and Angela Lanter, Eva LaRue, Roselyn Sanchez, and Celine Dion: Thank you for your time, generosity, humor, and beauty.

To Charlie Siem, Jeff Leatham, Iestyn Davies, Ed Michael Reggie: Thank you for being part of the 360bespoke story.

To Super P, Christopher Campbell, Virginia Bell, Joe Wilson, Ian Derry, Sarah Nash, Beth Tomkiw, Fred Petrovsky, Jim Colucci, Frank DeCaro, Beverly Byrd, Fabio Mercurio, Ron Sklon, Charles Mast, Angela de Bona, Matt Petersen, Ian Derry, Sarah Nash, Gilles-Marie Zimmermann, Cannon, Mark Mann, Christopher Rovzar, Crissy Poorman, Kate Betts, Loren Chidoni, Joanna Della-Ragione, Peter Greenberg, Ali Prato, Sarah Rose, James Hendry, Nick Teare, Jamie Kerr, Kate Betts, Hud Morgan, Sam Mittelsteadt, and Jeff Ficker: Thank you for an amazing journey through the printed page.

About the Authors

Author Jeremy Murphy. Portrait by Kim Myers.

Jeremy Murphy is a critically acclaimed author whose first book, *F*ck Off, Chloe: Surviving the OMGs and FMLs in Your Media Career*, received rave reviews when it was released in 2022. The book was called "hilarious" by the *New York Post* while the *Daily News* heralded, "Media mavens will love *F*ck Off, Chloe: Surviving the OMGs and FMLs in your Media Career*. The book is currently being developed into a TV series.

Murphy is also a screenwriter, and is developing the TV shows *House of Medici* with producers James Brolin and Scott Hart; *The Court* of *St. James* and *Python* with producer Faith Zuckerman; and *The Grapes of Matt* with actor/writer David Morton.

Now the head of his own New York PR agency, 360bespoke, he gained industry recognition when he created and edited the glossy magazine *Watch*, which redefined the perception of custom publishing. As its editor in chief, he built a respected masthead that featured top editorial talents. Working with these creative forces, he infused the magazine's pages with elegant and timeless features, including recreations of French impressionist paintings at the celebrated Hôtel Plaza Athénée Paris, homages to Christian Dior and Babe Paley, and a cover shoot with actress Julianna Margulies by Demarchelier at the Hotel du Cap in the Côte d'Azur. His strategy successfully transitioned *Watch* from a publication to a brand encompassing print, television, online, video and social media.

He began his career as a journalist for the *Boca Raton News*, *The Bradenton Herald*, and *Mediaweek* magazine.

Murphy is a graduate of Florida Atlantic University and was inducted into its Alumni Hall of Fame in 2010. He lives in New York with his cat, Champers, which is not at all creepy.

Co-author, Sophia Paulmier.

Sophia Paulmier is an actor, director, and writer from Germantown, Philadelphia, and is currently residing on New York City's Upper West Side. She has worked with many top creative talents, including the late director Joel Schumacher, who hailed her as "brilliant" on a filming project.

Her scripts are known to be female driven, as well as having an architectural framework and pink palettes. She is "always looking for stories that feel nostalgic in time and place." Paulmier's dark comedy, *Sisters*, about two sociopathic siblings, won her best director as well as several best web series and pilot awards. She is currently in the early script stages of a feature about the dark side of being an actress.